TESLA

Manhattan Dove to Queens Seagull

TESLA

Manhattan Dove to Queens Seagull

by

SHARON RICH & D. D. VUJIC

BELL HARBOUR PRESS
DUNEDIN, FLORIDA

Copyright © 2024 by Sharon Rich & D. D. Vujic

All rights reserved. No portion of this book may be reproduced in any form without written permission from the publisher or authors, except as permitted by U.S. copyright law.

Based on the script *Tesla* by D. Daniel Vujic & Sharon Rich © 2016

This is a work of historical fiction. While this book incorporates actual historical events, verified facts, and real persons from historical records, it also contains fictional elements, including but not limited to: fictional characters, imagined dialogue, dramatized scenes, and speculative interpretations of historical events. All fictional elements, including certain characters, incidents, organizations and dialogue, are products of the authors imagination or are used fictitiously. Any resemblance between these fictional elements and actual persons, living or dead, businesses, companies, events or locales is entirely coincidental and unintentional.

Published by Bell Harbour Press, www.bellharbourpress.com
Printed in the United States of America

ISBN: 978-1-7376812-8-1 (softcover)
ISBN: 979-8-9920227-0-4 (hardcover)
ISBN: 979-8-9920227-1-1 (ebook)
ISBN: 979-8-9920227-2-8 (audiobook)

Library of Congress Control Number: 2024924198

Book website: teslanovel.com
Author websites: sharonrich.com and ddvujic.com
Facebook page: facebook.com/teslanovel
Email: ntbook369@gmail.com

Dedication

D.D. Vujic: I dedicate this work, a tribute to the man who illuminated the world, Nikola Tesla, to my Mother, Vera Vujic. Like Nikola Tesla's mother, Georgina, whose ingenuity flowed through Nikola's veins. You, Vera, have been the electrifying force behind my own endeavors. You are the constant current that has powered my aspirations, the unwavering voltage that has transformed my ambitions into reality. With infinite gratitude and boundless love, this book is for you, Mom. May it serve as a testament to the enduring power of family, heritage, and the unwavering support that fuels a writer's journey.

Sharon Rich: For McKenna and Kinnison, my very young grandchildren. Before the age of one they were already wide-eyed with wonder at the innovations of Nikola Tesla: working magic with remote controls; making their robot dolls and trains talk or move; baking healthy treats with Grandma in the microwave oven; enjoying daily Facetime video chats with beloved relatives who live far away. All these skills have empowered them, making their toddler years easier, educational and fun. Despite his personal angst, Nikola Tesla shared the joy of a child in bending the physical universe to his liking. May my grandchildren and their generations know and appreciate the man who made all the above possible.

When wireless is perfectly applied the whole earth will be converted into a huge brain, which in fact it is, all things being particles of real and rhythmic whole. We shall be able to communicate with one another instantly, irrespective of distance. Not only this, but through television and telephony we shall see and hear one another as perfectly as though we were face to face, despite intervening distances of thousands of miles; and the instruments through which we shall be able to do this will be amazingly simple compared with our present telephone. A man will be able to carry one in his vest pocket.

–Nikola Tesla, 1926

FACT:

In the basement storage of the official Tesla Museum in Belgrade, Serbia lies a collection of artifacts hidden from the eyes of the world. This collection includes intimate letters exchanged between Nikola Tesla and his friend, Katharine Johnson. In addition to the letters, there is a fancy gold cigarette case given to Tesla for his birthday by George Westinghouse. And more ominously, there is a crystal whiskey decanter set with glasses gifted to Tesla by the original godfather of the Italian Mafia, Charles 'Lucky' Luciano.

But perhaps the most interesting artifacts in this secret collection are drawings that whisper secrets of time travel, and technologies that were a century ahead of its time, some of which could be weaponized. This was all part of the genius of Nikola Tesla. Only a few people have ever seen these contents. There are specific authorities who insist that it remain that way. These articles reveal a different side of Tesla than what has been publicly disclosed. He is remembered in history as a brilliant, eccentric inventor who was all but asexual, who did not smoke or drink alcohol and whose inventions were peaceful and never intended to be weaponized. This is how these certain authorities want people to remember Nikola Tesla.

While this book, in part, is a work of fiction, many of the details within its pages are rooted in truth. Many events including the various romantic references are true. Although Anya is a fictional character, she is actually inspired by a real person who was Tesla's first love, a Russian woman he held dear in his heart throughout his entire life.

The Time Radio is not a fictional invention but a real one, like all the other inventions mentioned in this book. Tesla did not assign a formal name to it. This book refers to it as the Time Radio. Tesla developed it in secrecy and as a result, no patents were ever filed. No one knows what became of that invention. All that remains of it are some early notes and incomplete diagrams and schematics. Whether Tesla successfully created it remains unknown.

Somewhere in Central Park, New York City, stands a majestic oak tree, its exact location a mystery. This is no ordinary tree, but the "Oak of Eternity," so named by Nikola Tesla himself. What makes this tree extraordinary is its role as a silent sentinel, an organic radio frequency receiver. A bridge between the past and future. Or perhaps it's just an oak tree favored by Tesla, we may never know.

In his last years, Tesla ordered "tea for two" almost daily at his last residence in the New Yorker Hotel. This standing order puzzled the hotel staff. He presumably was alone, yet a woman was heard by several of the hotel's staff. The FBI interviewed the staff after Tesla's death as to whether they had seen the woman coming or going, because the tea service platter that was always returned to the kitchen showed two people had used it. This was a mystery not solved in his lifetime and asks the question: was Tesla pretending to be two people and going mad towards the end of his life or had he been able to devise a way for his mystery mistress to come and go from the New Yorker Hotel unnoticed?

Part One

1

THE FUTURE IS MINE

New York City - November 18, 1942

A heavy silence blanketed New York City, a stark contrast to its usual restless pulse. A brooding storm on the eastern seaboard had cast an oppressive hush over the city. Even the ritzy New Yorker Hotel, a beacon of perpetual energy, had fallen eerily still.

Anxious whispers replaced the usual orchestra of laughter and swing. Guests cast glances at the darkening sky in anticipation of what promised to be the worst storm to hit the American east coast in decades.

The hotel's most eccentric permanent resident, Nikola Tesla, remained oblivious to the world outside his suite. Even on less ominous nights, he paid little attention to whispers of Hollywood royalty in attendance, like Spencer Tracy and Joan Crawford. Even the swinging rhythms of Benny Goodman and Tommy Dorsey echoing from the ballrooms meant nothing to him. His world had shrunk to the limits of his suite, his focus narrowed to a brilliance only he understood.

Tesla preferred near seclusion.

Each night a hotel maid, Alice Monahan, faithfully brought to his suite his standing order: tea for two.

On this night, Alice picked up the tray from room service, her heart thumping a little faster than usual. The elevator hummed its way upwards, the numbers ticking by with agonizing slowness. It was unsettling to be in an elevator during a night with lightning and thunder.

The hotel had forty-three floors, but tonight's journey led to the 33rd floor and down the hallway to room 3327. The tea tray heavy in one hand, she knocked on the door three times, which she knew was Tesla's preference.

"Mr. Tesla, I have your tea?" she called through the door, as a mere knock was not enough to get Tesla to answer. He paid heed to but a handful of people, Alice among them.

The door slowly opened. There standing before her was the great Nikola Tesla or the mad scientist, depending on who you asked. But at age eighty-six he looked neither great nor mad but instead, frail and beaten. Although he racked up a respectable age, he looked older and not like the suave Hollywood-ready hero that was expected.

Alice had been repeatedly told by other staff that the eccentric Mr. Tesla was the greatest living genius in the world, an icon still visited by a select few famous scientists, politicians, celebrities, authors and even mobsters. Alice had studied photographs of Mr. Tesla in his younger years and read many articles about him. She became privately fascinated by him but she would never admit as much to anyone. As far as everyone was concerned, to her, he was just another guest or resident of the glorious New Yorker Hotel.

Alice would often imagine what Tesla was like back in the day of his prime, when he first came to America as a young budding scientist. She had seen a few published photographs of him: a tall, dapper young man with naturally wavy dark hair that fell over his forehead and made him look boyish, a shy quality and soulful eyes that no doubt had once captivated women's hearts.

Even now, he still stood tall and with a gentleman's pride and stature. His once-dark hair was still thick, although white flecked with gray. But he was thin, so thin as to look almost skeletal. Age had whittled away his form. Once filled out, his suit now hung loosely, his gauntness a stark contrast to what he once was.

"Good evening, Mr. Tesla," Alice said cheerfully.

Tesla nodded and Alice entered the room, careful not to stand too close to him. She placed the tea tray on the table closest to the window. Then she made sure everything on the platter was neatly arranged as Mr. Tesla did not like disorder.

A gleaming teapot made from fine china formed the centerpiece of the tray. Two fragile teacups, a miniature milk pitcher, and a tiny bowl of golden honey flanked it. All complimented by a generous slice of Lady Anne cake, its layers of white and cream a study in perfection that sat alongside a few assorted cookies.

The final touch was the stack of neatly folded napkins.

Tesla was fixated on the number three, polishing his dining implements with meticulous care to a blinding shine and always keeping a precise stack of eighteen napkins on hand, using only three at a time.

Satisfied with the presentation, Alice turned to Tesla.

"Will there be anything more, Mr. Tesla?"

Tesla shook his head.

"Well then, I'll be saying goodnight, sir."

Tesla nodded. Alice headed back to the door and left.

As she retraced her footsteps to the elevator, Alice had reason to wonder anew about Mr. Tesla. She knew he was alone on this night and on most nights, yet he always ordered tea for two. That in itself was a puzzlement, as some time ago Mr. Tesla advised her he was quitting both coffee and tea. He had self-diagnosed that they were adversely affecting his heart and had explained this to Alice. Yet he did not seem fond of herbal teas, devoid of stimulants, that she could easily substitute for regular tea.

What was even more interesting was that when she collected the tray, Alice found both teacups had been used. And if not for the fact that she could swear she sometimes heard a woman's voice inside the suite, she might believe in the outrageous rumors that Tesla was truly mad.

But how did this mystery woman elude the entire hotel staff, entering and leaving the hotel without ever being seen?

Meanwhile, Tesla had been writing a letter before Alice arrived with the tea. He poured tea in both cups and carried his cup to the writing desk.

"Are you sure about this, Nikola?" A woman's voice asked seemingly from out of nowhere.

"Anya, I am offering peace to the world, but they want war again," Tesla replied and took a sip of tea, then resumed writing.

"This worries me so," Anya said with concern.

Tesla stopped writing and looked up at Anya as she stepped out of the shadows from the bedroom, approached the table, and seated herself in the chair opposite him.

A reluctant smile softened his features. Even after all this time, her concern for him stirred a warmth within him. Her beauty remained unchanged by the years. Yes, on closer inspection, he could spot a few threads of silver amidst her dark blonde waves, now swept up in a neat bun. But her figure remained slender, her wide hazel eyes still sparkled beneath long lashes, and her lips, full and delicately curved, held their familiar allure.

Anya added milk to her tea, stirred in a dollop of honey, and lifted the teacup to drink. She smiled back at him. A flicker of self-reproach crossed Tesla's face before he resumed writing. Anya's quiet presence was a gentle reminder of the world beyond his work.

He forced his focus back to the page, but a moment later another knock at the door sounded. The distraction tugged at him, but his words would not wait. His pen scratched out the last sentence.

The door swung open, revealing the bellboy. Henry Watt, with his auburn hair and freckled face, looked younger than his twenty-two years. He stood tall and slender. A genuine warmth in his eyes transcended the age gap between him and Tesla, a spark of honesty that had earned the old inventor's trust.

Tesla understood that trust was at times misplaced and came at a heavy price. Too often, smiles and honeyed words had masked the knives of back stabbers eager to steal his brilliance; but with Henry, there was no such falseness. Months of quiet observation had confirmed his initial impression: this young man's open nature held no hidden malice. That simple trust spurred Tesla's unusual decision, his mission for this trustworthy soul.

As Henry approached, Tesla merely gestured towards a small leather travel trunk beside the bed. There was a silent understanding in their exchange, a quiet choreography born of an unspoken agreement.

With a final flourish, Tesla sealed the letter, rose from his desk, and moved toward Henry. His movements were slow and deliberate, a stark reminder of the years etched into his weathered frame.

"We have discussed this." Tesla's voice was low with concern. "You understand the instructions. You understand the importance."

"Mr. Tesla, I won't fail you," Henry replied, his voice firm.

A brief smile touched Tesla's lips. He placed the envelope in Henry's waiting hand. "Conceal the letter in the trunk's lining."

"I understand, sir." Henry placed the envelope into his deep side pocket, picked up the trunk and left without another word. Tesla returned to his armchair by the window and sipped his tea.

Outside, the storm raged, a symphony of chaos against the rain-lashed glass. Tesla gazed at the fury unleashed outside his window, a reflection of his own restless energy.

Tonight, he had set time itself in motion. The trunk carried by Henry contained a weapon to upend the established order. Tesla's discoveries, the secrets whispered in that letter, would reverberate through the years, leaving a changed world.

He understood the magnitude of his life's work, the promise it held for humankind. So as he gazed out the window, accomplishment washed over him – a sense of finality, a quiet peace amidst the raging storm outside his window.

"The future," Tesla began, his voice barely a whisper yet charged with the weight of his vision, "belongs to me now."

His gaze through the window diverted to Anya, whose smile held a bittersweet understanding. Words were needless; she felt the shift in the air, the culmination of his relentless pursuit. After a lingering moment, she spoke, her voice soft and grounding.

"Drink your tea, dear."

2

GOING TO AMERICA

Liverpool, England – May 29, 1884

A raucous chorus of seagulls screeched overhead, their cries mingling with the mournful blare of the last boarding call.

Mist clung to the salty May air as a young Tesla, age twenty-eight, with meager belongings in hand, clutched the railing of the behemoth ship *City of Richmond* bound for a world he could only imagine.

With a mighty groan, the ship's massive propellers churned to life, sending tremors through its hull. Then, with a lurch, it tore itself from the familiar dock, each churn of its engines widening the gap between Tesla and the Old World.

Tesla navigated the crowded deck. Voices in a dozen languages mixed with the creak of wooden boards and the tang of sea spray. He ducked, sidestepped, and squeezed past preoccupied passengers, his progress a slow dance, until a sudden jolt sent him staggering into a gangly young man – Ernst Adler, just twenty-two.

"Pardon me!" Tesla exclaimed.

"Quite alright," replied Adler.

Adler, with a gesture of courtesy, stepped aside to let Tesla pass. The hallway here was less crowded than the deck.

Both young men scanned the doors, searching for their cabins. Tesla moved with a certainty that belied his unfamiliarity; Adler paused often, checking his ticket against the numbers on the doors.

"Been on this ship before?" Adler asked, a hint of curiosity in his voice.

"No," Tesla replied, his tone clipped.

"Strange," Adler persisted, "seems like you know your way around."

Tesla came to an abrupt stop before a cabin door. "I am familiar with the logic of the numbering scheme on this vessel," he said, tapping the worn brass '213'. "And this would be me."

Adler glanced at the number, then at his ticket. "Yes... this seems to be my room as well." He held out the ticket for Tesla's inspection.

Tesla shook his head. "Not at all."

"I beg your pardon, it says 213." Adler looked confused.

"Indeed, it does," Tesla agreed, "but it also specifies the upper deck. This is 213 on the primary deck. You'll find your cabin one level above."

"Hardly seems logical, numbering different decks the same way."

A faint smile touched Tesla's lips as he unlocked his door. "I'm sure you'll locate your room with ease. Each deck is undoubtedly laid out identically."

"I certainly hope so," Adler muttered. "My name is Adler. And you are...?"

"Tesla."

"Good day to you, Tesla." Adler turned and continued down the hallway.

Tesla entered his cabin. The ship swayed with a sickening rhythm and he lay down on his bed, staring at the single light bulb dancing a frantic jig on its cord. The room was a testament to stark utility: a table, a chair, all bolted to the floor. A chipped washbasin, a tarnished mirror, and the barest hint of a porthole offered a storm-tossed glimpse of the churning sea.

Comfort was an extravagance they did not offer on this crossing. No toilet, no running water, only the faintest pretense of privacy. He would have to adjust or endure for the next eight days and nights.

Tesla closed his eyes, the rocking motion mirroring the frantic pace of his thoughts.

A whisper: "Nikola."

His eyes snapped open. Anya's voice was soft but unmistakably real. He scanned the room, a jolt of adrenaline coursing through him. Yet he was alone.

Taking a moment to steady himself, he rose and rummaged through his meager bag. His fingers found the familiar coolness of his silver cigarette case. With practiced ease, he lit a cigarette and inhaled, collecting his rational thoughts. He surveyed the cabin again and then returned to the bed, exhaling a thoughtful plume.

"Auditory hallucination," he murmured to himself, the words a shield of sorts to protect his sanity. To calm his nerves, he immersed himself in deep thoughts of another distant time and place.

The depths of Tesla's vast mind held an exact date and location. Four years had passed since then, yet he could still vividly sense the phantom sensation of cobblestones beneath his feet and the mingling of fresh coffee with the scent of spring in the air.

∞

Paris, France – May 8, 1880

The morning sunlight dappled the cobblestones, turning them the color of old gold. A gentle breeze danced through the open-air café, carrying the scent of fresh pastries and roasted coffee beans.

At a small table sat Tesla. His lean form was silhouetted against the crisp pages of his newspaper, a picture of focused intellect.

He did not notice when the waiter, a weathered man with a knowing smile, seated Anya Ivanov at the adjacent table.

Her arrival was a symphony of color — the vibrant blue of her dress, the rich dark blonde of her hair swept up in a loose knot, the flash of emerald earrings adding a playful touch.

"Good afternoon. What can I get for you?" asked the waiter.

"Coffee with hot milk, please," Anya replied in French. Her Russian accent added a hint of exoticism to the ordinary order. "And a moment to soak in this delicious scene."

Tesla's focus momentarily wavered. He lowered the newspaper subtly, his gaze drawn to this unexpected burst of radiance beside him.

"What an exquisite moment, don't you think?" Anya breathed, her eyes sparkling as they met his.

Surprised, Tesla could only manage a startled, "I don't understand, Miss."

"The colors, the light!" She gestured towards the bustling street. "The coffee...the company. All so unexpectedly beautiful."

"Indeed," Tesla murmured, clearing his throat. "It is a fine day."

"May I introduce myself? Anya Ivanov. A painter, writer, an adventurer of sorts, visiting from Russia."

"Pleased to meet you," Tesla offered, the words feeling strangely inadequate. "I am Tesla..."

The waiter returned with Anya's coffee, breaking the spell for a moment.

"Thank you." She smiled and then turned her attention back to Tesla. "Surely, Tesla is not your given name?"

"Forgive me," he blushed faintly. "Nikola. I am Serbian. And..." He switched effortlessly into fluent Russian. "I hope your stay in Paris has been pleasant."

"You speak Russian!" Her eyes widened in delighted surprise.

Tesla nodded, a spark of amusement in his eyes. With a subtle shift of his chair, he edged closer, their shared language creating an instant intimacy.

"Absolutely delightful! And so inspiring," Anya declared. "I have visited your country. Belgrade has a... rustic charm that sets my imagination alight. And what is your vocation, Nikola? Why are you here in Paris, if it is not too forward to ask?"

"I am an engineer," Tesla replied, his voice softening. "I recently accepted a job here with Edison Continental."

"Edison? As in the Thomas Edison, the great American inventor?"

"Yes, the very same," Tesla answered proudly. "I even met him briefly when he was here in Paris."

Anya's smile widened. "Your work, then, is much like art. You are a creator, a builder of dreams."

"I suppose.... One could say that," he stammered, thrown off balance by her insightful observation. "And what form of art do you favor?"

"Oh, I adore poetry - Pushkin, Shakespeare, the passionate words of Goethe! But most of all, I love to paint."

"And what inspires you to paint?"

Anya rewarded him with a playful smile. "The present moment. Always the present moment! No matter where, when, what... or who."

Her voice faded to a near whisper as she reached into her oversized satchel, retrieving a small stack of sketches. Tesla felt his heart quicken.

"I made these yesterday," she said, handing them to him.

Tesla took the sketches, his fingers brushing against hers. He meticulously flipped through them, his eyes absorbing the delicate lines, the captured energy of street scenes and candid portraits.

"They are... exquisite," he murmured, warmth flooding his cheeks.

"Thank you."

"And what shall you sketch today?"

Anya's luminous eyes locked with his. "Perhaps," she began, a hint of mischief in her tone, "The memory of the moment I sat down here... And our most unexpected, delightful encounter..."

WHAM! A sudden jolt rocked the ship, brutally tearing Tesla from his sweet vision of Anya and startling him back to his present surroundings. His heart pounded, the fading remnants of her smile disappearing like wisps of smoke.

He struck a match, its harsh flare momentarily illuminating his cramped cabin, and lit another cigarette. Hands trembling, he forced himself to draw a deep breath as the ship groaned and steadied its course.

He tried to focus anew on his destination. America, a land of boundless promise and unknown perils, loomed in his mind. He reminded himself that he would make his fame and fortune there.

But it seemed impossible to relax — if such a concept ever existed in his mindset. Despite his attempted bravado, he knew in certain areas of life he was not a brave man.

He was commanding at the forefront of scientific discovery, with a mind that grasped the intricate workings of the universe. Yet Tesla felt a humbling sliver of fear and self-doubt as the storm raged outside on the open ocean. Did his audacity push him to chase after something that was destined to remain out of reach?

To calm himself, he forced his thoughts back to Anya.

3

Anya

Paris, France – May 15, 1880

The cobblestone streets of Paris were caressed by the warm May sun as Tesla left his simple accommodations. His heart raced with an unfamiliar anticipation, a feeling that both thrilled and unnerved him.

The previous day's encounter with Anya, their first date since they first met in the café a week earlier, had unfolded as Tesla had hoped. Tesla opened up to her, confiding his thoughts as he rarely did with others. Her acceptance without judgment made him feel safe with her. They agreed to rendezvous at the same restaurant the following afternoon.

As he made his way to the restaurant, the city seemed to pulse with a new energy. *Or perhaps it is I who am pulsing with a new energy*, he thought. He sensed he was overdressed for a simple daytime date, but what did it matter? He couldn't deny that he wanted to impress Anya.

He spotted her immediately as he arrived at the restaurant. She sat at a sunlit table, her dark blonde hair shimmering. Tesla's breath caught in his throat.

Anya's voice, musical and warm, echoed in the air. "Nikola!"

Tesla dashed over, a rare grin illuminating his face. "You're stunning!" he said as he sat down.

Anya leaned in, her mischievous hazel eyes sparkling. "My, my, Nikola, you certainly look dapper."

"Perhaps a tad overdressed," he confessed, blushing.

"Not at all, but in fact ... almost perfect, and I don't mean your attire." She gazed at his hair and then reached out, her fingers lightly brushing his meticulously styled hair. "But let's free these locks, shall we? There's a brilliant mind underneath that deserves to shine."

With a gentle touch, she tousled his hair, sending a shiver down his spine. The simple gesture felt oddly intimate, and he found himself leaning into her touch.

"There," Anya said, satisfaction evident in her voice. "Now you're perfect."

Tesla chuckled, a rich, deep sound that surprised even himself.

"Now, shall we order?" she asked, smiling. "I'm famished and I have plans for us today."

As they enjoyed their meal, Tesla found himself captivated by Anya's every move. The way her lips curved around her fork, the delicate arch of her neck as she laughed at his awkward attempts at humor.

"Tell me, Nikola," Anya said between bites, "what grand inventions are occupying that brilliant mind of yours?"

Tesla's eyes lit up. "Oh, Anya, if only you knew! I have visions of machines that could revolutionize the world. Imagine harnessing the very power of nature itself – electricity flowing freely, accessible to all!"

Anya attentively watched his animated face. "It sounds marvelous. I can see the passion in your eyes as you speak of it."

"But enough about my work," Tesla said, surprising even himself. "What shall we do today, my dear Anya?"

"I thought we might take a stroll through Parc Monceau. It's a hidden gem, full of beauty and tranquility. The perfect place to... get to know each other better."

As they walked through the magnificent gardens, arms linked, Tesla couldn't help but feel acutely aware of Anya's presence beside him. The soft rustle of her skirt, the warmth of her body so close to his seemed to engulf him.

They paused by a serene lake, its surface a mirror reflecting the azure sky above. Settling onto a bench, Anya boldly took Tesla's hand in hers.

"Look, Nikola," she whispered, pointing to a flock of seagulls circling overhead. "Aren't they magnificent? So free, so unburdened by the worries of the world below."

Tesla was amazed as several birds appeared to respond to Anya's voice by swooping down and landing near their feet. "It's as if they know you," he murmured.

"Perhaps they do," Anya replied with a cryptic smile. "Nature has many secrets, Nikola. Some of which even your brilliant mind has yet to unravel."

A couple of seagulls seemed to bow their heads to Anya as she gently spoke to them. She thanked them for visiting and complimented them on their beauty. The two birds pranced around, accepting her compliment before eventually taking flight.

As the afternoon waned, Tesla reluctantly explained that he had a business meeting to attend. "Some gentlemen are interested in my ideas for a flying machine," he said, sounding apologetic.

Anya's eyes widened with interest. "A flying machine? Oh, Nikola, you must tell me more about it tomorrow. You will see me again, won't you?"

"I wouldn't miss it for the world." His voice was husky with emotion. "May I take you to dinner tomorrow evening?"

Anya's face lit up with joy. "I should like that very much."

Despite his delight, Tesla couldn't help but feel concerned due to his lack of money. To secure funds for another outing with Anya, he found it necessary to engage in a card game, which resulted in him having a late night and of course, winning – as Tesla rarely lost.

That night when he arrived home and finally prepared for bed, his mind whirled with thoughts of Anya. Her laugh, her touch, the way her eyes seemed to see right through to his soul —it was all so new, so exhilarating. For the first time in years, his dreams were filled not with equations and inventions, but with visions of blonde hair and hazel eyes.

4

MIND GAMES

City of Richmond Ship - May 29, 1884

Tesla dined with his new friend Ernst Adler, listening to his excited chatter as they ate. Tesla found the food quality acceptable, but the surroundings were sadly less elegant. The ship's dining room was old and worn down, featuring faded chairs and mismatched wooden tables, their surfaces a testament to years of spilled drinks and gouges from careless cutlery. Tesla gazed up at the tarnished brass chandelier that dangled askew in the center of the room. Its crystal prisms, choked with dust, cast a dim, wavering light that scarcely reached the shadows in the dining room.

His disapproval of these shabby surroundings tainted whatever enjoyment he had from his meal. *A man should not have to live like this*, he thought, acknowledging a touch of arrogance.

Almost as an affirmation, he envisioned: *I will be a success in America and I must achieve the luxury I deserve, a lavish, wonderful lodging with staff to attend to me. My genius is, after all, just a tool to help make this world a better place...*

A voice broke through his inner contemplation.

"New York, Tesla!" Adler exclaimed, waving his fork for emphasis. "Can you imagine? The buildings, the inventions, the sheer energy of it all!"

Tesla offered a faint smile, his own gaze drawn to the window where the Atlantic Ocean churned beneath a gray sky. "Cities can be... overwhelming," he murmured.

Adler scoffed. "Overwhelming for those without ambition, perhaps. But for a man like you? And a lad like me, brimming with potential? New York is a banquet, and we shall have the finest seats at the table!"

Tesla was inevitably amused by Adler's unbridled optimism. The young man might not grasp the finer points of electrical engineering, but Adler had a fire in him that Tesla recognized.

"Speaking of banquets," Adler leaned in, lowering his voice to a conspiratorial whisper, "I learned about a most lucrative card game down in the boiler room. High stakes, they say. American dollars ripe for the picking. Care to join me, Tesla? A bit of fortune might ease our arrival in the land of opportunity."

Tesla considered the proposition and nodded his approval. A distraction might stave off the restlessness that gnawed at him, and a few extra coins would add a welcome layer of security.

"But remember, Adler, luck is a fickle mistress, as quick to leave a man penniless as she is to make him rich."

"And who better to charm a fickle mistress than two men bound for greatness?" Adler grinned, his eyes gleaming. "Now, shall we make our way to this game for which I have already reserved a seat for myself! I suspect there will be no resistance for you to join?"

They quickly finished their meal and headed to the ship's boiler room.

The belly of the ship throbbed with a relentless rhythm. In the depths of the boiler room, flickering flames cast monstrous shadows, and exposed pipes snaked like iron veins through the dimness. The air hung thick, a choking mix of coal dust and grease. If the Devil himself were to travel on this ship, this would be his suite.

Two men, Thomas, his face etched with years at sea, and Raymond, weathered hands stained with engine oil, presided over a makeshift card table wedged between towering boilers.

Tesla and Adler stepped into this chaotic inferno – Tesla with a detached curiosity masking a flicker of wariness, Adler with a wide-eyed eagerness that bordered on recklessness.

Thomas leaned forward, his bulk casting an imposing shadow. "Well, look what the tide's brought in. Gents, take a seat?" His voice boomed over the rhythmic clang of shovels hitting coal, but a hint of menace laced his words.

He motioned to two rickety chairs set uncomfortably close to a boiler radiating waves of heat.

Adler started forward but Tesla held him back with a quiet but firm touch.

Raymond cracked a smile that did not reach his eyes. "Pick your weapons, lads – red or blue?" He held up two greasy decks of cards, a predatory glint in his eye.

Tesla's gaze flickered not to the cards, but to a loose valve on a nearby pipe that hissed ominously. "The red deck, I believe."

Adler fidgeted, his eyes darting between the men. A bead of sweat traced a path down his temple.

"Red it is then," Raymond said with a note of amusement in his voice.

Thomas slammed a meaty fist on the table, the vibration rattling the cards. "Let's play. Five-card draw, aye?"

"Perfect," Adler squeaked, his voice a bit higher than usual.

"Just one small request before we start," Tesla interjected.

Thomas narrowed his eyes. "Oh? What's the problem?"

"Those chairs... rather close to the boiler, wouldn't you say?" Tesla gestured, his knuckles white where he gripped Adler's arm. "The heat, the noise – distracting for unaccustomed ears. Wouldn't want to give you gentlemen an unintended edge."

Thomas frowned, a muscle twitching in his jaw. "Suit yourselves. Noise is the same all over this blasted furnace."

"Then you won't mind if we take these seats over here?" Tesla motioned towards a less oppressive spot. A subtle defiance resonated in his words.

Raymond chuckled, a raspy sound that scraped across the tense air. "Now... let's play already!"

Tesla acknowledged Raymond's offer with a faint smile as he and Adler took their preferred seats.

Their chairs scraping the soot-covered floor, Tesla's fingers drummed lightly on the table. The rhythm, almost imperceptible, seemed to echo the increasing pressure building within the room. Time seemed to melt away in the haze of the boiler room. Each hand dealt, each bluff called, slowly tilted the tide in Tesla and Adler's favor.

Thomas's jovial mask slipped, revealing a scowl. Raymond's forced smile twitched with every lost pot and after a few hours, several more pots were lost. Finally, Thomas had enough and shoved back his chair.

"Gentlemen, Raymond and I must check in with the quartermaster. Excuse us for a moment, we'll be back shortly."

The two men rose. Sweat glistened on Thomas' forehead, and Raymond's hands trembled as they left the boiler room.

Adler leaned back with a triumphant grin. "Damn fine evening of poker, wouldn't you say?"

"This is not a legitimate contest," Tesla announced.

Adler blinked in surprise. "We're cheating!?"

"No, not at all. Well, not exactly. It's more the opposite, my dear friend."

Adler's brow furrowed. "If they're cheating, they're not very good at it. Perhaps we should let them continue."

Tesla chuckled. "Right now, they are trying to figure out why they are losing." He paused, then gestured around them. "Look around you. What do you see?"

Adler squinted. "A boiler room."

"Yes, but more specifically, a dimly lit room that is hot, loud, and, if I may be so bold, odoriferous."

Adler let out a startled laugh. "I beg your pardon."

"It smells in here," Tesla said bluntly.

"That it does," Adler agreed.

"All of this is a poor attempt to distract us." Tesla paused then added, "Oh, and the cards are marked too."

Adler's grin widened. "Not working out for them, is it?"

"It's the selenium, my good man."

"Selenium?"

"Yes, a chemical element found in metal sulfide."

"And this is why they are losing?"

"Selenium is red, and it becomes excited by electrical discharges which are emitted by that rather noisy generator directly in front of us."

Adler blinked again. "I don't follow."

"The pigments on the red-colored cards are likely made with selenium. With the electrical discharges, those cards have a subtle glow, invisible to the untrained eye. With proper focus and practice, one can make out the faint red picture on the other side of the card."

"And you, no doubt, can make out the pictures on the cards?" Adler asked, amused.

"Of course," Tesla replied.

Adler gaped. "My God, man! So we are cheating too!"

"That is a matter of perspective, Mr. Adler," Tesla said calmly.

Adler wiped a sheen of sweat from his forehead with his handkerchief. The temperature in the boiler room was stifling yet seemed to have no effect on Tesla.

"So everyone is cheating," Adler concluded.

"Yes."

"Might I ask what the plan is then?"

"To relieve the scoundrels of their money, of course."

"Any chance that these scoundrels might find us out?"

"My dear friend, they already have. They just don't know how we're doing it hence their quartermaster excuse to leave, so that they can discuss it."

"Does this not concern you?"

"It does indeed. That's why we will lose the next hand, and the ones after, until we've lost half of our winnings. Then we'll call it a night, a good take for us, leaving them perplexed, but not absolutely defeated."

5

High Seas Robbery

The night before the *City of Richmond* arrived in America, the otherwise uneventful passage erupted into sudden mayhem!

Tesla was ripped from his sleep by a deafening thud, followed by a bang that seemed to shake the ship's very core! The hallway erupted into terror - men shouting, women screaming in piercing tones, children wailing. Tesla bolted to the door, heart thundering in his chest.

The sight that met him was pure chaos. A hulk of a crew member, wild-eyed and spittle flying from his lips, swung an oversized wrench at Tesla like a madman.

It barely missed Tesla's head. The impact against the metal door sent flying sparks and a vibration through Tesla. He slammed the door shut, the lock clicking with desperate urgency.

The crewman pounded on the door, his blows rattling the thin metal. Tesla's frantic gaze swept the room. Nothing, no weapon, no way to defend himself.

His precious bag lay open on the floor. He grabbed it, shoving his bulky leather notebook, the culmination of years of work, into a desk drawer.

The door could hold no longer and burst open. Three crewmen, weathered faces twisted into masks of greed, swarmed inside.

The first man lunged, fingers like steel claws closing around Tesla's throat. He slammed Tesla against the wall and lifted him off his feet, his breath rasping.

"Don't like your fancy face," the man growled, drops of slimy saliva landing on Tesla's cheek.

His accomplices ransacked the cabin. An exultant whoop cut through the air as one triumphantly pulled out a thick wad of American bills before the other checked the desk drawer. "Got it!" he crowed.

The third man, a sneer marring his features, left the desk unsearched and gave the contents of Tesla's bag a final look. Unsatisfied with the remaining contents of the bag, he gave it a contemptuous kick. "Worthless trash. Let's get outta here."

A sliver of hope flickered in Tesla's chest as they turned to leave. But it died as the ringleader, his eyes still burning with malice, released his grip, letting Tesla drop to the floor with a choking gasp.

"I really don't like your face," the man muttered, pulling a steak knife from his belt. He moved with predatory grace, raising the blade for the killing strike.

As the knife began its descent, a blur of motion materialized behind the crewman - Adler, his face a mask of fury! His first slammed into the man's jaw with a sickening crack, sending him sprawling.

Before the fallen man could react, Adler rained down repeated blows, a whirlwind of righteous violence. Tesla scrambled up, his breath ragged, eyes locked on the brutal scene.

With a final, bone-jarring strike, the crewman slumped to the floor, blood flowing from his mouth. He was unconscious or dead. Adler stood amidst the chaos, bloodied but unyielding.

"Are you alright?" he wheezed, chasing his breath.

Tesla could only nod. In all his years, he had never witnessed such brutal violence. Despite his boxing training, he found himself ill-equipped to handle these critical moments of life and death. If Adler had not arrived when he did, Tesla would be dead.

"It was him or you," Adler said grimly. "Trust me, this was the better option."

Tesla began to speak, to ask, but his voice failed him.

"Don't worry," Adler said, a grim smile playing on his lips. "It's a shakedown by some of the crew. Saw a few of these thugs hitting the other rooms. You weren't the only target. It had nothing to do with our friends in the boiler room."

"These men..." Tesla whispered, his voice finally returned. "They must be stopped!"

"You think, dear man?" Adler smirked at the unconscious man on the floor. "But first..." He reached out and grabbed the steak knife from the floor. "Let's make sure our friend here stays friendly when he wakes up. I need something to tie him up."

"If he wakes up," Tesla responded pessimistically, removing his belt and giving it to Adler.

"He'll wake up and be none too pleased, I'm certain."

Adler kneeled down and secured the man's hands, searched his pockets, and found nothing.

A sharp bang abruptly shattered the air. A gunshot. Then another. And another! The ship was under rapid gunfire.

"Well," Adler said cheerfully, "seems like the ship's security finally woke up and brought their guns to this knife fight!"

He clutched the knife with a firm grip as he strode towards the sound of the continued gunfire. "This just got a whole lot more interesting! I think we may get out of this unscathed yet, my dear friend."

Adler turned back and surveyed the battered cabin. "Did they take all your money?"

Tesla nodded mutely and then remembered his most precious possession. He ripped open the desk drawer and pulled out his leather notebook. A flicker of relief crossed his face.

"What's that?" Adler asked, his curiosity piqued by Tesla's fierce protectiveness.

Tesla's voice, just above a whisper, rasped in the tense silence. "My... my research."

He held the journal to his chest like a lifeline. His eyes, wide and haunted, finally met Adler's. "It's everything I've worked for. Years..."

A flicker of understanding crossed Adler's face. "Don't worry." His voice was rough but reassuring. "You hear that? No more gunfire. I think it's over."

A sudden eerie silence befell the ship.

"Now, let's see about getting your money back, because this beast doesn't have it," Adler said with a smile, while Tesla still could not collect himself.

6

AMERICA

New York City — June 6, 1884

Despite the fog and distance, the New York skyline emerged in the hazy afternoon. A cheer rose from the shell-shocked and weary passengers gathering on the *City of Richmond* deck as they took in their first sight of the New World.

Tesla and Adler joined them. Adler's brimming excitement was in sharp contrast with Tesla's cool and mild persona.

Adler nudged Tesla, hoping to at least elicit a smile from his friend. "Here we are, we made it! You will stay in touch, yes?"

"Of course," said Tesla, his gaze fixed on the city skyline.

Adler chuckled, "My dear Tesla, your lack of excitement is curious."

"I am excited," Tesla replied dryly, breaking his gaze from the skyline. "Mostly to be alive."

"Hate to see your dreary look then." Adler burst out laughing and Tesla responded with the slightest of smiles. He turned out his pants pocket and pulled out all the money in it — precisely four pennies.

"I had hoped to arrive here with a little more money," he said with a rueful chuckle.

Adler frowned. "Where are you staying?"

"Liberty Hotel."

Adler nodded, reached into his pocket, and pulled out a wad of neatly folded bills, which he handed to Tesla.

Tesla had not expected this. "Why?" he asked.

"It will take weeks to get your money back from the ship. There's three hundred dollars there. That should help until then."

Tesla was speechless. But the grateful expression in his eyes was more eloquent than any verbalized 'thank you' that Adler might have expected.

The two men eventually said goodbye, disembarked the ship, and parted ways.

After going through his customs interview, Tesla carefully made his way to his hotel. The sights and sounds of New York City assaulted him, but not totally in an unpleasant way.

The streets were a chaotic mix of dirt and noise, with people rushing past in a determined manner. The air was filled with enticing aromas, ranging from exotic spices to the pungent scent of horse manure. Yet there was excitement, an energy to it all.

Here and there, as Tesla walked, he spotted green parks scattered among the tall, soulless buildings. Tesla concluded this was a city of life and vibrancy. A man could think and work here.

But not yet. He was too weary to do anything but check into his lodgings. The Liberty Hotel proved another culture shock for him. He approached the front desk, quickly filled out the paperwork and headed off, already envisioning in his mind a welcoming, comfortable bed.

Tesla put his key in the lock, entered and stood for a moment surveying his shabby dollar-a-day room with rickety furniture, a three-legged bed, and cracks in the wall. The odd cockroach might have completed the look but for now, Tesla was thankful there were none. These creatures were, after all, nocturnal crawlers, and the day was still young.

He set his belongings down and carefully positioned himself on the bed for a much-needed rest. At least there were no hoodlums here to potentially attack him.

The feeling of isolation weighed down on him, intensifying his sense of loneliness. Being accustomed to solitude, he thrived in working alone, finding solace in the silence and freedom to concentrate without distractions. But right now, his solitude offered no solace to him.

Under his breath, he whispered "Anya?", closed his eyes and let his mind take him back to Anya in Paris.

∞

Paris, France — May 16, 1880

Tesla escorted Anya to one of the better restaurants in the city, Le Petit Jardin, where gaslight chandeliers cast dancing shadows across the tables.

The waiter presented their first course with a flourish – a delicate *consommé aux truffes*. This was followed by the main course, a masterfully prepared *Canard à l'Orange*. Tesla cut into the duck with surgical precision, admiring how the knife conducted a slight static charge through the crispy skin. The meat practically dissolved on his tongue, releasing waves of flavor he experienced as distinct pulses of sensation — first the rich gaminess of the duck, then the bright citrus notes, followed by subtle undertones of lavender and thyme.

"Remarkable," he mused, dabbing his mustache with a pristine napkin. "The French have elevated cooking to an exact science. Notice how the sauce's acidity is calibrated precisely to balance the duck's richness – much like opposing electrical currents achieving perfect equilibrium."

"Only you, Nikola," Anya laughed musically, "could find electrical theory in a plate of duck."

"But isn't it wonderful?" His eyes lit up with their characteristic intensity. "Everything in our world is connected by invisible forces. Even this meal – these flavors dancing on our tongues – they're really just different frequencies of energy, manifesting as sensation."

The waiter appeared with a bottle of Château Lafite Rothschild 1875. They sipped the fine wine in concert with their exquisite meal, their conversation flowed effortlessly, touching on everything from philosophy to art to Tesla's latest inventions.

Anya rested her chin on her hand, watching him with evident affection. "I don't know anyone else who experiences the world quite the way you do, Nikola."

"Perhaps that is my blessing and my curse," he replied. "To see patterns and connections where others see only dinner. Though I must admit this particular dinner is enhanced considerably by the company." He smiled happily at her.

The evening concluded with a flawless *crème brûlée*, its caramelized top crackling under Tesla's spoon, reminiscent of miniature lightning. He savored each bite, appreciating the perfect balance of sweetness and richness, as he seldom could afford to indulge in such pleasures.

As the night wore on, a tension began to build between them. Their eyes met over the rim of wine glasses, lingering touches became more frequent, and their words took on double meanings.

After dinner, they strolled along the Seine. The gentle lapping of the river against its banks provided a soothing backdrop to their quiet conversation.

Finally, they arrived at Anya's apartment. Tesla's heart pounded as she turned to him, her eyes shining in the moonlight.

"Would you like to come in, Nikola?"

Tesla nodded, not trusting himself to speak. As they entered her small but cozy apartment, his eyes were immediately drawn to a beautiful piano in the corner of the living room.

"Do you play?" he asked, running his fingers lightly over the keys.

Anya smiled enigmatically. "I do. Perhaps I'll play for you someday. But tonight, I have something else in mind."

She eliminated the space between them as she stepped closer. Tesla's breath caught in his throat as Anya's hand came up to cup his cheek. As they gazed into each other's eyes, time seemed to stand still, with unspoken desire making the air thick.

"Anya," Tesla murmured, his voice rough with emotion. "I... I-"

Anya interrupted him, "Me too," and then kissed him long.

Tesla felt as though electricity was coursing through his veins. Anya reached out and took his hand. Intrigued by her boldness, Tesla allowed himself to be led down the dimly lit hallway, the sound of their footsteps muffled by the plush carpet beneath their feet.

They entered her bedroom, a sanctuary bathed in soft, golden light. The room came alive, as if it had been waiting for them. With eagerness and anticipation, Anya slowly shed her clothes, as did Tesla. They finally stood before each other completely exposed, both physically and emotionally.

The air crackled with a sweet tingle of electricity as they tumbled onto the bed, their bodies intertwined in a passionate embrace. The outside world ceased to exist; time no longer held any meaning.

Anya's hand reached out, her fingers entwining with Tesla's as they continued their exploration of one another. Their lips met in a fervent kiss, their tongues dancing with an intensity that expressed the depths of their unspoken need. Fleeting moments of hesitation passed as they locked eyes.

"Is this truly what you desire?" Anya whispered, her voice laced with a mix of vulnerability and urgency.

"More than anything," Tesla replied, his voice hoarse.

Unable to hold back any longer, he pressed himself against her, moaning with glee. They climaxed quickly, followed by a moment of repose before their longing for each other rekindled. His hand found its way back to her, as did hers to him; and their ceaseless passion consumed the night.

Eventually, Anya succumbed to a contented, exhausted slumber. Tesla watched her sleep, contemplating the profound effect she had on him. No woman before had evoked such a strong emotional and primal response from him. He hardly recognized himself, a man driven by passion, discarding all reason.

Throughout the years, Tesla had his share of encounters and intrigue with the opposite sex. He refused to visit brothels due to his phobia of germs and the fear of catching disease. Instead, chance encounters at parks or restaurants would occasionally blossom into short-lived passionate affairs.

He would sometimes spend afternoons courting pretty blondes on park benches, pretending to ponder scientific problems while stealing glances their way. Or have playful exchanges with waitresses as he dined alone, always drawn to the fair-haired ones. But these were mere flirtations, casual affairs devoid of deeper intimacy or connection.

Even back in his college days, he went through a wild period where his escapades with women got him into trouble at school. Word got back to some of his cousins, who were sending him money to support his higher education. Tesla was basically kicked out of one college for being an excessive "womanizer" and a compulsive gambler, with the result that his disillusioned cousins cut off their funding. Between both pursuits, Tesla was unprepared for his final course exams and faced further humiliation at his parents' disappointment with his behavior.

Thankfully, his parents reconsidered and renewed their support. He was subsequently given another chance at a new college, but for all his intrigue with women, Tesla finally understood that his greatest romance was with his work. Science consumed him, a mistress demanding total devotion. He was not one for a conventional domestic life. His brilliant and eccentric mind would not allow it.

No, he could never truly lose himself to a wife and family — his calling was to better humanity through technological progress.

Until Anya. Looking at her now, he felt the undeniable spark he had long thought impossible. This went beyond mere physical attraction. But it was the meeting of their minds that stirred his soul. Here was a woman who understood him, challenged him, stoked his passion to achieve the impossible.

For the first time, Tesla sensed his meticulously calculated life was about to be derailed by forces beyond his control.

∞

Paris, France — 1881-1883

The months passed. Tesla and Anya continued their relationship, spending time together as Tesla's busy schedule allowed. He loved living in Paris which for him, was indeed the city of love.

"I never can forget the deep impression that magic city produced on my mind," he later wrote. "Every morning, regardless of weather, I would go from the Boulevard St. Marcel, where I resided, to a bathing house on the Seine, plunge into the water, loop the circuit twenty-seven times and then walk an hour to reach Ivry, where the Company's factory was located."

At night after work, his habit had been to play billiards with his co-workers. That activity was often put aside for him to spend time with Anya. A free spirit, she insisted on maintaining her own residence, to which Tesla agreed for propriety's sake.

Tesla worked diligently for Edison's French affiliate company that first year. One of his projects was to work on the lighting at the Paris Opera House. Later, he was sent out to oversee electric and lighting problems in Bavaria and Berlin. Meanwhile, back in Paris, Anya began to make a name for herself, particularly as a portrait artist.

Their relationship was put to the test when Tesla was asked, in early 1883, to travel to Strasburg. It was their first lengthy separation and as Tesla wrote, "There is some trouble with the lighting plant which has been installed at the new railroad station in Strasburg, Alsace. The wiring is defective and on the occasion of the opening ceremonies, a large part of a wall was blown out thru (sic) a short-circuit right in the presence of old Emperor William I. On account of my knowledge of the German language and past experience, I have been entrusted with the difficult task of straightening out matters."

Tesla stayed in Strasburg for a full year. By the time he returned to Paris in March 1884, he determined that while he had a good job, working for Edison Continental did not have the advancement opportunities he craved. Also, he sensed his employers did not appreciate or fully understand his genius, and that he should forge ahead with his own inventions rather than always fixing the problems of others. He decided his future success might lie in the United States, a country that welcomed inventors and new ideas.

And so one night, he decided the time was right to discuss such a move with Anya.

The moonlight streaming through the window created a romantic ambiance. They had returned to Anya's place from a dinner out, celebrating her landing of a wealthy new client who commissioned a portrait from her.

Anya, who was a bit giddy from happiness and too much wine, sat at her piano, playing and singing for Tesla a song she had written.

Upon finishing, she jumped up, grabbed him and whirled him around, attempting to get him to dance with her. They laughed at his clumsy footwork and then shared a long kiss.

Tesla stopped dancing and, holding both her shoulders, looked at her with all seriousness. "Have I told you today how much I love you?" He took her hand and spoke nervously. "Anya, I am clumsy with words and perhaps a difficult man to live with. But you bring me such joy, such happiness. Can it be too much to hope that you feel the same for me?"

"You know I do," she replied.

He sighed in relief and mustered the courage to continue. "I cannot envision my life without you. Will you... will you do me the honor of marrying me?"

She hesitated and then softly answered him.

"Niko, I must remain in Paris, the art world is here. And you are moving to New York. How would it work?"

He had prepared himself for rejection, fearing he was unworthy of her. But he couldn't seem to help himself, he blurted out: "Don't you love me?"

"Yes, dear. But I have goals too. To have one of my paintings hang in the Louvre, which would be the ultimate honor. Please grant me a little time to at least try."

"Is it not enough to be my wife?"

What she answered next he knew to be true, but it didn't help the pain stabbing into his stomach and heart.

"You are married to your work. That is far more important to the world. And whether you work here or in America, you will constantly be traveling, as we have already seen this past year. Such separations are not healthy for a marriage. I am a distraction to you, Niko. That is not right."

He pulled away from her, hurt and disappointed.

"Then I shall never marry, because I could never love another as I love you."

They both stood motionless and silent for a moment. Then Tesla grabbed his coat and hat and headed toward the door.

Anya stopped him. "We can still be friends. You'll write to me about your successes, and I'll write back to you. And if you ever return to Paris—"

Without saying another word, Tesla opened the door and disappeared into the cold, dark night.

∞

Tesla and Anya did not see each other again, not even when Tesla departed for England. On that day, his heart broke and he feared he could never truly recover. The sting of rejection gnawed at him as he finalized his passage from Paris to Calais. The booking confirmation felt like a nail driven into his wounded heart.

As the train prepared to depart to Calais, Tesla found himself not in the comfort of his seat, but standing in the car hallway, his eyes locked on the shrinking platform. A flicker of desperate hope ignited within him — perhaps Anya would come rushing toward the train, breathless and apologetic, ready to embark on this adventure by his side. But the platform remained desolate, a mirror of his own despair.

He lit a cigarette, the harsh smoke doing little to soothe his raw nerves. Each inhale was a desperate grasp for composure, each exhale a silent plea for the pain to subside.

The train's whistle pierced the air and with a lurch, the train began its journey, carrying Tesla away from a life with Anya. He collapsed onto his seat, the weight of his grief threatening to crush him.

Though he prided himself on his usual unwavering resolve, on his ability to channel emotions into intellectual pursuits, the memory of Anya's rejection left him feeling raw and exposed.

A stray tear escaped and Tesla hastily brushed it away, disgusted by this display of vulnerability. He was a man of logic, of reason, not a weeping child clinging to shattered dreams.

Yet as the train rattled on, the tears continued to flow. The man who would one day harness the power of electricity now found himself powerless against the surge of his own heartache.

∞

Liberty Hotel, New York City — June 6, 1884

Tesla was suddenly jolted awake after a short sleep by a loud knock on the door. He was back at the Liberty Hotel; it was still his first day in America.

He opened the door and was met by one of Edison's engineers who rambled on about an urgent matter that required immediate attention. Apparently Edison sent the engineer to summon Tesla for help with repairing two high powered Dynamo engines on the ship SS *Oregon* – and this without even having a proper night's sleep or even formally meeting his new boss, Thomas Alva Edison! The Dynamos weren't working, and the ship was late in starting its next trip across the Atlantic.

Tesla agreed to oversee the crisis handling. He eagerly left with a team for the ship, and they worked through the night to ensure the *Oregon* was operational again. It was nearly 5 a.m. when Tesla and his helpers returned to Edison's Machine Works. As he walked through the business hallway, Tesla passed Thomas Edison but the two men didn't speak.

Actually, Tesla called out to Edison that he had successfully repaired the Dynamos, but Edison ignored him. This puzzled Tesla but he was heartened when his official job interview was scheduled for later that day.

He returned to the hotel to clean up, rest, eat and change into more appropriate attire for his meeting with the great inventor.

7

THOMAS EDISON

New York City — June 7, 1884

Tesla arrived for his interview, looking dapper and refreshed. But once waiting in Edison's office reception area, his confidence wavered. He clutched his worn briefcase, while his gaze darted towards the imposing double doors leading to Edison's office.

After an eternity, the doors swung open, revealing an older man who was Edison's assistant. Albert, in his crisp suit and ramrod posture, stood sentinel.

"Mr. Tesla, I presume?" His voice held a hint of formality. "I am Albert, Mr. Edison's assistant."

"A pleasure to meet you, Albert," Tesla replied with a faint smile.

"Mr. Edison will see you momentarily. Would you care to sit?"

"I prefer to stand but thank you."

Albert nodded, taking up his position beside the doors once more, his eyes fixed on a distant point.

Tesla, left alone with his thoughts, heard the faint hum of machinery echoing from somewhere within the laboratory. Suddenly, Edison's voice boomed. "Send him in, Albert!"

Tesla's heart pounded as he entered Edison's office. Albert closed the doors softly behind him, shutting out the rest of the world.

Edison sat behind a massive, ornate desk, his back to Tesla. He fixed his gaze on the window, where men could be seen busily assembling a tall wooden structure in the distance.

"My name is Nikola–" Tesla began.

"Yes, yes, Tesla, from Paris. You're our Parisian," Edison interrupted, a hint of amusement in his voice. "Got the telegram from France. Darn good day for making money, Tesla." He paused. "I understand you have a letter for me?"

"Yes sir, I do."

"Well, let's have it." Edison's back was still turned to Tesla. He extended his hand. Tesla handed it to him, feeling a strange mix of anticipation and trepidation.

Edison tore open the letter and scanned its contents, still not facing Tesla, and then he spun around in his chair, his piercing eyes locking on Tesla.

Tesla stood firm, a mask of composure hiding the panic inside him. His heart pounded; his throat choked. Never had he felt so overwhelmed by another.

Edison was a tall man, definitely a few inches shorter than Tesla but still an imposing presence with a heavier build, handsome features, and a shock of wavy hair already streaked with white. His authoritative, booming voice was intimidating.

Tesla feared it meant the great man's immediate disapproval of him. Tesla did not know Edison was deaf in one ear and nearly deaf in the other, thus his loud speaking voice. This was not common knowledge, and Edison went to great lengths to keep this handicap quiet.

Edison finished reading the letter. "Is any of this true?" he asked, a slight smirk on his lips.

"I should hope so, but I don't know what it says," Tesla replied honestly.

"Are you always this serious, Tesla?" asked Edison.

"I don't understand, sir."

"You lack a sense of humor!"

"It's not a trait I possess," Tesla admitted.

"All the way from France, and you didn't sneak a peek at the letter?"

"It was sealed, sir."

Edison chuckled. "Hmmm. It says here you're a man who can do the impossible. Can you walk on water?"

"I believe it could be possible to hover above water if not walk on it, sir."

Edison studied Tesla for a long moment. "Well, then, I want you to start working on that."

"Yes, sir," Tesla answered with a nervous smile.

His reply took Edison aback. "You're serious?"

"Yes, of course."

Edison stood abruptly, extending his hand. Tesla hesitated then accepted the handshake.

"You don't like shaking hands?" Edison had a touch of sarcasm in his voice.

"I have a certain... shall we say difficulty with that, sir."

Edison arched an eyebrow. "You have a lot to prove. Our manager in Paris thinks you're a genius."

"I do intend to prove it, sir," Tesla replied with quiet determination.

"Good. Your salary is eighteen dollars a week. Tomorrow, you start work on a problem I have. If you solve this problem, I'll give you a $50,000 bonus on top of your regular wages."

"That's quite generous, sir."

"Yes... well, it's a big problem."

"I shall endeavor to solve it."

"Right then, tomorrow you start. Eight o'clock sharp."

"Very good, sir," Tesla replied with a slight smile.

∞

Tesla arrived at work on time the next morning as instructed and began working right away. The date was June 8th, and it was only two days since he had arrived in New York City.

It took some time before Tesla felt fully recovered from his harrowing trip. A few decent nights of sleep, albeit on that uncomfortable bed, helped clear his mind.

In his free time, he ventured out of the hotel to walk the area and discover cheap restaurants and food stands offering fresh fruits and authentic, homestyle cooking, a tasty melting pot of the cultures that comprised New York City.

Tesla was a fussy eater and liked simple foods. Chicken soup was a favorite and so he made it his adventure to sample various affordable, hearty chicken soups found in his neighborhood.

The relentless pulse of New York City energized Tesla. He marveled at how quickly he adapted to this brash new world, a stark contrast to the quiet elegance of Paris.

As his schedule allowed, Tesla frequently strolled through Central Park, a sprawling oasis amidst the urban jungle. It was there he discovered the city's pigeon population.

He observed them with the meticulous eye of a scientist, noting their distinctive cooing, their intricate courtship rituals, and their remarkable ability to navigate in the city. Tesla's fascination soon blossomed into an obsession. In time he would come to spend many hours feeding the pigeons, scattering handfuls of seed with a childlike glee, marveling at their trust, their willingness to perch on his outstretched hand. He found solace in their gentle cooing, a soothing balm for his weary soul. Their unwavering loyalty and spirit spoke to him on a profound level, both as a source of comfort and inspiration, and a reminder of the importance of perseverance in the face of adversity.

But for now, he simply reveled in the simple joy of their company, finding a kindred spirit in these feathered inhabitants of the urban jungle.

∞

New York City — June 30, 1884

During his initial weeks at Edison Machine Works, Tesla worked diligently and tirelessly on his various projects.

Today an air of anticipation hung heavy in Edison's office as Albert, his posture as rigid as ever, entered and announced:

"Excuse me, sir, but Mr. Tesla insists on seeing you right away."

Edison, sitting at his desk, reacted with surprise. He was mid a business meeting with Robert Underwood Johnson and his wife Katharine. Johnson was an important figure in the New York City social world, an influential author, poet, and editor of a popular national magazine. For Edison, friendship with a positive member of the press was important in keeping the public updated on his latest inventions and news.

Johnson looked older than his years but his wife Katharine was strikingly attractive and curvaceous. Yet she was much more than a pretty face or eye candy. She had a high intellect and played an active role in her husband's life and work.

Edison glanced at Robert and Katharine. "He's back already? That project should have kept him occupied for months."

Johnson shrugged and looked expectantly toward the door.

Tesla entered, paid no mind to the Johnsons, and landed his eyes on Edison. But before he could say anything a melodious voice interjected.

"It's a pleasure to meet you, Mr. Tesla."

Tesla turned, and this time focused on Katharine Johnson. Her beauty was delicate. It radiated intelligence and wit.

Tesla experienced a fleeting moment of stillness in time, as if he had been momentarily winded. It was the first time he'd felt a stirring within himself since leaving Anya and for the moment, all thoughts of Anya flew out of his mind.

"The pleasure is entirely mine, Miss—"

"Mrs. Johnson," she corrected, a hint of a smile on her lips. "And this is my husband, Robert." She gestured elegantly to her husband.

"Robert is the editor of *The Century* magazine," Edison interrupted, a touch of pride in his voice.

Tesla tore his gaze from Katharine to acknowledge Robert. "Yes, a fine publication. I've enjoyed many of your articles, Mr. Johnson."

Robert nodded graciously, but Tesla's eyes were already drawn back to Katharine. "If I may, what is your given name, Mrs. Johnson?"

"Katharine."

"Katharine," Tesla repeated softly, savoring the word. "A lovely name for a beautiful woman."

Katharine's cheeks warmed. "Why, thank you, Mr. Tesla."

He finally looked away, meeting Robert's eyes with a touch of humor. "You are a fortunate man indeed, Mr. Johnson."

"That I am," Robert agreed, smiling.

Katharine cleared her throat, a subtle reminder of her presence. "Are you married, Mr. Tesla?"

"No." A flicker of regret crossed his face. "Sadly, I haven't been so fortunate."

Edison shifted in his seat, impatient. "Enough pleasantries, Tesla. Why are you here? Did the project prove too much for you?"

"On the contrary," Tesla replied with a spark of defiance in his eyes. "I solved it this morning." He opened his worn portfolio and pulled out a diagram. His gaze lingered on Katharine for a moment before returning to Edison.

"I doubt it!" Edison scoffed, eyeing Tesla's diagram.

Before Tesla could respond, Katharine interjected. "When you gentlemen have finished your business, Robert and I would be delighted if you would join us for dinner tonight, Mr. Tesla."

Robert looked surprised, as did Edison, but Tesla's face lit up. "I would be honored, Mrs. Johnson."

8

THE JOHNSONS

New York City — June 30, 1884

Later that evening, Tesla dressed in his best clothes, prepared to indulge in a delicious meal at the home of Robert and Katharine Johnson.

The Johnson's dining room, though built to host lavish banquets, felt intimate under the warm glow of the crystal chandelier. Robert and Katharine sat opposite each other at the long mahogany table, while Tesla occupied the seat at the head, subtly acknowledging his guest-of-honor status.

Robert cleared his throat. "Mr. Tesla, I'm fascinated by the reports of the Zephyr Avion. Do you believe the claims of a successful hundred-meter flight near Paris?"

Tesla leaned forward, intrigued. "Absolutely! In fact, I have been working on my own design for a flying machine for some time now."

"Well then, you must share with us the details," said Robert, excited.

"Indeed I shall when there are worthy details to share."

"Splendid! Katharine and I will look forward to it."

"Yes, very much so," Katharine confirmed.

Tesla beamed with a smile. "One day, man will soar not hundreds, but thousands of meters into the air. Even space is within our reach."

"Space travel?" Robert burst out laughing. "Now, that seems a tad ambitious."

"Not at all. The boundary of space is a mere sixty-two miles above us. Hot air balloons have breached the threshold. The true challenge lies not in conquering distance, but in surviving the thin, frigid atmosphere."

Katharine's eyes widened. "What purpose would man have in the vast emptiness of space?"

Tesla smiled at her. "The same purpose he has always had, Mrs. Johnson — to explore, to claim, to conquer."

A maid entered wearing neatly pinned hair and a starched apron, carrying a bottle of ruby-red wine. She poured each of them a glass, her movements practiced and unobtrusive.

Robert took a sip of his wine. "Speaking of innovators, Mr. Tesla, have you had the pleasure of meeting Henry Ford?"

"Our paths have not crossed," Tesla replied.

"A pity," Robert mused. "Mr. Ford serves as the chief engineer to Mr. Edison. Quite a visionary young man."

At that moment another servant, dressed in a neatly pressed black suit, arrived with a platter containing a tempting array of roasted meats and glazed vegetables. Katharine gestured for Tesla to serve himself first.

"We hosted Mr. Ford recently," Robert continued, "and his talk of carriages powered without horses piqued our interest. He has grand ideas about this German, Karl Benz, and his petroleum-fueled motor."

Tesla paused mid-bite, his brow furrowed. "Benz's design is ingenious but risky. Petroleum is far too volatile for widespread use."

"Henry argued the same about steam," Robert countered. "He believes in the potential to mass-produce these petroleum carriages."

"Mass production and petroleum seem like a recipe for disaster," Tesla scoffed. "Now, if he considered electricity — that's where the true potential lies."

Robert grinned. "You're speaking of fueling these carriages with lightning? Edison himself is struggling to keep his light bulbs from shattering."

"That, my dear Robert," Tesla declared, leaning back in his chair with an air of confidence, "is the fault of Edison's insistence on direct current. The bulbs themselves are not the problem. The direct current is. Alternating current, however, is the key to solving that problem and much more."

"Have you discussed this with Edison? " asked Robert.

"Not yet," replied Tesla. "But I plan to do so."

"Nikola, could you please elaborate on the distinction between these two currents?" asked Katharine.

Tesla smiled with excitement. "Of course. Direct current, as you know, flows in a single direction, much like a river. It is a reliable and steady source of power, but it has its limitations. It cannot be easily transmitted over long distances without significant loss of energy."

He paused, letting the weight of his words sink in.

"Alternating current, on the other hand, is a dynamic and versatile form of electricity. It oscillates rapidly, reversing direction multiple times per second.

"This allows it to be stepped up to very high voltages for efficient transmission over vast distances, and then stepped down to lower voltages for safe use in homes and businesses."

Tesla gazed into Katharine's eyes, as if probing to confirm that she understood his explanation.

She did; a quick glance at Robert confirmed the same, and then Tesla continued. "It is like a river that not only flows downstream, but also upstream, carrying energy back and forth with incredible efficiency, something that direct current cannot do."

His voice now filled with passion. "Imagine a world where electricity is plentiful and reasonably priced, where every residence and commercial establishment is illuminated with a radiance akin to that of a thousand suns. Imagine a world where machines are powered by invisible forces, where distance is no longer a barrier for communication and transportation."

Katharine's eyes darted towards Robert. "Perhaps," she said excitedly, "we should introduce Mr. Ford and Nikola. They are kindred spirits, each driven by a relentless pursuit of innovation."

Robert stroked his chin thoughtfully. "Indeed. It's curious that Edison hasn't done so himself."

"Perhaps Thomas sees the value in secrecy," Katharine remarked. "Though with someone of Mr. Tesla's brilliance, it might prove difficult."

The Johnson's dining room pulsed with continued conversation, the once subdued ambiance replaced by crackling energy courtesy of Tesla's bold pronouncements. Tesla's undeniable charm, while he basked in the limelight, captivated Robert and Katharine.

Robert ran a finger around the rim of his wineglass. "Mr. Tesla, you certainly don't lack ambition. Space travel, though?"

"The only limitation is our imagination," Tesla countered. "You recall those childhood nights spent gazing at the stars, Robert? Someday, we'll walk amongst them." He gestured towards the ceiling as though he could see a shimmering starry night sky just beyond the plaster.

"Now, now, Tesla," Robert chuckled, "let's not get ahead of ourselves. Right now, it's automobiles that capture the world's attention."

The maid, with her quiet efficiency, refilled Robert's wine glass. He thanked her with a distracted nod while Tesla seized the opportunity.

"Automobiles! Yes, Mr. Ford has the makings of a fine mechanical mind, but that petroleum of his..." Tesla made a dismissive gesture. "Mark my words, gasoline is the fuel of accidents waiting to happen."

"Mr. Tesla, you certainly don't mince words!" exclaimed Katharine. "What does our esteemed friend Mr. Edison have to say about this electric future you envision?"

Tesla paused, as if considering the full weight of his next statement.

"Let's just say, Mrs. Johnson, that Mr. Edison and I see power from very different perspectives. His fondness for direct current is, shall we say, a significant obstacle to progress."

The second servant placed a steaming plate of roasted lamb before Tesla. The savory aroma filled the air, momentarily easing an impending philosophical debate about to explode.

Robert, ever the voice of reason, interjected. "Tesla, with all due respect, Edison is a titan of innovation. It seems unwise to dismiss him so readily."

"And yet, titans can be blinded by their own light," Tesla retorted. "While Mr. Edison toils endlessly to illuminate rooms, I see the potential to illuminate minds, to move people at speeds they never imagined. To change the world." He sliced a generous piece of the lamb, the gesture mirroring the boldness of his words.

Katharine leaned in, captivated. "Thomas rarely speaks of his work. Mr. Tesla, your enthusiasm is... infectious. What other wonders are hidden within that brilliant mind of yours?"

Robert coughed, shifting uncomfortably in his chair. "Indeed, perhaps we could steer the conversation towards literature? I understand you admire *The Century*, Mr. Tesla. Perhaps you've encountered some of Mark Twain's work? Or rather, Samuel Clemens, his real name."

Tesla's focus wavered momentarily. "Years ago, I read *Tom Sawyer* and in fact it was the book that in part saved my life." Tesla's eyes darted between Katharine and Robert.

"Oh heavens, what happened?" asked Katharine.

"I had taken ill and lost my will to fight, but then I read that wonderful work and the fight in me returned."

"Thank goodness for Sam Clemens," Katharine replied.

"Do you know him?" Tesla asked with a sudden burst of excitement.

"Yes, of course," Robert replied. "I can arrange an introduction if you'd like."

Tesla nodded with a smile and then fixed his gaze on Katharine. "Mrs. Johnson, I'd wager your taste in literature is impeccable. A single recommendation to open those hidden worlds..."

He finished the last of his wine, and without his asking, his wineglass was refilled. He took a new sip, savoring its rich flavor and feeling his inhibitions relax under its influence. He locked eyes with Katharine, and she blushed ever so slightly.

"Well then," she offered, "Perhaps we should start with something by Jane Austen."

Robert leaned back in his chair. "Indeed, Mr. Tesla. Katharine's opinion on all things literary is held in the highest regard."

Tesla's gaze did not leave Katharine's. "As it should be. A woman of such exquisite taste must possess a beautiful mind to match." He gestured vaguely toward Robert with his wine glass. "Perhaps Robert, you could tell me more about your work at *The Century* magazine..."

Taken aback by the sudden dismissal, Robert sputtered, "Er, ah yes, well, we've recently commissioned a piece by Walt Whitman, a fine American poet..."

Tesla returned his attention to Katharine, deliberately ignoring Robert. "Whitman, now there's a man after my own heart! 'Electric body' he calls it – the spark of life, a current running through all of us. Imagine, Mrs. Johnson, if we could harness that energy..."

The lofty ceilings and gleaming wood paneling seemed to shrink around them as the conversation shifted. Tesla's declaration about the 'beautiful mind' hung heavy, the air charged with unspoken desires.

The servants, usually models of unobtrusive efficiency, lingered too long. Even their practiced masks of neutrality could not quite hide their amusement at witnessing this unusual exchange.

Katharine, her cheeks flushed a captivating shade of pink, fanned herself subtly, her gaze flitting briefly to Robert and then returning to Tesla.

"Mr. Tesla," she murmured, "Your boldness is quite disarming."

"And should you be disarmed, Mrs. Johnson?" he countered, leaning forward.

Their exchange was a dance, a delicate testing of boundaries. Tesla reveled in it, in the way Katharine mirrored his audacity, her outward composure hinting at the fire simmering beneath.

Robert, a keen observer, shifted in his seat. A gentle, almost frown creased his brow, not a sign of jealousy, but a faint wariness born of witnessing his wife's undeniable captivation. Yet with the good manners of a refined gentleman, he merely cleared his throat and smiled softly.

"My dear Tesla, it appears I've unwittingly stepped aside and allowed two brilliant minds to converge." Robert gestured between them, a touch of wry humor in his eyes. He rose with practiced nonchalance, realizing his role had suddenly been reduced to that of a spectator. Though not overtly threatened, he had a lingering concern. "Do forgive my retreat to the quieter realms of my study."

Tesla bowed slightly. "My deepest apologies, Robert." He fixed his gaze on Katharine. "However, even the most rigorous scientific disciplines can be swayed by an irresistible force."

Robert forced a faint smile and quietly left the room. Katharine met Tesla's gaze and spoke with a teasing challenge.

"Indeed, Mr. Tesla?"

"Yes," he declared with great intensity, "and then the challenge becomes all the more exhilarating."

A charged undercurrent lingered beneath their thin layer of polite conversation. But with Robert's departure, a shift settled over the room, the playful energy of moments before dissipating slightly. Katharine pulled back, a flicker of self-consciousness replacing the boldness in her eyes.

She smoothed a stray lock of hair behind her ear, a gesture that betrayed a hint of nervousness.

"Perhaps, Mr. Tesla," she offered, her voice regaining its usual composure, "we should steer the conversation towards less... unconventional topics. Robert is a fan of scientific advancements, I'm sure he would enjoy hearing about your latest work."

There was a hint of apology in her eyes, a silent acknowledgement she had perhaps indulged too far in this flirtatious exchange. A flicker of disappointment crossed Tesla's face.

"Of course, Mrs. Johnson," he replied, inclining his head in a gesture of respect. "My work is a source of endless fascination, even if I often find myself too captivated by the marvels of other disciplines."

Katharine blushed faintly. "Charmers like you are a dangerous distraction. Best to keep our focus, wouldn't you agree?"

Tesla's tone took on a more formal note. "Absolutely, Mrs. Johnson. Though I must admit, some distractions are far more captivating than others."

He let his gaze flicker towards her briefly before shifting his attention to the window, as though contemplating the world outside.

"But you are right, discipline is of the utmost importance. Perhaps I could share some of my ideas on alternating current with you and Robert another time?"

"I would like that very much," Katharine said sincerely. "Though fair warning, I won't let my enchantment with your eloquence distract me from understanding the technicalities."

"I would not expect anything less," Tesla replied, a touch of admiration in his eyes.

Their conversation resumed, a comfortable mix of scientific discourse and lighthearted banter. But the undeniable spark between them lingered, a delicate thread of possibility amidst the strict constraints of their era.

9

WORKING FOR EDISON

New York City — September 8, 1884

Thomas Edison pushed the heavy workshop door open, its hinges creaking against the hum within. The smell of ozone and hot metal assaulted his nose. He wasn't a man for surprises, least of all the kind Tesla might cook up.

After three months, Edison had grown weary of the rumors, the hushed awe surrounding this eccentric Serbian. Today was his first visit to Tesla's working quarters.

It was not in Edison's nature to leave an important employee like Tesla unmonitored in his work. A contributing factor was that Edison's wife, Mary, had died just two weeks ago. She had battled typhoid fever for nearly a month, which left Edison understandably exhausted, grieving and not in the best humor.

Sawdust crunched under Edison's shoes as he moved further into the room. Tesla's workshop was a tempest frozen in time. Blueprints swirled on the floor like autumn leaves. Components littered every workbench, and amidst it all, the Dynamo — a skeletal behemoth, wires snaking like veins from its iron heart. Tesla himself was bent over a workbench, smoke curling from a forgotten lit cigarette pinched between his fingers. He was oblivious to his visitor.

"Since when are you a smoker, Tesla?" Edison's voice crackled through the room.

Tesla was startled, nearly dropping the delicate coil he was adjusting. "Mr. Edison!" Surprise gave way to a tight smile. "I didn't expect... I mean, a pleasant surprise."

Edison stepped closer, surveying the controlled chaos with a seasoned eye. "Should I have sent word ahead? Perhaps you'd have found a broom."

Tesla flushed, extinguishing his cigarette. "My apologies. I am... immersed in my work, as you can see."

"That much is clear," Edison scoffed, nudging a half-disassembled motor with his polished shoe. "I must confess, Tesla, I've come seeking proof. Your reputation—" He paused, deliberately letting the judgment linger in the air.

Tesla's spine stiffened as he addressed the ever-imposing Edison across the cluttered room.

"Proof, Mr. Edison? Of what, precisely? My dedication? Or perhaps my results on assigned work?"

"Much more can be done if you didn't waste so much time as you do on your blasted AC. What have you got to show for all the time you spend on it?" Edison's eyes pointed to the Dynamo. "This monstrosity?!" He let a harsh laugh erupt, the sound echoing off the high workshop walls. He ran a hand through his white-streaked hair. "I'll believe in alternating current when pigs sing soprano, Tesla."

Before Tesla could respond, Edison continued to berate him while pacing. "Light bulbs are where the profits lie, Tesla. What have you done to prevent them from bursting? That's the issue at hand."

Tesla defiantly folded his arms. "As I have pointed out many times before, Mr. Edison, the light bulbs themselves are not the problem. The culprit is the direct current running through them. If you continue to insist on using DC, progress will indeed be impeded."

Edison snorted, dismissing the argument with a wave of his hand. "DC is reliable, Tesla. Your AC is a dangerous fantasy. Why should I gamble my investments on a theory?"

"The same reason you gamble on any invention, Mr. Edison — to advance, to improve, to lead. AC can power cities, reduce waste, and save costs." Tesla argued passionately, his eyes alight with the vision of his electric future.

Edison stopped pacing and leaned in closer, his expression intense. "I pay you good money to get things done. Fix the problem with the dammed light bulbs! I want to see progress!"

Tesla abruptly stood up and stepped back from Edison. "Progress that crawls when it could soar!" he said, his voice rising and with the hint of his Serbian accent thickening. "Your DC is a... a lumbering ox, Mr. Edison, when it could be an eagle! I am closer than you think with AC, but your focus on immediate profits blinds you to the larger picture."

"AC is dangerous," Edison retorted. "Your bird will crash and burn, leaving cities in darkness! A smoking splattered eagle on the ground will not pay the investors!"

Edison coldly locked eyes with Tesla. A lingering moment passed without another word from either man until Tesla finally broke the silence.

"Very well," Tesla answered, all but defeated.

Edison gave a slight nod, his triumph complete, then turned and walked out of the workshop.

Tesla sank back into his rickety wooden chair, the worn leather groaning in protest. He lit a cigarette and savored the tang on his tongue then let out a long, slow exhale, the breath escaping him in a ragged sigh.

The encounter with Edison still crackled in the air. Tesla could feel the lingering heat of the older man's anger, the sting of his belittlement. He tried to appease his bitterness by reminding himself that Edison was grieving for his dead wife. *I should have tried to be more understanding, more compassionate,* he scolded himself, but it did little to ease the sour feeling in his stomach.

He acknowledged there was truth in Edison's words, a truth that gnawed at Tesla even as he fiercely defended his alternating current theories. He was a foreigner in a land that often seemed resistant to his outlandish ideas. He depended on Edison's patronage, his dreams fueled by the man's dollars.

But beneath the frustration, a spark of defiance flickered. Tesla knew he was not just some starry-eyed dreamer. He was not some fantastic inventor peddling snake oil. He had the backing of science, of mathematics, of the laws of physics themselves. What he envisioned for the future was constructing empires and revolutionizing cities with a brilliance far beyond Edison's comprehension.

As he sat there, eyes closed, he forced his thoughts away from today's disappointment and allowed his mind to wander to a more pleasurable place. A familiar warmth bloomed in his chest, a counterpoint to the lingering tension.

∞

A memory, a refuge he often sought in stressful times.

He was a child again, all of eight years old, back in Smiljan, a small village nestled in the foothills of the Austro-Hungarian Alps. Lightning cracked across the vast canvas of the night sky, illuminating the snow-capped peaks in a glow. Eyes brimming with boundless curiosity, he stood mesmerized, the raw power of the storm resonating deep within him.

He felt there was a reason behind his affinity for lightning because he was born during a fierce lightning storm.

As he grew up, he loved to hear his mother relate the story of his birth when, while she struggled with her final labor, the midwife wrung her hands and declared the lightning a bad omen. "This child will be a child of darkness," the woman unkindly predicted. Tesla's mother replied, "No, he will be a child of light."

Experiencing lightning was a feeling both terrifying and exhilarating for Tesla, a connection to something primal, something far grander than himself.

In those moments, the world seemed to hum with a hidden energy, a symphony of unseen forces. It was a language he innately understood, a language that resonated in the fabric of his being. And it was this connection that fueled his passion, his relentless pursuit of unlocking the secrets of electricity.

The memory, vivid and potent, washed over him, a soothing balm on his frayed nerves. He could almost feel the crisp mountain air on his face, smell the pine needles damp with rain. The anger, the frustration, the self-doubt; they all receded, replaced by a renewed sense of purpose.

Tesla heaved a huge sigh and opened his eyes. He was back in his workshop, working for Thomas Edison. He forced himself to look around the place, at all his equipment, blueprints, and everything else that made this current world so special to him.

Another deep breath and then mustering up new determination, Tesla reached for a half-completed diagram, his fingers tracing the intricate lines with renewed focus.

The workshop, no longer a cramped space, became his laboratory, his cathedral. He was no longer just Nikola Tesla, the foreigner, the dreamer. He was a conductor, a conduit, channeling the unseen forces of the universe into a tangible reality.

Edison's direct current was powering the city lights of New York for now, but Tesla knew with certainty that the future belonged to alternating current and to him.

∞

The next two months bled into each other, a blur of tinkering and sweat. Tesla meticulously improved the DC generators, but the fundamental flaw remained. Edison's precious light bulbs, fragile glass hearts fed by direct current, continued to burst in blinding flashes, mocking Edison's vision with each failure. Tesla's mind raced, searching for a solution that would not require a radical departure from Edison's entrenched system.

In his heart, Tesla had to admire Edison as a visionary, a trailblazing inventor of a wide range of amazing products. Even if his technical genius was not up to Tesla's abilities, Edison was a marketing genius.

Tesla tried to remember Edison's positive qualities rather than dwell on the negative. During these months, his contributions to Edison's other projects were undeniable successes. New machines sprang forth, more efficient, more powerful, bearing the unmistakable mark of Tesla's touch. Newspaper headlines praised Edison while Tesla remained the unseen genius in the background.

Perhaps it was inevitable but the tension grew, a slowly tightening wire between the visionary immigrant and the self-made American titan. For Tesla, it wasn't about being recognized. He yearned for the opportunity to unleash the true power of his ideas and reshape the modern world. Yet he was bound, for now, to the constraints of Edison's empire.

∞

New York City — December 6, 1884

The rift between the two men had steadily widened as the months passed. The culmination of their simmering tensions came sharply into focus over a promise not kept.

The $50,000 bonus Edison had casually promised, a fortune to the young inventor, had become a bitter symbol. Tesla had delivered his work, but Edison refused to pay him the money.

Edison had laughed it off. "It was a joke, Tesla, don't you understand American humor?" Instead, he offered Tesla a paltry raise. The insult burned hotter than any electric arc.

The sting of that betrayal and Edison's continual belittling lingered in Tesla's mind, a bitter reminder of how his revolutionary ideas had been dismissed, his genius reduced to little more than a moderately compensated set of skilled hands.

Edison's world, once full of potential, now felt narrow and oppressive.

Tesla realized that to actualize his vision and unlock the complete potential of his AC theory, he had to depart from Edison's realm. Still, he forced himself to grit his teeth and tough it out at his job.

But his last inkling of patience vanished when Edison yelled at him as they argued once again about DC versus AC.

"Tesla, just make it work!" Edison's voice boomed through the workshop. "No more theorizing!"

Tesla's jaw clenched. "Your DC system is clumsy, inefficient!"

Edison's face hardened, his shrewd eyes narrowing.

"Dreamer! Your 'currents' are impractical, dangerous! People want light bulbs that work, not flights of fancy. Edison Electric will illuminate the world, not Tesla's theories."

"Theories? These are the laws of physics, Mr. Edison! I envision a world where energy flows effortlessly, a network of power blanketing the globe—"

"Enough!" Edison roared, his voice silencing the workshop. "You'll improve my existing systems or you'll find yourself back on the streets of Paris, an immigrant, peddling those useless patents of yours!"

The humiliation of that moment was the final spark. Tesla announced his resignation and stormed out.

His employment with Thomas Edison in America had lasted exactly six months.

Tesla was now resolute in his endeavor to discover an alternative method of leaving his mark, to manipulate nature to conform to his desires. And perhaps, one day, topple the self-proclaimed Wizard of Menlo Park.

10

Manual Labor

Two and a half years had passed since Tesla, a whirlwind of wounded brilliance, stormed out of Edison's bustling empire.

At first, he was exhilarated by his new freedom. But in the solitude that followed his departure, Tesla's resentment simmered as he replayed in his mind the confrontations, the belittlements.

He had a fierce determination to prove not just to Edison, but to the entire world, that his ideas could transform the very fabric of modern society.

He formed his own company, the Tesla Electric Light and Manufacturing Company, and landed two major investors. His first goal was to introduce necessary improvements to arc lighting, such as creating a stable light with no flickering.

His inventions in this area proved to be a success. But lacking a practical business sense, Tesla registered his patents for this and additional inventions under the company name.

At first, all seemed well, especially with his new system of arc lighting. It was sold and used in Rahway, New Jersey, to light up some of the town's streets and factories.

But then, to his surprise, his mentors focused solely on expansion in New Jersey, selling arc lighting systems. They were not supportive of his ongoing improvements and inventions. And same as Thomas Edison, they were not interested in his progressing work with alternating current.

With breathtaking speed, Tesla lost the rights to his own inventions, his company folded, he lost his patents and found himself virtually bankrupt.

It was a bitter blow and one his somewhat naïve and trusting nature found difficult to process. Once again, he had been betrayed. Humiliated, he withdrew from his friends and social life as he tried to figure out his next move.

Tesla eventually found himself a new job. He was now working in the trenches, wielding a pickaxe!

The hot summer sun beat down on New York City, turning Fifth Avenue into a shimmering mirage, the elegant carriages and rustling finery blurring into an indistinct backdrop for the work at hand.

Tesla, clad in rough laborer's clothes, swung his pickaxe alongside a crew of burly men, their synchronized grunts and groans the soundtrack of the day. Sweat stung his eyes, and his muscles burned with an unfamiliar, relentless ache.

Ditch-digging was hardly a scientific pursuit, a jarring fall from the lofty realm of laboratories and schematics. A cruel twist of fate, some might say, for a man who'd envisioned a world transformed by the power he understood so intimately.

Yet there was a certain brutal honesty to his current predicament, a defiant satisfaction in the tool's weight, in the tangible way the earth yielded with every strike. Tesla had never shied away from work, even when his mind soared to celestial heights.

"Ain't seen a college boy swing a pickaxe like that in a long time," a grizzled foreman remarked, the first grudging hint of approval Tesla had received in weeks.

Tesla offered a faint smile, a flicker of his usual charm beneath the grime.

Though his circumstances were a far cry from the pristine laboratory he craved, there was a freedom to this hard labor, a sweat-soaked dignity he hadn't found amidst the polished veneer of his previous jobs. Yes, his hands were calloused, but his mind remained ablaze. Between the heft of the pickaxe and the bite of the noonday sun, plans blossomed and circuits danced behind his eyes.

This labor, as backbreaking as it was, was merely a means to an end. He was biding his time, regrouping, and hardening his resolve.

One day, the world would transform under his visionary touch. Until then, he'd dig ditches if he had to, fueled by the unyielding force of his own ambition.

$$\infty$$

With his change of profession, Tesla had vacated the Liberty Hotel and moved downtown to somewhat better quarters. His room in the Universal Hotel on the Bowery was a testament to his singular focus. Nothing hinted at the vibrant social life he had experienced the previous years — instead, the space was as meticulous as Tesla's mind: a small, functional bed, a writing desk overflowing with precisely arranged schematics, and a single worn armchair positioned to catch the fading evening light. Books on physics lined a modest shelf, their spines cracked and faded from countless readings.

Life in the Bowery was never dull, with various ethnicities and foods to explore. Nearly every street in the area was lined with fresh fruit, vegetables, meat, and fish stands. Tesla could walk a few blocks east to find a hearty chicken soup in the Jewish neighborhood.

A few blocks south found him in Little Italy, where the strong coffees, espresso, and delicious pastries pleased his palate. Further south and west was Chinatown, offering inexpensive soups and dumplings.

He had not yet become finicky and nervous about where he ate his meals, as he would be in later years. However, he insisted on drinking only boiled or purified water; this after viewing untreated water under a microscope.

The Bowery neighborhood provided a slice of life, giving Tesla a glimpse of the world that someday soon, he knew, would benefit from his efforts.

Despite often feeling bone weary from his job, he was driven to press forward with his research during almost every free hour of the day or night. Consumed by work, he had no remaining time, energy, or inclination for anything else in his life. Yet sometimes he allowed himself to remember the warmth of having a cup of coffee with Anya, and the joy it brought him.

∞

Parc Monceau, Paris - August 11, 1882

The exquisite grounds unfurled around them, a tapestry of green and gold under the warm afternoon sun. The successful French artist, Claude Monet, had already captured the park's beauty in three famous paintings.

Tesla and Anya had found a secluded spot by the pond, a mirror reflecting the rustling leaves and dappled clouds. The air was alive with the soft symphony of birdsong, and the scent of damp earth and wildflowers clung to the breeze. A basket lay between them, the remains of their picnic lunch spread out on a white cloth.

"For you, my feathered friends," Anya cooed, tossing a handful of breadcrumbs toward the water's edge. A flurry of pigeons descended, their wings a whirring blur of gray and white. Anya giggled, her eyes bright.

Tesla watched the birds, a thoughtful crease furrowing his brow. "Why do they always gather, like a little army?"

Anya shrugged. "I think they like being together. Maybe it feels safer." Her gaze landed back on Tesla. "Do you ever wish you could just... sprout wings and fly away?"

"I don't wish," Tesla said slowly, as if considering the very concept for the first time. "I wonder... how it would work. The physics of flight, the currents of the air."

Just then, one bird walked trustingly over to Anya, eating out of her hand. Tesla observed with interest as Anya spoke silently to the bird, and it seemed to listen and respond to her. Watching them, it was evident to him that telepathic communication between people and other life forms was possible, transcending the need for verbal language.

After a time, the bird wandered off and Anya snuggled up to Tesla, who gently kissed her hand. Anya rested her head against his chest and looked soulfully into Tesla's eyes, then said:

"These are the moments that dreams are made of."

11

GOOD FORTUNE

New York City – July 8, 1887

The scent of stale coffee and the tang of ozone from some recent experiment permeated the air in the apartment.

Yes, Tesla had moved yet again to a small garden apartment.

He much preferred hotel living; it was an easier lifestyle overall, but his finances couldn't sustain it. And here, even in this small space, he'd been able to set up a makeshift laboratory.

Hunched over his cluttered workbench, Tesla's pen scratched a steady rhythm against the hum of a nearby transformer. Lost in the tangle of equations filling his notebook, he barely registered the insistent rapping against the door.

Only when the sound cut off abruptly did he jerk his head up. He snapped the worn leather notebook shut. Years of honed instinct had him concealing the contents with practiced ease.

He opened the door. Katharine Johnson stood on the threshold with a soft smile and a familiar warmth in her eyes. They hadn't seen each other for over eighteen months.

She looked as beautiful as he remembered her. Beside her, radiating quiet power, stood a man with a broad frame and an imposing mustache, the kind that spoke of wealth and influence.

"Nikola, how have you been?" Katharine's voice held a thread of concern.

"Well enough...." He hesitated, a prickle of guilt surfacing. "I apologize for disappearing, Katharine. I needed..." He gestured vaguely, unable to articulate the mix of frustration and restless energy that had possessed him.

"Robert and I assumed as much," she replied gently. "We hoped you'd reach out when you were ready."

"I should have," he conceded.

With a smile, Katharine turned towards her companion. Tesla followed her gaze and something within him stilled. A sense of recognition gripped him, but nothing to do with introductions. He knew this man, not personally, but by reputation.

"Nikola Tesla, this is Mr. George Westinghouse."

"Mr. Tesla." The man's voice resonated with confident authority. "It's a genuine pleasure to finally put a face to the name that's been swirling like a storm through the electrical world."

The warmth Tesla felt for Katharine extended to her companion. "And I to you, Mr. Westinghouse. Please, come in, both of you."

As they squeezed into his cramped, dingy apartment, Tesla felt a flicker of self-consciousness. Despite Westinghouse's portly figure and the extravagant mustache that dominated his face, there was something open in his demeanor. The man exuded sincerity and whatever his purpose in seeking Tesla, it felt genuine.

"I must confess," Tesla began, "I'm familiar with your work, Mr. Westinghouse. Your air brake system... brilliant." Tesla paused, a thoughtful expression on his face. "You've revolutionized the railroad industry, making travel safer, faster, and more efficient, using air pressure to control motion. It is a testament to the power of human ingenuity, the ability to harness the forces of nature to our will."

A moment of surprise flickered in Westinghouse's eyes, swiftly followed by warmth. Katharine, however, seemed to bristle.

"Nikola, Mr. Westinghouse has a proposal, something we'd very much like to discuss with you. Over dinner, perhaps? Tomorrow evening?"

If Tesla felt a jolt of surprise, he concealed it beneath a practiced calm. But a flame sparked in his eyes, a hunger he'd desperately tried to contain. Westinghouse was not blind to it.

"A proposal? One that, I trust, involves the future of electricity?"

"Precisely," Westinghouse affirmed. "And if you're amenable, a good meal would be an excellent setting to explore the potential... the potential for a revolution, shall we say?"

The word 'revolution' hung in the air, heavy with unspoken possibilities. Tesla, ever the master of restraint, finally met Katharine's gaze and offered a slight smile. "Then consider your invitation accepted."

Tesla ushered them out, a strange mix of excitement and apprehension churning in his stomach.

As the door closed behind them, Katharine and Westinghouse exchanged silent glances. There was shared thought in their lingering looks — this brilliant, complicated man deserved far better than this.

Katharine felt an ache, a sense of unwitting betrayal for introducing Tesla to the realm of wealth only to have it snatched away again.

Westinghouse, however, saw something more: a fire in Tesla's eyes, a steely determination etched on his face. This, he realized, was a man who burned with more than mere ideas. Tesla was a force starved for fuel.

And perhaps, Westinghouse mused as their carriage pulled away, he could be the one to provide it. This, he sensed, could be the start of a partnership that would change the course of technological history.

∞

The grandiosity of Delmonico's engulfed Tesla the moment he stepped through its gilded doors. No mere restaurant; this was a cathedral of wealth and privilege, a stark contrast to his own humble apartment. Crystal chandeliers, colossal and shimmering, showered the room in a starburst of light. Their brilliance ricocheted off the gleaming silver and the fine china. The delicious aroma of roast pheasant mingled with the intoxicating bouquet of vintage wines, while the flow of affluent conversation painted a symphony of exclusivity that Tesla found both alluring and intimidating.

Tesla took a seat beside Katharine, who wore a striking sapphire gown. Westinghouse was on her other side. She was a graceful conduit between the visionary and the industrialist.

"Nikola," Katharine's voice was like fine silk, "I trust roast pheasant is satisfactory?"

"Indeed," he replied with a rare, full smile.

Westinghouse seconded the suggestion. A bear of a man with a shrewd glint in his eyes, he observed Tesla over his champagne flute.

Tesla's spine straightened ever so slightly. Years of struggle and doubt echoed within him, but he settled himself down. Katharine leaned forward, lifting a glass of champagne.

"Gentleman, a man convinced against his will is of the same opinion still."

"I concede." Tesla lifted his glass of champagne.

"As do I," Westinghouse agreed. And the three clinked glasses. Then their meals were served, and Tesla tucked into his food as if a man starving. In a way, he was, as it had been far too long since he'd enjoyed fine cuisine. Katharine and Westinghouse watched in silence and exchanged concerned glances as Tesla eagerly cleaned his plate and then requested a second helping.

∞

The remnants of their meal long cleared away, the dinner meeting carried into the late night.

A half-empty bottle of champagne hinted at earlier toasts, and their conversation wound down.

"...two dollars and fifty cents per horsepower," Tesla repeated, impressed. "I must confess, Mr. Westinghouse, the boldness of your offer takes some getting used to."

Despite his usual composure, Tesla carried a hint of nervous energy beneath his charm. The past two years had taken its toll, leaving faint shadows under his eyes, but his gaze still burned with the intensity of a man on the cusp of realizing his grandest ambitions.

"Mr. Tesla," said Westinghouse, "I have made my fortune by recognizing not just good ideas, but the drive behind them. You possess both in abundance. Risk is the currency of progress, and I have no doubt your system holds the potential to transform far more than just our lighting grids."

Katharine's excitement mirrored Tesla's. "Nikola, this is precisely why I brought you two together!" She leaned in conspiratorially. "Imagine, entire cities illuminated by your system..."

Tesla gazed into the distance, finding it still hard to believe that Westinghouse's offer was for real. "Yes! Not just cities but all of New York State," he murmured and paused, choosing his next words carefully. "Edison will be a troubling obstacle to overcome."

"Leave Edison to me," Westinghouse replied with quiet authority. "His direct current is... well, let's just say it lacks a certain flexibility. The future, Mr. Tesla, belongs to those who can harness power on a grander scale. With you designing the system and my resources behind it, Edison will be no factor."

"Very well then, Mr. Westinghouse," Tesla said joyfully, all doubts vanished. "We have a partnership!"

"Excellent!" Katharine raised her glass. "Gentlemen, shall we toast to this momentous occasion? To innovation, to progress, and to light up the entire state of New York and beyond!"

Westinghouse chuckled as they clinked glasses. As the champagne bubbled, their laughter seemed to echo a greater promise, a symphony of ambition and audacity. It was the start of a partnership that would change not just their fortunes but the course of history.

∞

Tesla could hardly believe his good fortune as, almost overnight, his life changed for the better. What a remarkable transformation! Only a day prior, he had been wrestling with the typical uncertainties and the daunting shadow of obscurity. Yet now, he sensed a profound shift in the winds of fate. America was truly the land of opportunities.

He was both amazed and grateful for how swiftly George Westinghouse evolved into a figure of immense importance in his life. A titan of industry known for his integrity and innovation, Westinghouse saw the potential in Tesla's groundbreaking ideas, recognizing the spark of genius so many others had dismissed. Westinghouse was not merely a businessman but a visionary in his own right, one who valued honor and commitment above the mere calculus of profit.

And so the two men sealed their partnership with an earnest handshake. Tesla marveled about it all. And then remembered it was all possible due to Katharine.

Westinghouse wasted no time settling Tesla into better lodgings. Eventually he would move Tesla into the newly built, prestigious Waldorf-Astoria Hotel, a sanctuary for the affluent and notable. Westinghouse also attempted to pay Tesla's hotel bills for the next many years until his death.

This proved to be a daunting challenge, as Tesla racked up huge expenses. Increasingly fussy about the quality of his food, he preferred to eat his meals in the expensive hotel restaurant or have meals delivered to his room. Many other assorted bills were also charged to the room.

The hotel was partly owned by the famous Astor family and thanks to Westinghouse's introduction, Tesla also became friends with John Jacob Astor IV, one of the world's wealthiest men. Astor was so impressed that he invested $100,000 into Tesla's new business, becoming a majority shareholder in the Nikola Tesla Company.

Tesla's new grand suite at the Waldorf-Astoria epitomized the luxury of the era. The spacious living room, with its plush carpets and heavy drapes, offered breathtaking city views. Velvet-upholstered furnishings surrounded an oval coffee table adorned with fresh flowers – a gift from Katharine. A grand writing desk stood sentinel near the window. Art graced the walls, and an enormous fireplace with a decorative mantle dominated one wall, topped by a sparkling crystal chandelier.

The bedroom boasted a stately four-poster bed dressed in luxurious linens, flanked by reading tables. A vanity and wardrobe completed the elegant ensemble. The bathroom, a marvel of modern convenience, featured pristine white tiles, a luxurious bathtub, and a separate shower stall. Shiny fixtures and a mirrored medicine cabinet added the finishing touches to this opulent living space, reflecting the refined tastes and status of its illustrious occupant. The Waldorf-Astoria was, at that time, the largest hotel in the world, and the first to offer private bathrooms and electricity throughout.

Tesla felt comfortable enough to envision living there forever. Additionally, Westinghouse gifted Tesla his own laboratory, rent free. Tesla meticulously ordered equipment, wiring, transformers, and glasswork for his vacuum tubes. It was a fine laboratory. He had finally gained what he always wanted.

After he settled into his new living and work quarters, Tesla arranged a lunch meeting with Katharine at the hotel's restaurant, to thank her properly. He wanted this meeting alone with her, but not in his private residence.

He inevitably wondered if her attraction to him was still as strong as his own to her and felt it too risky to place them in a situation where temptation could be easily acted upon.

He was correct in his assumption of her feelings. Their conversation was lighthearted and general at first, but then she startled him by abruptly changing the subject.

"Nikola, if I may be so forward, may I ask you, are you seeing anyone... romantically, that is?"

"No," he replied, wondering where this conversation was leading. "Why do you ask?"

She delicately and carefully chose her words. "I've heard rumors, that you say you've never touched a woman..."

He bowed his head then looked back up at her. "Perhaps that is true during these last years here in New York. My circumstances fell to such — a man digging ditches — who would want such a man?" He gave a rueful chuckle. "I did love someone once and hoped to marry her, but she refused me."

"Why? If you don't mind me asking—"

He shook his head. "She wanted to remain in Paris for her career. And I came here."

"I'm sorry, Nikola. Do you still care for her?"

He did not directly answer. After a long moment he said, "I shall never know the joys of being married or having children. As an inventor, it's not in my nature. A man has needs, of course, but I don't have the soul of an artist, a writer, or musician for which wild, passionate love heightens one's creativity."

"I would beg to differ, Nikola," she said softly. "I think you have a great capacity for wild, passionate love."

"I did experience it once and it was all-consuming," he replied. "When I lost it, it left me drained emotionally and I could not focus on my work." His face flushed as he met her gaze. "I apologize if our conversation has become too intense for your sensibilities."

"Not at all," she said, touching his hand in reassurance. "I appreciate your honesty. You're an honorable man, Nikola."

"Not always," he replied, again with a rueful glance. "Yes, there is a thrill that goes through me when I work through one of my experiments or inventions, and I finally triumph because it works the way I knew it should. That is a kind of ecstasy in itself. But there are times when I confess, I long for the other."

His gaze fell on her hand, still on his. There was an intense moment between them, and then he gently pulled his hand away.

"I think I could love again, if I let myself," he said, half believing it himself. "But you and Robert are dear friends. He's like a brother to me. I could not betray him. I had a brother who I betrayed, and I never forgave myself–"

Their waiter approached them, bringing dessert and more coffee. This broke their intimate mood, and lunch was hastily finished. They said their goodbyes as Tesla helped Katharine into her carriage. He watched her driven away and wondered, since he had done most of the talking, what she might have wanted to confide to him. Instead of dwelling on it, he returned to his laboratory and continued with his work.

∞

George Westinghouse was an amazing promoter and under his sponsorship, Tesla's fame and fortune grew.

With his new life as a celebrity, Tesla had women throwing themselves at him, chasing a romantic encounter with him. This was a pride to his ego and on a very few occasions he indulged in fulfilling their fantasy and his own. His private lust, though, was for Katharine Johnson, but he knew a liaison was impossible.

Though Robert Johnson tolerated their flirting, Tesla would never take it further. Yes, he had seduced and had sexual relations with other married women, but Robert was his best friend.

Theirs was a relaxed, informal friendship. Whereas Tesla usually addressed most men by their formal names, now Robert Johnson was "Bob". In return, Robert was the only one to call Tesla "Nick." In speaking with women friends, Tesla always called them "Miss" but of course, Katharine was the exception. That Tesla dared to call her by her name even in public was startling.

Tesla understood that his sleeping with Katharine would cross a line that might destroy their friendship. Sincere, loyal friends were scarce, and Tesla cherished that friendship. He respected Robert too much to be such a cad.

And then there was Anya. She had kept her word, encouraging their continued friendship. She sent Tesla long, newsy letters about her life in Paris, or sometimes congratulatory telegrams when she learned of a new success he had.

Tesla now found himself responding to her, and they corresponded by mail and telegram. He would take her latest correspondence and sit in Central Park to open and read over and over, remembering their precious time together in France.

Despite the distance, his joy surged when he realized she was back in his life. She invited him to visit her should he return to Paris. Tesla found himself excited at the prospect of seeing her again and discussed with Westinghouse possibly embarking upon a European tour.

Part Two

12

AH, SWEET MYSTERY OF LIFE

Manhattan, New York City - August 2024

The great city was still standing tall, albeit shaking in its boots.

While the nation faced difficulties in the last few years, New York seemed to endure an even greater struggle. The city was shut down because of a worldwide pandemic just four years earlier, and the streets remained eerily silent for an extended period, reminiscent of the aftermath of the year 2001 terror attack on The World Trade Center.

As the lockdown was lifted, the city gradually came alive again with the sounds of people chatting and cars honking. Movie and Broadway theaters opened their doors, and the streets came alive with the hustle and bustle of people returning to their favorite businesses.

There was a welcoming back of the chaotic roar of taxis, honking cars and overfilled street traffic. Yet the city still had not fully returned to its former glory. Where New York had once scoffed at national chain stores and restaurants, they were now the norm, as small mom and pop places were forced to fold shop permanently after the pandemic income losses.

Additionally, recent months had seen a heightened increase in both political and religious turmoil, which led many formerly loyal residents to a mass exodus from the city, moving to Florida and other warmer states.

The world was at war again: Ukraine and Russia, Israel and Palestine and other Arab nations. World War III, whispered the fearful.

Yet even amidst this storm, New York was the epicenter in America with riots, marches, protests, and a surge in homelessness. Even more disturbing were crimes fueled by hatred, a grotesque echo of Germany's darkest days leading to World War II.

Despite such unrest, the younger generation still viewed New York as their sacred training ground for pursuing the American Dream. The highly acclaimed universities and specialized schools still smacked of prestige, dedicated hard work, and talent. A degree here still meant something and prepared one for a respectable career.

Such was the dream of John Watt, age twenty-two. He was a tall, lean, good-looking fellow, with a shock of brown hair flecked with auburn.

Today he was working diligently on building a computer server at his school of choice, the Sterling School of Technology. Several other students did the same.

Their teacher, Mr. Ortega, hovered around the room, observing their progress. Sensing his presence, John picked up his pace as Mr. Ortega neared him.

"Mr. Watt," said Mr. Ortega as he studied John's machine. "Are you forgetting something?"

John stopped his hurried work and examined the partially built server. "I don't know, sir."

"Take a better look."

And then John saw it. "The power supply," he sighed.

Mr. Ortega nodded.

As John quickly installed the power supply, Mr. Ortega commented, "This exercise is not about speed, Mr. Watt. Slow it down and think about the order of the components."

"I will," said John as his teacher moved on to another workbench.

Before the end of class, John had completed building his server and received a high grade plus a pat of approval on the shoulder from Mr. Ortega.

John was happy with his school day's work. He drove out of the city in his old Toyota Corolla clunker, heading over the bridge into Queens to check in on his grandmother, Ruth Watt.

Earlier in the day, she had called him on his cell phone and asked him to stop by.

Now widowed and in her early nineties, Ruth lived in an older part of town where small single-family houses still stood, a neighborhood perhaps looking a bit worn but otherwise seemingly untouched by time. Ruth lived alone but had a housekeeper come in every couple of days to help her with chores and shopping.

John pulled into her driveway and parked. He spotted his grandmother asleep in a comfortable chair on her porch. She was a petite woman whose figure still looked trim and despite her gray hair, she had sweet features. Time had been kind to her. It was obvious she'd been beautiful in the years gone by.

Grabbing his cell phone, John made a quick call to his girlfriend Sara and then glanced back over at Ruth. Sudden terror gripped him as she was slumped in her chair, motionless.

He aborted the phone call, jumped out of his car through the front passenger seat and then stood frozen for a long moment, his heart in his throat. Ruth was the only family he had left. An only child, he'd lost both parents years ago and his grandfather more recently.

Ruth was more than just a grandmother that one dutifully visits. She had raised him half his life. She loved him, understood him, and championed his life goals and achievements.

He knew the day would come when his grandmother would leave him, but he hoped to God it wasn't today.

John hurried over to Ruth, calling her name. She still had not moved, so John picked up her hand and checked her pulse.

To his immense relief, she opened her eyes and gave him a gentle smile. "I assure you, young man, I'm still alive," she said.

John's face flushed red and he choked back tears. It took a moment to compose himself then he smiled back at her.

"You shouldn't be sleeping out here."

There was no fooling Grandmother. Ruth embraced him with a comforting hug until he relaxed again.

"Who's sleeping?" she joked. "I just dozed off for a moment. Help your grandmother up. You'll stay for dinner, of course."

John had planned to eat with Sara, but just now spending time with his grandmother seemed far more important.

They went inside and after eating dinner, moved to the living room for tea and dessert. John sat down on the sofa, curious why Ruth had requested he stay for dinner. Normally he visited her on weekends when there was no school. Obviously, she had some news for him. He hoped it was good news.

Ruth returned to the kitchen to prepare the dessert platter of homemade lemon poppyseed cake and tea. John offered to help but she declined it.

So he sat alone and glanced around the tidy living room, with dated but well-kept furniture and almost no clutter. His grandmother was a romantic; she had put on a music CD that played softly in the background. It was of her two favorite movie stars singing "Ah, Sweet Mystery of Life", a famous old song about eternal love.

Ruth knew about true love; her long marriage to John's grandfather had been happy till his death. John couldn't recall them ever having a fight or argument. Sometimes he wondered whether that kind of everlasting love and devotion could even exist anymore in the fast-paced world of his generation.

Above the fireplace on the wall there were several framed photographs, some of John's parents and of him as a child growing up, but many featuring older photographs of Ruth and her husband Henry. Yes, he was recognizable as the same young Henry Watt who began his career as a bellboy, assisting Nikola Tesla at the New Yorker Hotel in 1942.

Something different in the room caught John's eye. On the floor beside the fireplace was an old leather travel trunk. Curiosity compelled him to approach for a better view. The trunk was dusty, as if in storage for many years.

Ruth returned with the tea and cake and placed the dessert tray on the table. She took a seat on the sofa.

"What is this?" asked John, still studying the old trunk.

"You know Grandpa was friends with Nikola Tesla toward the end of his life," Ruth said.

"Yes," John nodded.

"Mr. Tesla gave Grandpa this trunk for safekeeping."

"Why would Tesla trust Grandpa? He was just a kid, like me."

"I can't answer that," Ruth said. "It's been in the attic for as long as I can remember. We never allowed your father, God rest his soul, up there when he was a child. Henry was afraid he might open it."

"What's in it?"

"I don't know, dear. Henry made me promise never to open it."

"And you listened to him?"

Ruth smiled. "Of course. We never broke promises to each other."

John kneeled down to the trunk and brushed off the dust. "Why take it down now?" he asked.

"Because your grandfather wanted you to have it soon after your twenty-second birthday."

"Why?"

"I don't know, dear. He was specific about it being sometime this year. That was the last thing he said to me." Ruth fought back her tears. She picked up her cup of tea and took a sip of the soothing liquid.

"It doesn't make sense," John argued. "Why not give it to Dad when he was alive?"

Ruth shrugged. "No idea, John."

"Should I open it?"

"I don't see why not."

"Because he said not to open it."

"He said for me and for your dad not to open it."

John looked over at Ruth and after a long moment of deliberation, attempted to open the trunk. But found he couldn't because it was locked.

"Grandma, I don't suppose you have a key?"

Ruth shook her head and John continued, "I could break the lock. It's pretty rusted."

There was no argument from Ruth, so John slammed the lock with his heel, breaking it off. Ruth got up from the sofa to get a better look.

They scarcely breathed as John slowly opened the trunk, revealing a cotton sheet slightly discolored because of time. It was tightly wrapped around some bulky object. He pulled off the sheet, and they stared at what looked like a radio.

Whatever they had expected, it wasn't this!

John studied it for a moment and finally said, "Cool, it looks like a nineteen thirties Hi-Fi system!"

"I have never seen this before." Ruth seemed puzzled. "He was so adamant that you get this sometime after your twenty-second birthday."

"What am I supposed to do with it?" asked John.

"I don't know, dear. But I know it was very important to him."

"Alright, I'll take a better look at it at home."

And with that, they both turned their attention to their tea and Ruth's delicious lemon poppyseed cake, and ate in silence.

Still, John couldn't help but sneak glances at the trunk, wondering whether he should feel disappointed or happy.

He downed a second piece of cake, hugged Ruth goodbye and lugged the trunk to his car. He felt a sense of excitement building. The trunk and its contents were a mystery for sure, and he couldn't wait to get home to solve it.

An hour later, John slumped back into the worn leather of his desk chair. His small one-bedroom apartment, cramped and cluttered, was home for him the past two years. The living room, with its faded floral sofa and mismatched tables, held the dual purpose of home office and relaxation space. A stack of unopened bills teetered on the corner of the desk, a grim reminder of being a part-time worker and full-time student.

His gaze settled on the weathered trunk, a relic of a bygone era. Inside lay the radio. He kneeled on the carpet.

The trunk's musty scent, a mix of old wood, leather, and something vaguely sweet, prickled his nose as he lifted the radio out. The polished wood felt cool beneath his fingertips. Too large for his desk, he set it carefully on the carpet.

It was surprisingly light, a meticulously crafted mahogany cabinet measuring two and a half feet in each direction, shaped like a cube. There were also some knobs and switches, and what looked like a built-in microphone and speakers. The power cord was long, at least eight feet. The plug was unusual. John examined it closely and realized it would not fit into today's modern electrical outlets.

He would need to replace it with a modern plug. And then a flash of white inside the trunk diverted his attention from the plug. There was an envelope at the bottom of the trunk. His stomach suddenly in a knot, John carefully picked up the envelope and opened it. With trembling fingers, he pulled out the letter inside and began to read the handwritten words.

∞

John now had two letters in front of him on his desk. He had read the first one then discovered another one hidden under the trunk's false bottom. That one was quite yellowed and fragile with age, the handwritten ink somewhat faded. The more recent letter appeared to be in better condition.

After reading them both and absorbing their information, he now sat staring at them with a wondrous expression. He did not notice the sound of a key turning in the door lock.

Sara Roberts, John's girlfriend, entered with an exasperated expression on her face. She was a pretty brunette, also twenty-two, and unmistakably a New Yorker. She had a brash and impatient demeanor, slamming the front door behind her and folding her arms while tapping her foot in annoyance.

"Hey, you!" she shouted across the room to John. "You were supposed to pick me up at work and take me out to dinner!"

John, now completely absorbed in the radio, barely glanced at her. "I was busy. I lost track of time. Sorry."

"You could have called. Lucky for you, I went to Trader Joe's and found something delicious to nuke in the microwave! What was so important that you forgot about me?" Sara noticed the radio and sighed. "This is the reason you forgot?"

John finished removing the old power cord and plug from the radio. He jumped up from the carpet, grabbed Sara and kissed her passionately.

Despite her initial anger, she quickly responded. He finally released her, leaving her dazed but in a much better mood.

"Sara!" he said excitedly. "I have something amazing to tell you! But first, I need to find something."

"Okay," Sara said agreeably. "Amazing is good."

John guided Sara to his desk and sat her down in the chair. He pointed to one of two letters lying side by side on the table.

"Read these letters. Start with this one."

"What is this?"

"That one is from my grandfather. The other one, you won't believe who it's from. I'll be right back."

John hurried out of the room. Curious now, Sarah picked up the letter John had pointed to and began reading Henry Watt's letter aloud.

To my dear grandson John Watt, time has made a fool of me. This letter finds you on the cusp of my own departure.

Inside this trunk, hidden within a false lining, lies another letter — penned not by my hand, but by that of Nikola Tesla himself. I don't know its contents other than that they are instructions.

Tesla entrusted me to ensure his radio and the letter were safeguarded until 2013 or later — at least 70 years after he wrote it — which meant passing it on to a soul I deemed worthy of the task he outlined in his instructions.

Unfortunately, God saw fit to take your father from us before 2013 and you were much too young to take on such a monumental task that Tesla surely has in store for the recipient of this radio, which now, my dear boy, is you. I never understood why he chose me to safeguard his radio and choose the soul to undertake this task, whatever it is; but he did, and I swore to him and myself that I would not let him down.

At the time of writing this letter, you are not yet in your teenage years, but only 10.

I have instructed Ruth to give you this trunk sometime after your twenty-second birthday, which I hope is old enough for this enormous responsibility you are about to undertake. I was 22 when Tesla entrusted me with the same responsibility.

The sands of life have nearly run out for me. I can only wonder how Tesla knew I would live to such a ripe old age and be able to execute his task by the date he gave.

Whatever Tesla wants you to do, it is surely important. I trust in you that you will do well by him.

John returned to the room as Sarah finished reading the letter. She looked at him, bewildered.

"Is this for real?" she asked.

John nodded with solemn seriousness. He was holding another cable, one with a modern plug. He carefully placed the cable beside the radio, picked up Tesla's letter, and gave it to Sara.

"Now read this one."

She nodded. Because of its age, she held it delicately as she read Tesla's words aloud.

You have by now set your eyes on my time communication machine, or radio as Marconi loyalists would call it. Whatever you wish to call it is irrelevant.

What is relevant is that according to all my calculations, the Time Radio shall work. What lies beyond the veil of normal matter and space time is now rendered mutable.

Should anyone transgress the laws of causality, even born of benevolent intent? Can man's mind fathom or govern the ripples in time and space? I have emplaced safeguards and counterbalances, quantum entanglement keys, and barriers to prevent abuse of this technology. But I wonder if I have only birthed a new, more insidious Pandora's Box? Regardless, there is no turning back. Ahead lies only the abyss of potentiality…and hope against hope this machine shall never be needed. That I may disassemble it one day in which case you would not be reading these words.

However, should this machine be needed, you will be reading this letter now.

I have built into the machine radical countermeasures, designed to reach across the very sea of chronology itself.

If the unthinkable transpires and the nefarious capture the machine for weapon purposes, the Time Radio could mean the end of the future as you know it. The one true and only purpose of this machine is for the recipient to beam warnings back through time to me in 1913. With this foreknowledge from the future, I could make the pivotal adjustments to safeguard my present scientific trajectory, course-correcting the timeline to avert global calamity. You have before you the power to right the wrongs of my inventions. Simply contact me in 1913 by pressing down on the left switch to activate the radio, and speak into the microphone the key code: 'Queens Seagull' to 'Manhattan Dove'; then wait briefly for me to respond from the past. The other switch powers the machine on and off.

Why 1913? This is the year I still have the power to make changes. Know that you now bear the terrible responsibility of hindsight across the cosmic abyss of time. My faith and trust in you is strong, as I remain a friend solely in service to help mankind.

Nikola Tesla, November 18, 1942.

∞

John tossed anxiously in bed, unable to sleep. A persistent buzzing filled his head, as if being called by Tesla's strange radio. It was impossible to ignore. Not even the warmth of Sara's naked body beside him or the gentle rise and fall of her breathing could lure him to peace.

He had sworn to himself he would wait until morning to investigate the radio further, but that promise was now wavering.

With the cautious movements of an escape artist, he eased himself from the tangled sheets. Sara let out a muffled protest. John froze in place and the protest faded.

He quietly made his way to the living room, where the radio gleamed in the faint light filtering through the curtains. With John's new power cord now attached, it was obviously in working order.

He had taken the time to carefully study the radio. Its polished wooden surface gleamed under direct light, its finish the result of careful hand-rubbing with shellac by a Serbian craftsmen Tesla had specifically commissioned for the project. The front of the radio showcased a woven cotton mesh speaker grille cleverly concealing a specialized temporal-quantum microphone array, engineered to capture cross-dimensional voice patterns through quantum entanglement, voices from the future through temporal resonance.

The central control panel housed six Bakelite knobs, each calibrated with precision to tune through chronological wavelength frequencies.

Between these controls sat an Analog VU meter, illuminating its glass face with a glowing green light boosted by radium paint — a common practice of the era that Tesla had reluctantly adopted despite his concerns about radiation. The radio's dual speakers exposed, without grill, on the right side of the radio were made from treated lamb's leather chosen for its unique ability to reproduce time-shifted harmonics. To complete the aesthetics, they were painted black.

The true marvel of the device lay in its transformers, exposed on the outside of the radio, their copper windings hand-wrapped around iron cores and mounted in brass fixtures that Tesla had designed. These weren't merely for power conversion — they generated precise electromagnetic fields capable of opening microscopic bridges across time itself. A thick rubber-wrapped copper cable encircled the cabinet to stabilize the electrical field around the radio.

John hesitated at turning on the radio, in part because he sensed the entire assembly represented impossible pre-war era engineering. Maybe Tesla had used physics principles that weren't formally discovered until quantum mechanics matured all these decades later. Or perhaps it even utilized technology more advanced than what was invented by this year of 2024!

John pulled Tesla's faded and aged letter closer, the ink clinging desperately to the paper. He reread the erratic scrawl, Tesla's instructions littered with cryptic hints like breadcrumb clues on some baffling trail.

As absurd as it seemed, he intended to follow those directions to the letter.

Clearing his throat, he leaned in close to the built-in microphone. "Queens Seagull to Manhattan Dove. Come in, please. Over..." His voice was swallowed by the radio's static. "Queens Seagull to Manhattan Dove. Over..." he repeated. But again nothing, just static.

Sara's voice sliced through the static hiss. "I'm going home. Over!"

John jolted, startled by her sudden appearance in the doorway. He blinked, adjusting to the sight of her standing there, naked and none too pleased.

"Sara, it's three in the morning," he mumbled in frustration, "Go to sleep."

Her response was a huff of indignation. "If I wanted to sleep alone, I'd be at home!"

John slapped the side of the radio, instantly wishing he hadn't. The relic came to life with a piercing shriek from its speaker, a high-pitched whine that made John's ears ring and sent Sara scrambling back through the doorway with a startled cry.

He heard the rustle of bed sheets as she burrowed under the covers, seeking refuge from the invasive noise. John followed her, feeling the tremor of her body as she clung to him in bed.

"What the hell did you do?" she whimpered, her breath hot against his skin.

"I... I just tapped it," he confessed.

The room was filled with the low, resonant hum that seemed to pulsate through every object, as if each item was alive with its own unique vibrancy. The air itself thrummed with an unsettling energy.

"Well, it clearly doesn't like that." Sara's voice was muffled against his chest.

"So it seems..." John agreed.

Sara pulled back, her eyes wide with alarm. "And what makes you so sure this thing isn't going to explode?"

"It's not a bomb, it's a radio, Sara," he reassured her, though even he could hear the uncertainty in his voice.

She gave a derisive snort. "Not much of a radio..."

Despite the growing unease in the pit of his stomach, John felt a stubborn curiosity taking hold. He gently disentangled himself from Sarah's embrace and crept back towards the living room. "Queens Seagull to Manhattan Dove," he said loudly. "Come in, please..."

And then an impossibly clear voice crackled from the aged speaker.

"Q-Queens Seagull...?"

"Yes, yes!" John exclaimed, his heart pounding in his chest.

A loud thud echoed from within the radio housing, abruptly cutting off the power and plunging the room into dead silence.

Part Three

13

MOTHER

New York City - January 1892

During his first years in New York, Tesla had also stayed in touch with his family in Serbia.

Writing mostly to his older sister Milka and now that his financial status had improved, he invited her to bring Mother and his other sisters to New York. But Milka advised him that their mother was not in good health and not up to a lengthy sea voyage.

In early 1892, Tesla alerted Milka he was planning a lengthy European lecture tour and would come visit the family.

Despite the frigid weather, a crowd of fans cheered Tesla as he boarded the SS *Britannic*, ready to sail across the Atlantic once again. He turned back to give George Westinghouse, Katharine and Robert Johnson a last wave and then disappeared inside the ship as the ship's horns loudly sounded for final boarding.

The trip overseas was less eventful and definitely more luxurious and relaxing than his last experience on a ship.

The first night at sea, Tesla came to grips with how very exhausted he was, stressed nearly to the point of collapse. He bolstered his morale and inner strength by taking long walks around the ship.

During the daytime, instead of cooping himself up in his stateroom, he forced himself to sit out in a deck chair, observing people, the ocean, the sky — anything to extrovert his attention and return his focus onto his upcoming plans.

After a day or two at sea, Tesla realized he might have suffered some sort of mental failing. He seemed to have blanked out memories of much of his personal life for the last year or so. He could recall almost nothing of his day-to-day interactions! Was he repressing memories or was he suffering from actual partial amnesia? He did not know but thankfully, his memory loss did not affect his work. "I could recall the smallest details and the least significant observations in my experiments," he claimed, "and even recite pages of texts and complex mathematical formulae."

Over the next months, Tesla struggled to make sense of his mental confusion. In time, he was able to recapture some personal events in his mind — but not all. A fear nagged at him that he had forgotten something terrible; or maybe it was a premonition of a disaster about to happen soon. He wasn't sure which.

This would not be the last such strange episode of long-lasting amnesia, but it was definitely the first.

∞

Tesla spent February 1892 first in London, giving lectures to members of the Association of Electrical Engineers and the Royal Society. He was feeling much improved and hopeful about the future.

Next, he traveled to Paris. Once safely settled in his hotel there, he took some time to prepare for his conference with the Société Francaise de Physique and the Société International des Electriciens. He tried to contact Anya but couldn't reach her, so he attended his first lecture alone.

To an enthusiastic and fascinated group, Tesla delivered his speech, demonstrating a hand-held ultrasound device. Speaking to them in French, he explained,

"There are healing effects from the high-frequency vibrations. The warmth of electric stimulation brings blood to the area and concurrently relaxes muscles, reduces pain and promotes healing."

His lecture was an overwhelming success, and as soon as it ended, a swarm of press surrounded Tesla eager for interviews. However, he politely declined.

"I offer my apology but have another engagement and cannot be late," he explained. "I bid you good afternoon, gentlemen."

And with that he was out of there and off to the Louvre, as speedily as possible. He quietly slipped into a gallery room where an excited press had gathered. All eyes focused on President Carnot, France's fifth president, and his honored guest from Serbia, King Aleksander. The event was to unveil a new painting for the Louvre.

With a dramatic flourish, King Aleksandar lifted the cloth and revealed a painting of a young lady holding an umbrella while rain descended on her. The work was called *Sky Tears*. All gasped and studied it, and then applause broke out.

Smiling, the King turned to the artist and congratulated her as did President Carnot.

Tesla's heart skipped a beat — it was Anya!

She had made it. She fulfilled her life's dream and Tesla was there just in time to witness it. The audience applauded warmly and Anya graciously bowed multiple times. *She has never looked more beautiful than she does in this moment,* Tesla thought, beaming with pride.

As the President and King left and the crowd thinned, Anya spotted Tesla. With a cry of joy, she ran over to him. He welcomed her into his arms, smiling proudly.

The next few hours were pure bliss. They found a restaurant serving delicious food. Anya was too excited to have much appetite but Tesla ordered her a bowl of steaming hot onion soup. She could hardly eat a spoonful so Tesla himself finished it, savoring the intoxicating flavors of the caramelized onions, cognac, heavy cream, melted gruyere cheese and a pinch of thyme; a hearty meal in itself. He was ravenous so ordered one of his favorite entrées from his previous years in Paris: a thick broiled steak sandwiched between two thin steaks.

After their meal and well into the evening, they walked and talked, soaking up the moonlit sights of this romantic city. It was evident they were both aching with desire, but there was sweet suffering and anticipation in their continued leisurely strolling.

Tesla was content for some time in dragging out the inevitable, but finally he insisted they go to his hotel.

Once they were lying naked in his bed, he kissed her lips and then her neck, her breasts and down her body. Each delicate kiss took his breath away until he could not wait anymore. He took her hand and placed it on his own body where he needed it most.

The touch of her fingers entwined with his own, slowly stroking him, was too exquisite to bear and moaning in anticipation, he pulled her onto him with a fierceness he'd long forgotten he possessed.

Their bodies moved frantically together as if one until the release came and they fell back on the bed, happily exhausted. In time, Tesla recovered sufficiently to smoke a cigarette, and they shared some wine. They rested, but it wasn't much later when Anya snuggled back into his arms and whispered in direct, somewhat unladylike words, what she wanted him to do next.

Her uninhibited manner fueled Tesla's mind, and he felt free to explore any fantasies he had with her, just as she wanted with him. His hand followed hers and returned to where they had started before, and they progressed from there. Their lovemaking lasted well into the night, leaving them both emotionally fulfilled and physically exhausted.

Tesla finally gave Anya a tender kiss goodnight and fell into a deep but surprisingly restless sleep.

∞

Tesla remained in Paris for the next month and held several important meetings. One was with Prince Albert of Belgium, who wanted solutions for finding the most economical way to power his country's electricity. Tesla also met with and sold his alternating current patents to a German representative for use in that nation.

Along with work, there were more intimate nights at his hotel with Anya. One morning they went downstairs for a late breakfast. As Tesla sipped his coffee with hot milk, his adoring gaze at Anya turned serious.

"I had a strange dream last night, that mother came to me. She was trying to tell me something."

Before Anya could respond, the waiter approached and handed Tesla a telegram. He hesitated, lacking the courage to open it. He knew he had intuitive powers, a sixth sense as it were, to predict or know what was happening before it happened. He felt this ability was a perception of the spirit that did not follow the normal laws of the physical universe. He did not understand this sense, but experience had taught him that a telegram could either bring great joy or, as he felt in this moment, overwhelming dread.

He sat frozen, holding the telegram. His hands shook with fear and blackness swam before his eyes. He realized he was about to faint and so, not to make a spectacle of himself, put his head down into his hands on the table and tried to steady his breathing.

"Are you alright, Niko?" he heard Anya say, as if from far off.

"Yes," he mumbled and thankfully, his vision began to clear.

Anya finally gently took the telegram out of his hands, read it and then looked up at him with concern.

"It's from your family. Your mother is very ill. You need to go to her now."

Tesla was distraught. "I have to pack my bags and cancel the rest of my tour and stay with them until Mother is better." He took a shaky, deep breath. "Will you come with me?"

Anya hesitated. "Darling, you know I want to, but I can't. There's that official party tonight in my honor; I can't not show up. I had hoped you would attend with me... but of course, you must go to your mother; that is far more important."

Tesla's eyes welled up and Anya squeezed his hand in an effort to comfort him. "It seems I am at the peak of my career," she said quietly. "This last month, receiving important commissions for my work, with more to come. I must remain here."

Tesla's shoulders slumped in defeat.

"It was so hellish for me before," Anya continued. "I wanted so much to reach my goals. And now finally, I have achieved what I worked so hard for. Let me enjoy it and ride it out, as fame can be fleeting. And maybe then, when all the hurrahs are over, I promise you, I will rethink the future..."

Tesla could not argue with her.

They went back upstairs and Tesla hastily packed. He checked out of his hotel and they headed to the train station. A quick, emotional goodbye and then Tesla took the next train to Lika, in Serbia.

Looking out the window as the scenery flashed by, Tesla couldn't help being affected by the change of environment. The lengthy trip involved leaving France and traveling through two other countries before arriving in Serbia. One minute he was in Paris, the city of love; now he was heading back home to the Austro-Hungarian Empire. Such change was a rude jolt to his sensibilities and he found it hard to relax, despite the normally soothing motion of the train.

His breath came in gasps and his mind, usually so analytical, seemed to trigger early memories of other, mostly terrible events in his life. He couldn't seem to regain his self-control as these events loomed large in his mind and choked him with fear.

He forced himself to focus only on memories with his mother, who had been his rock throughout his childhood. He loved her; she protected him. Her influence on his life, habits, and beliefs had made him the man he was today, for whatever good he was.

∞

Smiljan, Austro-Hungarian Empire — April 15, 1862

The worn tabletop was young Nikola Tesla's battlefield. At five years old, while his siblings clamored and tumbled like kittens, he'd sit rigid as a statue, scrawling out mathematical calculations. The scratching of his rough chalk against the slate tabletop was a kind of music in the lively Tesla household.

He knew, even in his childish heart, that his mind was different. A peculiar furnace burned within him, throwing off sparks the others didn't seem to see. Already, a fine thread of isolation separated him from the world, a sense of living on a different plane. He rarely spoke as a child and when he did, it was most often with his mother, Georgina "Djuka". She saw the fire within him and while the other family members sometimes teased or misunderstood his intensity, her eyes held a deep understanding.

"My little thinker," she would say, smoothing his hair as he scribbled, "The world might not catch up with you for a long time, but never doubt yourself."

"They think I'm strange, Mama," he replied, eyes not leaving his numbers. "Why can't I be like the others?"

She'd kneel beside him then, her homespun dress rustling softly. "Strange is just a word for what people don't understand yet. You'll build things with that mind, Nikola – things that will change how we all see the world."

And with those words, a flicker of pride would light his eyes, banishing the shadows of loneliness, if only for a moment.

He stopped writing his math sums to watch with admiration as she put the finishing touches on a crude homemade iron walnut cracker. His heart warmed as she smiled back at him, as if reading his thoughts and feeling his love for her.

Mother set a walnut in and neatly cracked open the shell.

"See, Nikola?" She said. "Neat and organized, as all inventions should be."

Little Nikola ran to give her a hug as his siblings - older brother Dane and three sisters - all filed in for lunch.

While young Nikola was already seriously minded, his sisters Angelina, Milka and Marcia were playful. However, their merry laughter subsided as their father Milutin now joined them at the table.

Father was an Orthodox priest.

His stern, seemingly unloving demeanor dampened the mood as he sat down and offered a prayer before eating. The girls dutifully looked down at their plates and ate in silence.

Young Nikola looked over at Mother and saw her natural gaiety subdued as well. It broke his little heart to see this. Oh, how he wanted to jump into her lap, to hug and comfort her until she was smiling again.

∞

Smiljan, Austro-Hungarian Empire — 1863

The sun was a pale, deceptive orb in the sky, a stark contrast to the vibrant laughter echoing from the meadow. Dane, the eldest Tesla child, sat astride the family's Arabian stallion, his grin as wide as the frosted field.

His sisters chased after him, squealing for him to ride slower, their cheeks flushed pink against the unforgiving wind. Even from a distance little Nikola could feel that familiar pang of envy twisting in his gut. Dane always got to go the furthest, the highest, the fastest.

A flash of premonition struck Nikola then.

An image of Dane's horse rearing, eyes wild, and Dane himself - a crumpled heap against the unforgiving ground. Tesla opened his mouth, a cry forming in his throat. But it was too late.

A sharp whinny sliced through the air. The stallion bolted, his hooves barely skimming the snow-dusted earth. A loose stone, a patch of black ice... and it happened.

Nikola watched as though through a thick fog. Dane's body, so full of life a moment ago, now sailed through the air with sickening grace. Time seemed to freeze as the earth rushed up to meet him.

The horrific thud of bone against frozen soil echoed around the field, followed by a scream so piercing it seemed to split the very sky in two.

His sisters were already sprinting towards their fallen brother, their joyful cries replaced by wails of terror.

But Nikola couldn't move. He felt the blame coiling within him like a venomous snake — he'd known he should have stopped it. Now, Dane...

Dane was broken, his twisted body sprawled on the frozen ground. He was still breathing, but just barely.

When Nikola finally found his feet, his oldest sister Angelina sat cradling Dane's limp head, whispering his name as though that alone could mend him. Tears streamed down her face, hot and relentless, even against the biting chill.

But for little Nikola, the world had gone numb and distant. All he could feel was the weight of what he hadn't done. He had betrayed his brother. His failure to find his voice in time to warn Dane was unforgivable in this young child's mind.

By midnight, Dane had died of his injuries. Nikola was awakened by Mother, who held him close and insisted he come kiss his dead brother goodbye. Into the late hours of the night, their home was a tomb, the air thick with grief. Mother huddled by the hearth, clutching Dane's lifeless form to her chest as though she could will him to breathe. Her sobs, once sharp with pain, now dissolved into raw, animalistic moans.

Nikola, sitting numbly nearby, wanted nothing more than to offer comfort, to take just a sliver of her pain onto himself. But the guilt was an abyss inside him, threatening to swallow him whole.

His father, ever stoic, ever devoted to God, reached for the worn leather Bible.

Nikola braced himself for the familiar words, the forced stoicism that grated against his mother's despair like sandpaper on an open wound.

"God's will," Father intoned, the words as cold as the air seeping through the cracks in the walls. "He rests in the arms of the Lord now, in a place beyond our suffering..."

"NO!" Mother's shriek sliced through the room. "His place is here! With me, with his sisters and brother, with his family!" She glared at her husband, her eyes blazing with a fury and contempt that Nikola had never seen before. "You speak of God... what kind of God steals a child?"

Father's hands tightened on the Bible, knuckles white. "Do not question His plan! This is a test of our faith."

"Damn your faith! And your God!" Djuka screamed.

Milutin was so taken aback by his wife's blasphemous announcement that all he could do was close his eyes and bow his head in silent prayer.

Nikola buried his face in his hands. He couldn't watch this. He rocked helplessly, trying to block out the pain and sound of his mother's sobs and his father's cold pronouncements. Eventually, Mother noticed her remaining son was ashen-faced and severely traumatized. She turned her attention to him, taking him back to bed, tucking him in and weeping, "God gave me one at midnight and at midnight he took away the other one."

That statement was obviously of little comfort to Nikola, who could not forget the shock of Dane's ice-cold lips as he kissed his brother goodbye. Nikola never really recovered from the horror of his brother's death and soon after, even ran away from home overnight in an effort to escape his parents' rejection and his own perceived guilt.

∞

Smiljan, Austro-Hungarian Empire — November 22, 1873

Tesla was seventeen. A lightning storm raged as he lay in bed with eyes closed, near death from cholera. A pile of his various inventions sat on his night table.

As Mother gently soothed his forehead with a wet cloth, young Tesla felt himself drifting out of his body, if that were possible. He seemed to rise above the bed and viewed Mother as if from above. Her voice seemed foggy and far off, but he tried to focus on it because somehow, he sensed it was important to do so.

"My darling Nikola," he heard her say, "you must hold on. Love is stronger than death. Let my love give you strength. Hold on dear boy, can you hear me?"

Yes, he could hear her. But he could not speak or let her know. She kept talking to him and he listened as best he could. As he contemplated letting go and drifting away, he couldn't bear the thought of the immense anguish it would cause Mother. He did not want to cause her pain, to have her to have to grieve for another dead son.

And so suddenly he felt he made a conscious choice and was back in his body. He knew this because he felt not pain but an extreme weariness, beyond anything he'd ever felt before.

He tried to lift a finger or otherwise give Mother a hopeful sign but could not. Yet it was a comfort to reconnect with his body and feel anything.

This memory had a happier ending. Some time passed. He was awake and smiling weakly at Mother who spoon-fed him some broth.

"Boiled vegetable soup," she said, smiling at him. "The food best for you, no germs." She explained to him how most of his childhood ailments, cholera, malaria and the like, came from contaminated water and one must be very careful to avoid germs as they had made his body frail.

Well-meaning as Mother may have been, she had ingrained into her son such a fear of germs and poor hygiene that he would be haunted by such worries throughout his adult years.

When he'd eaten all the soup, Mother set down the bowl, washed his hands with soap and water, and said:

"Father has some wonderful news he wants to tell you. He will support your desires to be an engineer, to study abroad and become a brilliant inventor." She held his hand and continued, "But first you must become well, my love."

Tesla felt a surge of vitality and hope. His Mother recognized this in his eyes and gave him a kiss on the forehead.

This was not Tesla's last youthful brush with serious illness. He would later relate how a few years later, when deathly ill and being tended by Mother, she came to his bedside and handed him a book.

"From your sisters."

Tesla looked at the title: *The Adventures of Tom Sawyer* by Mark Twain. He quickly thumbed through the book; it looked interesting. He eagerly read and enjoyed it, never dreaming that someday he would be good friends with the author.

∞

With this last memory ending on a positive note, Tesla's mind returned to the present.

The train's iron wheels screeched against the rails as it crawled into Gospic station, belching steam across the crowded platform. Tesla stood rigidly by the door, his heart pounding with a mixture of anticipation and dread. As the train shuddered to a halt, he took a deep breath, bracing himself for what lay ahead.

The moment the doors swung open, Tesla was swept into the bustling crowd. He weaved through the throng, his eyes scanning frantically for familiar faces. Suddenly, a voice cut through the crowd.

"Nikola! Nikola, over here!" Tesla's head snapped towards the sound. There, pushing through the crowd, was his older sister Milka. Behind her, he glimpsed the faces of his other sisters and Uncle Petar, the local priest.

Relief washed over him, quickly followed by a wave of guilt that threatened to knock him off his feet. As Milka drew closer, Tesla was struck by how much she had aged. At forty, her face bore the lines of worry and hardship, a stark reminder of the years he'd spent away, pursuing his dreams while his family carried on without him.

"Milka," he breathed, his voice barely audible above the noise of the station. She threw her arms around him, pulling him into a tight embrace.

"Oh, Nikola," she whispered, her voice thick with emotion. "Thank God you're here."

Tesla returned the hug, his mind reeling. As Milka pulled away, his other sisters surged forward. Angelina, the eldest, cupped his face in her hands, her eyes searching his and Marica, the youngest, clung to his arm, as if afraid he might disappear again.

"Mother?" Tesla gasped, dreading the answer but needing to know.

Milka's face crumpled and she shook her head. "She's... she's dying."

The words were like a blow to the head. Tesla staggered, darkness creeping into the edges of his vision. He felt a firm hand grip his elbow, steadying him.

Uncle Petar's voice came from somewhere far away. "Come, nephew. We must hurry."

The journey to the family home passed in a blur. Tesla sat rigid in Uncle Petar's wagon, his mind a storm of regret and fear. How many years had he wasted? How many letters had he left unanswered, too engrossed in his work to spare a thought for the woman who had given him life and made him who he was?

As they approached the house, Tesla's heart sank. A small crowd had gathered, their curious faces staring at them. He felt their eyes on him as Milka and Uncle Petar helped him from the wagon, his legs trembling beneath him.

"Nikola," Milka murmured, her arm around his waist. "Be strong. For her."

Tesla nodded mutely, allowing himself to be led into the house.

The familiar scents of home — wood smoke, herbs, and something indefinably mother — assaulted his senses, threatening to undo him completely. And then he saw her.

Djuka Tesla lay in her bed, her once-vibrant face now pale and drawn. But as Tesla entered the room, her eyes flickered open, and a spark of recognition lit them from within.

"My boy," she breathed, her voice a whisper. "My pride."

Tesla fell to his knees beside the bed, clasping her frail hand in both of his. "Mother," he choked out, tears streaming down his face. "I'm here. I'm so sorry. I should have come sooner. I should have—"

Djuka shook her head weakly, cutting off his torrent of apologies. "You're here now," she murmured. "That's all that matters."

For hours, Tesla sat vigil by his mother's bedside, holding her hand, wiping her brow, murmuring words of love and comfort. His siblings came and went, urging him to eat, to rest, but he refused to leave her side.

As night fell, Djuka's breathing became labored. The local doctor arrived, his face grim as he examined her.

"There is nothing more to be done," he said softly. "It's a matter of hours now. We wait... and we pray."

Tesla's anguished cry echoed through the house. He rocked back and forth, his mother's hand still clasped in his. "No," he moaned. "No, please. I can't lose you. Not now. Not when I've only just returned."

Milka knelt beside him, wrapping her arms around him. "Nikola," she whispered. "You need rest. There's nothing more you can do here."

But Tesla shook his head vehemently. "I won't leave her," he insisted. "Not again. Never again."

Tesla burst into tears, his body convulsing with the force of his sobs. He doubled over, nearly falling from his chair as he rocked back and forth in anguish. His fingers dug into his scalp, pulling at his hair as if the physical pain could distract from the emotional torment tearing him apart.

"No, no, no," he moaned, his voice raw and broken. "This can't be happening. Mother, please... please don't leave me."

The doctor exchanged a worried glance with Uncle Petar.

He approached Tesla cautiously, placing a gentle hand on the distraught man's shoulder.

"Mr. Tesla," he said softly, his voice laced with concern. "You need to rest. There's nothing more you can do here, and your mother wouldn't want you to destroy yourself like this."

Tesla's head snapped up, his eyes wild and bloodshot. "How dare you?" he snarled, his grief momentarily transmuted into rage. "How dare you presume to know what my mother would want? I abandoned her for years, and now you want me to abandon her again?"

Uncle Petar stepped forward. "Nikola," he said, his deep voice resonating with authority and compassion. "Listen to me. Your mother loved you more than life itself. She was proud of your accomplishments, but she would be devastated to see you like this. You need to rest, to gather your strength for the difficult days ahead."

Tesla's anger deflated as quickly as it had flared, leaving him slumped and trembling. "I can't leave her," he whispered. "I've already lost so much time."

The doctor nodded to Uncle Petar, and together they lifted Tesla from his chair. He was surprisingly light, his body frail despite his tall frame.

"No," Tesla protested weakly, trying to pull away. "Please, I need to stay with her. Just a little longer."

"Shhh, Nikola," Uncle Petar soothed, as they half-carried, half-dragged him from the room. "We'll come back soon. I promise."

Tesla's sisters watched with tear-stained faces as their brother was taken away, their hearts breaking anew at his pain.

Outside, the cool night air hit Tesla like a slap in the face, momentarily clearing the fog of grief from his mind. He blinked, looking around in confusion as Uncle Petar and the doctor maneuvered him into a waiting carriage.

"Where... where are we going?"

Uncle Petar climbed in beside him, wrapping a protective arm around his shoulders. "There's a small inn just down the road," he explained gently. "You need to rest, Nikola. You're exhausted, and grief can do terrible things to a man's mind and body if he's not careful."

The short journey passed in silence, broken only by Tesla's occasional hiccupping sobs. When they arrived at the inn, a middle-aged woman was waiting at the door, her face etched with sympathy.

"I've prepared a room," she said softly. Uncle Petar nodded gratefully as he and the doctor helped Tesla inside. They navigated narrow stairs and a dimly lit hallway before entering a small, cozy room with a single bed and a sofa chair.

"Here we are, Nikola," Uncle Petar said, easing his nephew onto the bed. "Let's get you comfortable."

Tesla allowed himself to be tucked in like a child, his eyes vacant and unfocused. As Uncle Petar pulled the blanket up to his chin, Tesla suddenly gripped his arm with surprising strength.

"Promise me," he rasped, his eyes suddenly clear and intense. "Promise me you'll wake me if... if anything changes. I can't... I can't not be there at the end."

Uncle Petar's eyes glistened with unshed tears. "I promise, Nikola. Now, please, try to sleep."

As Uncle Petar made himself comfortable on the sofa by the window, Tesla whispered, "Uncle, do you think... do you think she knew how much I loved her? Even though I was away for so long?"

Uncle Petar's face softened with compassion. "Oh, Nikola, she never doubted it for a moment. Your love was as constant to her as the stars in the sky."

With those words hanging in the air, exhaustion finally pulled Tesla into a troubled sleep.

Uncle Petar sat vigil on the sofa chair, falling in and out of sleep. Barely three hours later Tesla suddenly jerked awake, startled by a strange sense that overcame him.

He felt his mother's presence; in a way, he could almost see her energy standing before him with a glowing sad smile. Was it a hallucination, an angel, or was it indeed her spirit? If so, it could only mean she had died and felt this was her last task, to contact him directly to say goodbye.

"We must go back!" he alerted his uncle, who snapped out of sleep, disoriented. They left the inn and returned to the family house. Milka immediately wrapped her arms around Tesla. He jerked away, a sense of urgency gripping him.

Angelina glanced at the clock on the wall. "It's Easter Sunday," she said softly.

"Just past 3 am," confirmed Marica.

Tesla scarcely heard them. He rushed into his mother's room and leaned over her, searching her face. Djuka lay still, her hands folded on her chest, her eyes closed. The rise and fall of her chest had ceased.

"No," Tesla breathed, his voice breaking. "No, no, no!"

He gathered her lifeless body into his arms, rocking her as he had longed to be rocked as a child. Sobs wracked his body, years of pent-up guilt and grief pouring out of him in a rush.

"I'm sorry," he wept. "I'm so sorry, Mama. I worked so hard, I thought I was doing it for you, for all of us. But I lost sight of what truly mattered. I wasn't here when you needed me. I wasn't here to say goodbye."

His sisters surrounded him, their own tears flowing freely. Milka stroked his hair, murmuring words of comfort that fell on deaf ears.

"Your work must continue, Nikola," Angelina said softly. "Mother would want that."

But Tesla shook his head, still clinging to Djuka's body. "No," he said, his voice hollow. "It's too much. The price is too high. What good are my inventions, my dreams of the future, if I lose everything that matters in the present?"

Marica wrapped her arms around him. "Dear brother, you have not lost everything. You have us and we love you; please do not belittle that. Yes, you live across an ocean but in our hearts, there is no distance at all."

"You don't understand," Tesla murmured tearfully. "Too late, too late ... How many times have I hesitated when I should have acted quickly? A wise man learns from his mistakes; I am not a wise man but a disappointment to those I love... and to myself."

His sisters gathered around to comfort him. Milka said softly, "You are a man who carries the weight of the world on his shoulders, and that is a tremendous responsibility. But you are here now, so why not take some weeks and visit with us before you return to New York?"

There was a long pause as Tesla considered her offer. Finally he made his decision. "Yes," he nodded, "I will do that. Thank you."

As the first light of Easter Sunday crept through the windows, Tesla remained by his mother's side, bolstered somewhat by his sisters' presence but still a broken man facing a future suddenly without a guiding light.

14

THREE DAYS IN SERBIA

In the weeks that followed his mother's funeral, Tesla surrounded himself with his sisters, even visiting their homes and spending time with his relatives. It was an effort to seek comfort and support from loved ones who shared his loss.

He also sent a telegram to Anya in Paris, alerting her to his mother's passing. She replied, offering her condolences to him and his family.

Much to Tesla's surprise, toward the end of May he received yet another telegram from her. In her message, she explained how she had been entrusted with creating a painting for a wealthy client who lived in Belgrade. In fact, she was in Serbia now, and if he had time to come visit her, she would take time off to spend with him.

Tesla found himself briefly conflicted. His impulse was to catch the next train and go right to her. He pondered on what the implications of their reunion would mean. Did this mean she was open to changing her mind about marriage? Did she love him as deeply as he loved her? After the pain of losing his mother, he wasn't sure he could endure another loss if either answer was no.

In the end, his decision of whether to make the trip was taken out of his hands. Some of his concerned acquaintances, fellow Serbian scientists, took it upon themselves to help arrange two important events for him in

Belgrade: receiving a special title by the King and being honored by the mayor. His friends expected his spirits would be lifted by such praise, and they even accompanied him on the train to Belgrade to ensure he arrived safely.

During the lengthy train trip, Tesla tried to focus on his upcoming speech – about being a Serb and his sincere goal in life, to benefit all humanity. But losing his mother still weighed heavily on his heart, a dull ache that seemed to permeate every corner of his being. He looked through the train window, gazing out at the passing landscapes. The sun was setting, painting the sky in hues of orange and pink that reminded him of Anya's favorite dress.

"What game are you playing, my dear?" he whispered to the absent Anya. "Do you truly wish to see me, or is this merely a consolation for my loss?"

Tesla's mind, usually so adept at unraveling the mysteries of electricity and magnetism, found itself hopelessly tangled in the complexities of human emotion. *Nikola, you fool,* he thought. *You can map the currents of the earth, but you cannot fathom the currents of a woman's heart.*

In just a few hours he would meet with Anya again. And now all he had to do until then was to convince himself it wasn't madness.

The journey to Belgrade was mostly a blur. He hardly noticed the hills and quaint villages that slipped by outside his window. His mind was consumed with thoughts of Anya — her laugh, her scent, the way her eyes sparkled when she spoke of her art.

As the train pulled into Belgrade station, Tesla's heart raced. Once he completed his official duties, he declined any further socializing with his friends for the rest of his stay.

He arrived at the designated café before sunset, an hour earlier than the agreed meeting time with Anya. The waiter observed him with curiosity as he requested his third cup of coffee, his fingers nervously tapping on the table.

And then there she was. She had arrived.

"Niko, my darling!" Anya's voice rang out across the café, causing heads to turn. She rushed towards him, her cheeks flushed from running, a few stray curls escaping from beneath her hat.

Tesla stood, his breath catching in his throat. She was as beautiful as ever, perhaps even more so. "Anya," he breathed, drinking in the sight of her. "I've missed you," he said softly as he helped her into her seat.

Anya's eyes softened. "I've missed you too, Niko. More than I care to admit." She paused, her hand going to her ears. "Oh! I forgot..." She quickly removed her earrings, remembering his aversion to them.

Tesla smiled, touched by her thoughtfulness. "Thank you. I know it's a strange quirk of mine."

"One of many," Anya teased, her eyes twinkling. "But they're all part of your charm."

As they ordered lunch, the conversation flowed easily between them. Tesla found himself relaxing, the tension of the past weeks easing from his shoulders.

"Tell me about your mother," Anya said quietly, reaching across the table to take his hand. "I was so sorry to hear of her passing."

Tesla's throat tightened. "She was... extraordinary. Strong, brilliant, the backbone of our family. I fear I'll never meet her equal."

Anya squeezed his hand. "But you already have, my darling. It's you, she raised an extraordinary son. She lives on in you, Niko."

They talked for hours, the café emptying around them as afternoon faded into evening. When Anya suggested he stay with her, Tesla's heart leapt.

"Are you sure?" he asked, searching her eyes for any sign of hesitation.

"Of course," she replied with a smile. "We have so much catching up to do."

As they walked to her hotel, they passed a street fair. The air was filled with the scent of roasted chestnuts and the sound of laughter. Anya's eyes were drawn to a jewelry stand, where a delicate silver bracelet caught the light.

"It's beautiful," she murmured, picking it up.

Tesla watched her, a warmth spreading through his chest.

"Let me," he said, taking the bracelet and slipping it onto her wrist. "A gift, to commemorate our reunion."

Anya's eyes widened in surprise. "But Niko, you don't like jewelry..."

"I find that I like this one, very much indeed."

∞

During his trip to Belgrade, Tesla found himself immersed in an array of passionate and sensual encounters that surpassed any other previous sexual experiences he had ever had.

He spent most of his three days in Serbia in room 327 at the Moskva Hotel. And then, on his last night with Anya, reality intruded.

"Niko," Anya said, her head resting on his chest. "What are we doing?"

Tesla sighed, running his fingers through her hair. "Living in a beautiful dream, my love."

She propped herself up on one elbow, looking into his eyes. "But it can't last, can it? My work, your inventions... we're both married to our careers."

"Perhaps," Tesla mused, "there's a current that could unite us, a force stronger than our individual pursuits."

Anya smiled sadly. "You and your forces, Niko. But love isn't electricity. It can't be harnessed or controlled."

As Tesla prepared to leave on the final day of his visit, he felt a familiar ache in his chest. Anya stood in the doorway of her hotel room, watching him gather his things.

"Will you tell anyone about us?" she asked softly.

Tesla shook his head. "No. This... this is ours. Sacred and secret." He cupped her face in his hands, memorizing every detail. "Anya, I..."

She placed a finger on his lips. "I know, Niko. I feel it too. But sometimes, feeling is all we can do."

As he walked away, Tesla's mind was already turning to his next invention, his next breakthrough. But his heart... his heart remained in room 327 at the Moskva Hotel in Belgrade, Serbia with a woman who understood him better than anyone else in the world.

Later that day, a reporter recognized him before his departure from Serbia. He asked Tesla about the purpose of his visit to Belgrade. Tesla's thoughts flashed to Anya's smile, to the warmth of her embrace. He gave the only answer he could.

"I feel much more than I can say."

And in those words, lay a universe of unspoken truths, of paths not taken, and of a love that defied all his attempts at rational analysis.

15

Call Me Kate

Tesla finally took his leave of his homeland. Made the long trek across central and western Europe, across the English Channel, and on to the familiar city of Liverpool where he boarded the SS *Germanic* for the voyage back to America.

When the ship finally arrived in New York Harbor on June 2nd, 1882, thousands of people gathered to see Tesla. The owners of the SS *Germanic*, the White Star Line company, had informed the New York newspapers via telegram that the famous scientist Nikola Tesla was onboard. The newspapers announced the same in their papers.

No one could imagine that such a large crowd would materialize to welcome Tesla back to America. Tesla himself was taken aback by the sight of the sizeable crowd.

At the foot of the gangplank stood Katharine, Robert, and Westinghouse, watching anxiously as the passengers debarked.

Finally, Tesla made his way down the gangplank, looking shell-shocked and disoriented. Katharine rushed to Tesla and embraced him.

"So sorry about your mother, Nikola."

Tesla broke down in grief while Katharine, Robert, Westinghouse and a half dozen policemen surrounded him to escort him away from the cheering crowd and forming chaos.

∞

Tesla threw himself back into his work and in time, the love and support of his friends, and encouragement from George Westinghouse, helped Tesla regain his footing in life.

He resumed working such long hours he usually averaged about three hours of sleep a day. But he was productive and happy.

Then, without warning, all his pride and achievement turned to horror.

There was a raging fire. The date was March 13th, 1895.

The once-bustling laboratory on Grand Street lay in ruins. Charred beams and shattered equipment littered the floor, bathed in the light of dawn. The air hung heavy with smoke; a bitter echo of dreams devoured by flames.

Tesla stood amidst the wreckage, his silhouette a haunting picture of despair against the devastating backdrop.

His eyes, usually alive with brilliance, held only a dull reflection of the destruction.

The fire marshal, a grizzled veteran of such tragedies, approached cautiously. "A damn shame, Mr. Tesla. No accident, this. The way it spread... someone meant to burn you out."

"Not just someone." Tesla's voice was laced with fury and despair. "Edison. He couldn't defeat me with his 'demonstrations', so he resorted to this.... Coward."

Amongst the ashes, Tesla's gaze fell on a miraculously intact extra-large light bulb.

He remembered the day it was manufactured, the press photograph where it had illuminated his face, a perfect symbol of his work, now a cruel reminder of all he'd lost.

Clutching the bulb, he fell to his knees, the weight of the night finally crushing him.

∞

Losing his laboratory left Tesla feeling unnerved. Once again, as happened with other heartbreaking traumas in his life, he temporarily lost his memory. Normally he would have thought this strange amnesia an unacceptable development, but for now, it served as welcome oblivion.

He took to his bed, staring at the ceiling while memories of the ruined building insisted on flooding his mind.

His devastation was further strengthened by the knowledge that such evil could exist, that a devious person could order a match to be lit and boom! In the blink of an eye, a man's entire life's work could be obliterated, leaving him with nothing. Tesla's efforts had always been driven by his genuine desire to help his fellow man, and this work had brought him immense joy. But now — it was all ripped away from him.

Such were his haunted nights that followed, beset by restless dreams. The days were even worse. His most painful memories would kick in as if, in his mind, he was watching before him a strip of moving motion pictures. The visuals went back to early childhood and then jumped forward to the next scene of horrors. Repeatedly, these memories played before him.

He had faced terrors in the past, and always pulled himself out of the abyss and carried on.

This time, he doubted he had any remaining strength or sanity to do so.

∞

New York City - March 21, 1895

Katharine Johnson burst through the revolving doors of the Waldorf-Astoria Hotel, her usual grace momentarily forgotten.

The lobby fell silent as heads turned to watch her entrance. Her emerald silk dress, usually a perfect complement to her poised demeanor, now seemed to accentuate the worry etched across her face. The click of her heels against the polished marble floor echoed through the cavernous space as she made her way to the front desk. The scent of fresh-cut flowers and cigar smoke hung in the air, a stark contrast to the worry on her face and tension radiating from her every movement.

Charles, the impeccably dressed front desk manager, mirrored her alarm.

"Mrs. Johnson!" he exclaimed in a hushed tone, glancing nervously at the other patrons. "We've been hoping you'd come. It's about Mr. Tesla."

Katharine's heart pounded harder. "What's happened, Charles? Tell me everything."

Charles wrung his hands, his usual composure slipping.

"It's been a week now, ma'am. Mr. Tesla has barricaded himself in his suite. He won't let anyone in, not even to clean or deliver fresh linens."

"Good God," Katharine breathed. "But surely he's been eating?"

Charles shook his head. "That's just it, Mrs. Johnson. The food trays we've left outside his door remain untouched. It's as if..." He trailed off, seemingly unwilling to voice his fears.

"As if what, Charles?" Katharine pressed.

The manager leaned in closer, his words coming out in a rush. "As if he's lost his mind, ma'am. We hear him at all hours, pacing and muttering to himself. Sometimes... sometimes he shouts the most terrible things."

Katharine's blood ran cold. "What sort of things?"

Charles looked around furtively before responding. "Curses, ma'am. Ravings about electricity and invisible forces. The maids refuse to go near the room now. They are afraid."

A chill ran down Katharine's spine. The idea of Tesla being reduced to a raving madman was almost too much to bear.

"But he's alive?" she asked, clinging to hope. "You're certain of that?"

Charles nodded. "We hear him moving about, ma'am. Shuffling papers, muttering to himself. Sometimes there are strange flashes of light, like lightning beneath the door. The management is very concerned."

Katharine straightened her back. "I need to see him. Now."

"Mrs. Johnson, I'm not sure that's wise," Charles protested. "Perhaps we should call for a doctor or the authorities..."

"No!" Katharine said firmly. "Nikola needs a friend, not a stranger. Take me to his room immediately."

Charles hesitated for a moment before nodding in resignation. "As you wish, ma'am. Please, follow me."

As they made their way to the elevator, Katharine's mind raced. What could have driven Tesla to such a state? Had his genius finally pushed him over the edge into madness?

The elevator operator, a young man named Thomas, greeted them with a nervous smile. "Eighth floor, Mrs. Johnson?"

"Yes, Thomas," she replied, forcing a calm she didn't feel. "And quickly, please."

As the elevator began its ascent, Charles leaned in close. "Mrs. Johnson, I feel I should warn you. The... noises coming from Mr. Tesla's room have been most disturbing. Are you quite sure you want to do this?"

Katharine met his gaze with determination. "I've known Nikola for years, Charles. He's one of the most brilliant minds of our time. If anyone can reach him, it's me."

The elevator came to a stop with a gentle ding, and the doors slid open to reveal a deserted hallway. The plush carpet muffled their footsteps as they made their way to suite 813.

As they approached, Katharine could hear it — a low, constant muttering punctuated by occasional outbursts in a language she didn't recognize.

She placed her hand on the door, feeling it vibrate slightly beneath her palm.

"Nikola?" she called out softly. "Nikola, it's Katharine. Please, let me in. I want to help you."

The muttering stopped abruptly. For a moment, there was complete silence. Then, a voice that barely resembled the Tesla she knew responded.

"Katharine? Is it really you?" The words were slurred, heavy with exhaustion or something worse.

"Yes, Nikola. It's me. Please, open the door."

There was a shuffling sound, then the click of multiple locks being undone. Slowly, the door creaked open, revealing a sliver of the darkened room beyond.

Katharine turned to Charles. "Thank you. I'll take it from here."

The manager looked uncertain. "Mrs. Johnson, are you sure—"

"I'm sure," she said firmly. "I'll call if I need anything."

With a deep breath, Katharine stepped into the darkness of Tesla's room, the door closing behind her with a soft click. Whatever she found inside, she was determined to help her friend — no matter the cost.

She turned on the lights and gasped. The once-luxurious suite was in utter disarray. Papers covered every surface, scrawled with incomprehensible equations and diagrams. The curtains were drawn tight, and the only light came from a single guttering candle on the desk. In the center of the chaos stood Tesla, a shadow of his former self. Unshaven, unwashed, his eyes hollow and haunted, he looked as if he had lost considerable weight. The smell of stale sweat and tobacco hung heavy in the air.

This wasn't the genius Katharine knew. This was a man on the verge of total collapse. He paced frenetically, muttering to himself and occasionally stopping to scribble something on the wall with a piece of chalk.

"Nikola?" Katharine called softly, her heart breaking at the sight of her brilliant friend in such a state.

Tesla's head snapped up, his eyes focusing on her with an intensity that made her take a step back. "Katharine! You're here! You must see, you must understand!" He grabbed her arm, pulling her towards the wall covered in chalk scribblings.

"Nikola, what's happened to you? We've been so worried—"

"No time for that!" he interrupted, waving his hand dismissively. "Look, look! The power of 3, 6, and 9! It's all here, the key to the universe!"

Katharine stared at the wall, trying to make sense of the jumble of numbers and circles. "I don't understand, Nikola. What am I looking at?"

Tesla's eyes gleamed with a fevered light. "It's so simple, yet so profound! The circle, Katharine, 360 degrees! And what is $3 + 6 + 0$? It's 9! Always 9!"

He began to pace again, his words tumbling out faster and faster. "Divide the circle, divide it again and again. What do you get? 3, 6, 9! Always! It's the secret rhythm of the universe!"

Katharine watched as he scribbled frantically on a nearby piece of paper. "Look! $360 \div 2 = 180$. $1 + 8 + 0 = 9$! Divide again! $180 \div 2 = 90$. $9 + 0 = 9$! It never ends, Katharine! The pattern is eternal!"

He whirled around, grabbing her shoulders. His eyes were wide, pupils dilated. "Don't you see? These numbers - 3, 6, 9 - they're not just numbers. They're the keys to free energy, to communication with other worlds, to the very fabric of reality itself!"

Katharine gently took his hands, trying to calm him. "Nikola, please. You're not making sense. You need to rest, to eat something-"

But Tesla was beyond hearing. He broke away from her, rushing to the window and throwing open the curtains. The sudden influx of light made Katharine blink.

"The world isn't ready, Katharine! They can't see the truth!" Tesla pressed his forehead against the glass, his breath fogging the pane. "But I see it. I see it everywhere now. The city, the people, the very air - all vibrating to the rhythm of 3, 6, and 9!" He turned back to her, his face a mask of anguish and ecstasy. "I've touched the mind of God, Katharine. And it's beautiful and terrible and I can't... I can't..."

Suddenly, Tesla's legs gave out. Katharine rushed forward, catching him before he hit the floor. As she cradled his head in her lap, she could feel the heat radiating from his skin. He was burning up with fever.

"Oh, Nikola," she whispered, tears forming in her eyes. "What have you done to yourself?"

Tesla's eyes fluttered open, a moment of clarity shining through the madness. "Katharine?" he murmured. "Is it really you? I've been lost in numbers... so many numbers..."

"I'm here, Nikola," she soothed, stroking his hair. "I'm here and I'm going to help you. We'll figure this out together, I promise."

Katharine looked around the room, taking in the extent of his obsession. Somewhere in this chaos of numbers and theories lay the brilliant mind of Tesla, her dear friend. She was determined to bring him back, to make sense of his ravings about 3, 6, and 9.

But as she gazed at the complex equations and diagrams covering every surface, a chill ran down her spine. What if Tesla's madness wasn't madness at all? What if he had truly discovered something beyond their understanding? And if so, at what cost to his sanity?

She suddenly changed gears, and her eyes began to dart around the chaotic room, her mind racing to formulate a plan. The brilliant inventor before her was a far cry from the dashing, enigmatic figure she knew. Tesla's disheveled appearance and wild eyes spoke volumes about his deteriorating state.

"The shower," Katharine murmured to herself, her voice barely audible above Tesla's continued ramblings about the mystical properties of numbers. "That's the first order of business. Nikola," she said softly, placing a gentle hand on his arm. "Let's get you cleaned up, shall we? A hot shower will do wonders."

Tesla's gaze, previously fixed on some invisible point in the distance, snapped to her face. For a moment, confusion clouded his features before a flicker of recognition sparked in his eyes.

"Katharine? Is that really you?" His voice was hoarse, as if he hadn't used it for normal conversation in days. "But the numbers... I was so close to unraveling the universe's secrets."

"The universe will still be there after you've had a shower," Katharine replied, a hint of her usual wry humor creeping into her tone. "Come now, let's get you sorted."

With gentle persuasion and surprising strength, she guided him towards the bathroom. Tesla's protests were weak, his body realizing its need for basic care even as his mind continued to race with theories and calculations.

"But Katharine, you don't understand," Tesla insisted as she maneuvered him through the door. "The power of 3, 6, and 9 – it's everywhere!"

"I'm sure it is," Katharine soothed, reaching past him to turn on the shower. The sound of running water filled the room, a hopeful counterpoint to the stagnant air. Steam began to rise, carrying with it the faint scent of sandalwood from the hotel's luxury toiletries.

"Now then," she said, adopting a tone one might use with a child, "in you go. There's soap and shampoo there, and I'll lay out some fresh clothes for you. Can you manage on your own, or shall I call for assistance?"

This seemed to snap Tesla out of his fugue state. "I am not a handicap, Katharine," he said, a flash of his old pride shining through. "I am perfectly capable of bathing myself."

Katharine smiled, relieved to see a glimpse of the old Tesla. "Of course you are. I'll be right outside if you need anything. And Nikola?" she added as she turned to leave. "Do try not to solve all the mysteries of the universe while you're in there. Some of us enjoy a good puzzle now and then."

She closed the door behind her, leaning against it with a sigh. The sound of water splashing and Tesla's muffled voice — still expounding on his theories, but with notably less fervor — filtered through the thick wood. e heavy curtains to let in the late afternoon sunlight.

She rang for service, ordering a light meal to be sent up — nothing too heavy, but nourishing.

By the time Tesla emerged from the bathroom, Katharine had transformed the chaotic suite into something resembling order. The inventor himself was a transformed man — showered, clean-shaven, and clad in a luxurious set of silk pajamas that Katharine had found in his wardrobe.

"Well," Katharine said, unable to keep a note of approval from her voice, "You look much more like yourself, Nikola. How do you feel?"

Tesla ran a hand through his damp hair, his movements slow and deliberate, as if he were reacquainting himself with his own body.

"I feel... clearer," he admitted, a note of surprise in his voice. "As if a fog has lifted. But Katharine, the things I saw, the connections I made – they were real. I'm certain of it."

Katharine gestured to the small table by the window, where a tray laden with light food awaited. "Why don't you tell me all about it over some food? I daresay your brilliant mind will function even better with some nourishment."

As Tesla took a seat, his movements still somewhat unsteady, Katharine couldn't help but notice the gleam in his eyes. The madness seemed to have receded, but the spark of genius — that dangerous, brilliant spark that had always defined Nikola Tesla — burned as brightly as ever.

"Now then," she said, pouring him a cup of strong, fragrant tea. "Start at the beginning. Tell me everything about these mystical numbers of yours, and we'll see if we can't make sense of it all."

Tesla's hand trembled slightly as he reached for the teacup, but his voice was steady as he spoke.

"Katharine? Everything... gone, only 3-6-9 remains."

"Not everything. You have your mind; you have your friends. And now you have this 3-6-9 whatever it is. George will help you rebuild." She reached across the table to cover his hand with hers, the gesture filled with unspoken support.

He looked up, his eyes moist with tears. "Edison did this. He couldn't defeat me with science, so..." His voice trailed off, replaced by a bitter laugh.

He poured himself another cup of tea, the steam obscuring his features for a moment. "I had passion, once, for my work... for my love," he confessed, his voice thick with a sorrow that went beyond his recent loss.

Katharine leaned forward, intrigued and a little surprised.

"The interviews always paint you as a man married solely to your work."

He offered a ghost of a smile. "Do not believe everything you read, even when they quote my words." His voice took on a melancholic note. "My work has made me... a solitary figure. Now I am left with nothing."

A subtle silence hung in the air. Katharine studied his downcast eyes. He carried the weight of the world on his shoulders. Yet underneath it all, she sensed a flicker of something else... vulnerability, perhaps?

"A solitary figure can become lonely," she murmured, her tone soft and thoughtful.

His gaze snapped to hers, surprise lacing his features. He hesitated for a beat then lowered his defenses slightly.

"Indeed. Though loneliness is not a thing one can speak of readily. It exposes... a certain weakness."

She smiled. "Solitude is not a weakness. But perhaps... sometimes it longs for a companion."

He watched her and for the briefest moment, the mask seemed to slip. "And yet, what value does a fleeting connection have when one's life is built around one's work?"

"Can't a fleeting connection be like this coffee? A brief, beautiful moment of flavor and taste."

"Dangerous words, Katharine. Suggesting life should be savored and hold moments of pleasure, not simply be a ledger of tasks."

"Perhaps it's time you savored something," she replied boldly, the challenge hanging subtly between them.

He held her gaze for a long moment then slowly, he stood. His expression was one of longing. "You are so..." He paused and took a shallow breath. "Beautiful." Moving closer, his hand touched her cheek with tenderness. It sent a delicious thrill coursing through her body.

"But perhaps... dangerous is exactly what I need," she said in a soft voice. Then their lips met. It was as if the air itself caught fire. He'd forgotten this, the intoxicating rush of claiming another person so completely, of losing himself in the sweet oblivion of shared desire.

It was not just hunger, though that was undeniable; it was a desperate yearning for connection, for proof that he was still capable of feeling, not just thinking.

Katharine met him with an urgency that surprised and thrilled him. Her hands were everywhere — in his hair, on his shoulders, tracing the line of his spine with a touch that set his nerves alight. She was all warmth and silken skin.

He found himself clumsy, fumbling with buttons and clasps. Years and decades of solitude seemed to melt away, replaced by a frantic need to touch, to taste, to possess.

When they finally tumbled onto the bed, it was less a deliberate act and more a surrender to inevitable forces. The room filled with gasps and soft cries, their bodies finding an instinctive, desperate rhythm.

There was no time for tender exploration, only a frenzy of sensation — of skin against skin, the exquisite ache of building pleasure, the shared moans and gasps of release.

Afterwards, they lay entwined, the echoes of their passion reverberating in the stillness. Then Tesla found himself suddenly overcome with emotion and sobbed in her arms, as if his physical release had opened the floodgates of repressed pain, sorrow, and ecstasy.

She comforted him until he was calm again. A profound silence settled over them. Tesla now felt a strange mix of exhilaration and shame wash over him, battling for dominance in his aching heart.

Katharine drew a finger across his chest, her touch as light as a whisper. "No regrets, Nikola," she murmurs, the words tinged with a vulnerability she seldom displayed.

He sighed, knowing it was a lie, even a well-meant one. How could there be no regrets when their actions betrayed a trust, however unspoken? "Bob is my friend," he began, but his voice faltered.

This was not just about Robert; it was about a code of honor he'd upheld all his life, and now lay in tatters in the soft light filtering through the curtains.

The silence stretched between them, heavy with unspoken truths. There was a profound understanding between them, an unspoken recognition that they were not simply two individuals in a moment of vulnerability, but kindred spirits who had found each other amidst the chaos of life.

He traced the line of her jaw with a shaking hand. "We should never have..." he began, but the protest died on his lips. Despite his scientific and rational nature, certain forces surpassed logic.

Katharine turned her head, pressing a kiss to his palm. "Perhaps," she whispered with a ghost of a smile, "some things are so fated, we are merely players caught in a grand, inevitable design."

"A dangerous design," he admitted, a wry chuckle catching in his throat. She propped herself up on one elbow, gazing lovingly into his eyes. He lightly traced patterns with his finger on her bare breast.

"Dangerous, perhaps. But tell me, Nikola Tesla, do you dare deny it was... glorious?"

Her smile was both a challenge and a balm. He cupped her breast with his hand. He could not deny the truth. It had been beautiful and destructive, impulsive and profound.

"You are a temptress, Katharine Johnson," he managed to say, a spark of his usual humor returning to his eyes.

"Call me Kate," she whispered, snuggling closer into his arms.

He instantly tensed up. "Is that what he calls you, when you—"

"No, it's my name for those dearest to me, close family and friends. And surely you qualify in that regard."

He relaxed again and she leaned in, their lips almost brushing. "Perhaps," she added, the hint of mischief returning to her voice, "we deserved this burst of lightning."

He inevitably laughed, the sound surprisingly carefree. And as she kissed him again, this time with lingering sweetness, he allowed himself to believe that perhaps, just perhaps, the consequences were worth the exquisite risk. Fate, it seemed, had dealt them a complex hand, and they, with a mixture of trepidation and undeniable anticipation, played it.

"Even so..." Katharine countered, "You're the great Nikola Tesla. And like a phoenix rising, you will come back stronger and better than before. Your inventions make Edison look small. Now explain again what this 3-6-9 theory is all about."

16

Phoenix Rising

Three months passed. Tesla, with the generous help of Westinghouse, rebuilt his laboratory. This was not merely a reconstruction, it was a rebirth, bigger and better than the one reduced to ashes.

The new laboratory was a technological marvel, surpassing anything Edison had in terms of sophistication and equipment. Gone was the cramped, haphazard feel of the old laboratory. This space was built for purpose.

Westinghouse understood the value of Tesla's groundbreaking work and ensured that no expense was spared. Around the clock armed watchmen secured the perimeter, remaining vigilant against any threat. High walls and a gated entrance added an extra layer of security, projecting a fortress-like protection for the treasures of intellect housed within.

Upon entering the laboratory, one was immediately struck by sparkling new generators humming steadily, and arrays of electrical components lining the clean, well-organized workbenches. Glass cabinets filled with meticulously arranged tools and materials reflected the glow of electric lamps, illuminating the laboratory in a clear, steady light that was a luxury of the era.

Tesla's personal office was a contrast to the industrial ambiance of the main laboratory. It was an enclave of comfort and reflection, designed to suit his unique working habits.

The office featured a large oak desk, cluttered with blueprints and papers. Bookshelves lined the walls, filled with scientific texts and notebooks.

In the room's corner, a lavish soft leather sofa invited brief rests. Here, Tesla would indulge in his famous twenty-minute power naps, recharging his mind.

Tesla viewed the laboratory as more than a mere workplace. The air buzzed with the electricity of potential, both literal and metaphorical, as Tesla continued to push the boundaries of what was possible.

Another joyous triumph was a visit to the new laboratory by Mark Twain. The famous author's white hair was a wild halo around his weathered face, and he sported his trademark bushy mustache as he entered the premises.

There was no fear in Twain's face, only a childlike wonder. His gaze darted from the towering coils to the intricate contraptions that whirred with an alien purpose. His calloused writer's hands, usually wielding a pen, twitched with a suppressed urge to touch the impossible.

Twain slowly moved through the building, absorbing everything in sight, so it took some time to reach the office. When he did, Tesla already had a glass of whiskey prepared for him.

"A wizard's den, Nikola!" quipped Twain. He chuckled, accepting the whisky that seemed to glow in the dim light. "Tell me, are you harnessing lightning itself?"

Tesla flashed a grin, the warmth in his eyes a stark contrast to his usual intensity. "Something like that, my friend. But the truth, as always, is stranger than fiction." Tesla's voice turned hard. "Edison would have the world believe my work is dangerous folly."

Twain's expression became serious. "I hear our friend Mr. Edison let you work out of his New Jersey laboratory while all this was being rebuilt. Surely that was kindness on his part?"

"Kindness... or guilt, perhaps," countered Tesla. "It is difficult when you want to like and admire your rivals, even work together with them, only to learn that behind their kind gestures that provide you hope, they are stabbing you behind your back. I remain too trusting, I fear."

Twain quickly changed the subject to lighten Tesla's mood. "Dangerous folly, Nikola? Tell me more. Time travel, perhaps? Like my Connecticut Yankee found himself in King Arthur's court! I must write a sequel!"

Tesla's eyes sparkled. "Sam, you just—" He paused and then continued, "But perhaps you're closer to the truth than you realize..."

He launched into a whirlwind explanation of wireless communication, harnessing the energy of the Earth itself, concepts so far ahead of their time that even Twain's fertile imagination struggled to grasp them.

As the night wore on, the air crackled with shared enthusiasm. Two of the world's sharpest and most creative minds dueled not with weapons, but with ideas. They laughed and toasted to audacity, to the power of the human spirit, and, as the whisky flowed, to a future they were determined to shape.

∞

New York City, Columbia University - July 20, 1888

The heat of the day was oppressive, mirroring the simmering rage in Thomas Edison's gaze as he addressed the crowd at Columbia University.

The grim spectacle before them was no scientific demonstration, but a theatrical act of cruelty. Chained in the unrelenting sun, a magnificent Newfoundland dog whimpered, its eyes wide with terror.

"Behold!" Edison's voice cut through the murmurs of the crowd. "The unchecked madness of alternating current! Tesla would have you believe his system is the future, but it is chaos given form, a tool of destruction masked as progress!"

He gestured dramatically towards the trapped animal, his cronies standing grim-faced beside him. "This is the price of innovation without conscience!" Edison snapped at the crowd.

A switch clicked, and the dog convulsed and foamed at the mouth as the lethal current coursed through its body. The air crackled with electricity as the stench of burned fur struck the crowd. Some sobbed, others turned away, but Edison watched coldly, his point made in the most brutal way possible.

∞

Tesla was duly dismayed at the cruel lengths Edison took to discount the superiority of alternating current. However, Tesla did not crash emotionally as he might have done in the past. He kept his attention on his work, knowing all too well that this was a war that Edison could not win.

Edison would finally have to retreat with his unworkable direct current and focus instead on other viable inventions such as sound recordings and the earliest motion pictures, including his first successful efforts to colorize film.

Tesla was enjoying both a professional and emotional, even keel. He and Katharine chose to discreetly continue their affair, as time and logistics allowed. Their intimacy provided a stabilizing influence in his life, and he accepted the reality that there was no chance of her seeking a divorce. Nor would he have wanted that. At heart, when his mind and body did not demand physical enticement and release, he remained a stoic whose attention was fixated only on his work.

In her own way, Katharine became obsessed with Tesla, perhaps for the very reason of his unique personality. She came to understand why he could not maintain a "normal" relationship. His idiosyncrasies were such that most women would have found him too problematic to deal with.

He explained to her how his germ phobia had come about from his childhood illnesses and near death from drinking tainted water. He further detailed how his mother subsequently ingrained in him the urgent need for cleanliness. He had other phobias too, but his fear of germs seemed to ebb and flow, depending on his stress level.

While Katharine observed that Tesla could eat normally at their home, she was all too familiar with watching him eat at a restaurant, where he demanded eighteen napkins placed before him, in groups of three. He meticulously used one napkin after the next to clean his silverware, plates and glasses, all while deep in conversation with his dining companions. Then, once the food arrived, he carefully organized and rearranged it on his plate to his liking before eating.

His fear of germs interestingly did not extend to the act of sex. To Katharine's delight, when the moment came, all his uncertainties and fears were forgotten as his need overcame logic. It thrilled her and urged on her own response to see this usually rigid, sexually repressed man lose control and become an eager lover.

During their pillow talks, she came to understand more about him. He shared with her information about his life that he rarely spoke of to anyone. He even discussed his father, Milutin Tesla, who came from a military family, had a brilliant mind and was all about helping others at the expense of being a nurturing parent to his own children. Tesla admitted his stern father smacked him a few times as discipline, and he never really felt adequate around him. But overall, he admitted Milutin's abuse was fundamentally emotional, not physical. Tesla confessed to Katharine that when his father died, he felt a loss but hardly hysterical grief as he had for his mother.

Even now, as a middle-aged man, Tesla still felt driven to prove his worth, not to the world that already valued him, but to himself.

Katharine realized Tesla was gripped by a mother fixation and that what attracted her to him was a mixture of both sexual compatibility and a need for motherly comfort and understanding. She accepted this and, in a way, his almost childlike trust in her only endeared her more to him.

In time, Tesla opened up even more to Katharine. Again, over pillow talk, she brought up the subject of marriage and why Tesla had avoided it all these years.

"After all, Nikola, many of our gentlemen friends who are older now and widowed or divorced are taking younger wives. Having new families and children and finding joy in their golden years."

"No, this will not happen."

"But why?"

Tesla chuckled, "Is this why you are always introducing me to young, available women at your parties? In hopes that I will fall madly in love with one of them and be swept off my feet?"

"It wouldn't hurt if you did, and I would surely understand. Perhaps it would be a cure for your great loneliness."

"I can't," Tesla replied. "These young women of today, they are different. Challenging men, dressing like men, wanting to take their jobs, and in all ways be equal—"

"We are equal," Katharine argued. "For too long we have lived in the shadow of men, been possessions of our husbands with few rights of our own. I am looking forward to being able to vote in the next election, finally!"

"In truth, women are more than equal," Tesla admitted. "I find them natively brighter, wittier, and a source of strength. Men can emotionally be as children. Can you see a man enduring the pain of childbirth without whimpering like a coward?"

They both laughed heartily then Tesla continued, "What I admire in you, Kate, is your skill at making Bob feel important and useful. With his professional ups and downs, you are always there to encourage him, to suggest solutions. The power behind the throne, as the saying goes."

"I'm sure there's a woman out there who as a wife would do the same for you," Katharine mused.

"No, it cannot be. I am not fit to be a husband; a wife would demand my attention and would come to hate me as my work would always come first."

"But what about children? Mine are a blessing; Owen has become a writer like his father. And Agnes is a wonderful mother. They both have given me grandchildren and watching the little ones grow up is a delight. I have tried to teach them some wisdom about life and hope that they will carry on some memory of it as adults. And then pass it on to their own children."

"Please, no more discussion of this," Tesla said, looking agitated.

"But why? Help me to understand."

Tesla sighed. "Yes, I flirt with these women. I take it as far as I can and then I force myself to stop, despite my attraction and desire. Because if I give in–"

"They might end up with child?" Katharine interrupted.

"Yes. And that is my fear."

"What fear?" She tried to be lighthearted. "That you will need to marry the woman and live happily ever after with your new family?"

Tesla was quiet for a long moment, and she saw his eyes fill with tears.

"That a child of mine would be... different. Like me. They call me a genius, but it comes at a dear price. My mind is not... normal. Maybe that is the price of genius but from my earliest childhood, I understood my mind was unusual. At school they laughed at me, taunted me, hit me. It is why I took boxing lessons and learned to fight. There was a certain satisfaction in hitting these bullies back."

Katharine said gently, "Even if your child was... brilliant, he could carry on your work and legacy."

Tesla shook his head. "He would face a life of pain and depression, as I do. I would not wish that on a child of mine. And I would be an old man, unable to protect him when he was an adult. No, Kate, in the cards of life, I am destined to remain alone. Surely you understand that now."

"Yes," replied Katharine. "But you have me and I hope my love is a comfort to you."

"More than I deserve," replied Tesla, pulling her into his arms.

∞

Katharine was aware of continuing society gossip. Whispers circulated suggesting a secret romantic involvement between her and Tesla.

The affair with Katharine tested Tesla's religious beliefs, or rather his spiritual beliefs that were influenced by Buddhism. In simplest terms, as he explained to Katharine:

"Perhaps it's true that the spirit or soul has potential power and strength to belie the laws of the physical universe. Maybe this is the reason for my visual memory, my telepathic awareness, how I can predict things and have visions of the future."

"I believe in God," said Katharine, "and I understand your viewpoint. All mainstream religions believe in a Supreme Being — whatever name they assign it. And we know that man was created in His image."

"That is my point," agreed Tesla. "And if such a God could pull off miracles that follow no laws of the physical universe, could not Man's life force also have the potential to create miracles? In this case by harnessing the potential energy of physical matter?"

This all made mathematical sense to Tesla, and after consulting with a Swami, he was determined to adopt a stricter ascetic lifestyle to strengthen his mental powers.

However, as many who choose celibacy have found, such is easier said than done. Tesla lived in his head, but at times his needs were distracting to where he needed an outlet.

At such times, Katharine found their subsequent liaisons fascinating, as Tesla would request of her to undress before him as he looked on, his eyes watching her intently, his hands kept to himself. Katharine obligingly and slowly shed her clothes most seductively. Without fail, Tesla's excitement rose, and she felt a thrill when he was hastily forced to remove his own clothes. Whether they satisfied their own needs or brought it about for each other, the quirkiness of such lovemaking proved far more enticing to Katharine than the rather mundane activity found at home. Over the years, their relationship was never exclusive but remained meaningful to both.

17

THE WESTINGHOUSE YEARS

In the years after his partnering with George Westinghouse, Tesla was learning to embrace and enjoy his fame again. He granted many interviews and posed for the newspapers alongside an ever-supportive Westinghouse.

"For the future of alternating current!" Westinghouse proclaimed to the press, raising a glass.

"And for the future of humanity," Tesla replied softly, a glimmer of excitement in his eyes.

The American Institute of Electrical Engineers became the stage for Tesla's triumphant resurgence. He ascended the podium, spine uncommonly straight, and delivered his speech with fervor. It wasn't just about coils and capacitors; his voice resonated with a near-forgotten passion, painting a vivid picture of cities thrumming with his clean, boundless energy.

When the applause swept the auditorium, he saw the faces of not just colleagues, but believers. Westinghouse beamed from the front row, eyes shining.

Invitations poured in, each more prestigious than the last — esteemed societies, industrial titans, even heads of state hungry to meet the man who spoke of reshaping the world.

Chicago World's Fair – May 1, 1893

Another triumph for Tesla was attending this magnificent event. It was a mesmerizing spectacle, an explosion of sights, sounds, and wonders; a dazzling microcosm of the rapidly changing world; and the birth of the American industrial age.

Amidst the many pavilions, exotic exhibits and the marvels of modern technology, one spectacle stood out, drawing the crowds with an irresistible allure: the Westinghouse Company's demonstration of Nikola Tesla's Polyphase Alternating Current 500-horsepower generator!

It was not just the imposing size of the generator itself that commanded attention, nor the intricate network of coils and wires that promised a display of unprecedented power.

It was the aura of the man behind it — Tesla, the enigmatic inventor whose name whispered of both brilliant promise and the potential for electrifying danger. The tales of Tesla's experiments and the rumors of his fierce rivalry with Edison had become the stuff of legend, adding an undercurrent of thrill to the anticipation of the coming spectacle.

The crowd pulsed with whispers, speculations, and hushed predictions. The air thrummed with an energy that seemed to echo the very current poised to surge through the generator. As the appointed hour drew nearer, every eye was fixed on the Westinghouse Pavilion, breaths held in collective anticipation! The fair was about to experience a moment that would either illuminate a new era or be a sensational failure.

As the last slivers of daylight faded, the crowd craned their necks, their faces a canvas of awe and bewilderment, their eyes wide with expectation as George Westinghouse, the maestro of this symphony of science, took the stage. The murmurs of the crowd softened to a hush.

"My friends!" Westinghouse's voice boomed over the whispers. "Tonight, we bear witness to a revolution in the very nature of power! Mr. Nikola Tesla's Polyphase Alternating Current 500 horsepower generator stands ready to illuminate our fairgrounds with a radiance surpassing even the noonday sun!"

As the applause swelled, Tesla offered a slight bow. Then Westinghouse, with a dramatic flourish, motioned for the generator to be activated. With a surge that set the air crackling, the generator roared to life! One by one, two hundred thousand bulbs glowed into existence, casting the fairgrounds in a dazzling web of light! Gasps turned into cheers, swelling into a roar of approval.

Westinghouse beamed, exchanging a triumphant look with Tesla. This was more than just a display; it was a declaration that the future was electric, and Tesla was its sole architect.

∞

Niagara Falls Power Plant - November 18, 1896

Then came the ultimate vindication: Niagara, the world's most famous waterfalls between Canada and America.

The thundering falls, an awe-inspiring testament to nature's raw power, were to be tamed, their energy harnessed and transformed. For Tesla, it was a sacred duty, one he had dreamed of since his childhood. Here, his visions of alternating current, once dismissed as impractical dreams, would become a glorious reality.

The day Tesla finally made his mark and bumped Edison from the world's stage was unlike any day he had known. The air crackled with nervous excitement as dignitaries and engineers gathered near the massive generators. Tesla stood tall in a long raincoat that later became immortalized with countless statues, the most notable one on display in Niagara itself.

When the moment came, he threw the giant lever with a sense of destiny fulfilled. For a heart-stopping second, there was only silence. Then, as if echoing from the great falls themselves, a surge of energy roared through the lines!

Niagara was no longer merely a force of nature, but a monument to human ingenuity — Tesla's genius. The cheers drowned the roar of the falls out, but Tesla scarcely heard them. That unyielding torrent of water was no longer an adversary, but a collaborator, its boundless power channeled through his designs.

Newspapers, once filled with Edison's exploits, now blared Tesla's name. They hailed him as the prophet of a new electrical age, no longer the obscure assistant.

Lectures and demonstrations filled his calendar, grand events where he was the star attraction, not a shadow lurking behind another man's success. Westinghouse, ever the shrewd businessman yet also a steadfast ally, was now a reassuring presence amidst the whirlwind. Their shared vision was no longer a hopeful gamble, but a revolution in the making.

Then came Madison Square Garden in New York City, drawing over fifteen thousand souls for a science demonstration, unimaginable until the day Tesla's name appeared on the marquee.

"Tonight, ladies, and gentlemen, we defy the laws of physics themselves!" Tesla crowed, an impish grin on his face.

He gestured towards a water tank where a miniature boat bobbed innocently, a tiny antenna jutting skywards. With a flick of his wrist, a bulky remote control appeared in his hand.

The boat lurched forward then turned in a tight circle, its lights winking merrily at the crowd's astonished gasps. Tesla smiled and took a bow as the exuberant audience applauded and roared its approval.

Another night, another breathless crowd. The American Museum of Natural History buzzed with journalists and influential patrons.

Tesla, meticulously dressed, strode to the center of their semicircle. A glass bulb glowed in its stand, and with a theatrical flourish, Tesla heated it until it became pliable, twisting it expertly until the tube spelled out a single word —"Clemens." The room erupted, flashes from a hundred cameras illuminating the prototype of the world's first neon sign.

Amidst the clamor, Tesla's newfound celebrity made him an object of fascination. On Grand Street, Tesla's laboratory became a shrine to innovation, and carefully orchestrated public tours fed the public's appetite for the wondrous and bizarre.

One evening demonstration included his friend Mark Twain acting as his assistant, as Tesla unveiled his latest masterpiece.

"Behold, the Thought Camera!"

A hush fell over the gathered reporters as Twain settled into a chair, positioned before a typewriter. At Tesla's signal, a beam of light speared the darkness, painting a blank canvas upon the wall.

"Mr. Clemens, if you will," Tesla murmured.

Twain grinned, fingers beginning to clack against the keys.

Tesla gestured, shifting the focus from the typewriter to Twain's brow, and finally to the shimmering projection. Murmurs of astonishment rippled through the room - for there, flickering in uncanny synchronicity with the clack of keys, were letters, words, a sentence taking shape!

"A glimpse into the mind itself!" Tesla announced, his face alight. "Instantaneous communication, the birth of a new age of unfettered thought!"

Was this a parlor trick, many reporters wrote, or is Tesla beyond genius?

Tesla's innovations, which sparked a revolution in the realm of science and technology, fascinated the world. His achievements didn't just catch the eye of the common man; they drew the attention of one of the most renowned figures of the era — the successful Harry Houdini himself.

Houdini who had just started to make a name for himself as the master of illusion and escape at just twenty-five years old, found himself skeptical of Tesla's impossible feats. The magician's natural inclination was to uncover secrets and expose frauds. He became determined to reveal Tesla as nothing more than a clever trickster, a man whose "miracles" were mere smoke and mirrors.

In his quest to unmask the brilliant inventor, Houdini found an unlikely ally in William Randolph Hearst, a titan of the publishing world. Hearst was no ordinary newspaper man; he was a media mogul who had built an empire from the ground up. His influence stretched across the nation through Hearst Communications, the largest newspaper chain and media company of its time. Hearst later became Orson Welles' inspiration for the movie *Citizen Kane*, which coincidentally was one of Tesla's all-time favorite films.

Hearst's reputation preceded him, for he was known as the pioneer of yellow journalism — a controversial style of reporting that prioritized sensationalism over substance. His papers were filled with lurid tales and exaggerated news, all designed to captivate readers and send circulation numbers soaring. It was a tactic that had proven wildly successful, if ethically questionable.

For Hearst, Nikola Tesla was a godsend — an enigmatic figure whose work straddled the line between science and science fiction. Furthermore, Hearst's mother Phoebe was a good friend of Tesla's, and so Hearst and Tesla were also on good terms. The inventor's radical ideas and fantastic claims were perfect fodder for Hearst's brand of journalism. Tesla became a recurring character in the pages of Hearst's nationwide newspapers, his exploits often embellished, and his failures magnified for maximum effect.

Perhaps it was no surprise when Houdini and Hearst forged a partnership in the fires of mutual interest.

Houdini saw an opportunity to leverage Hearst's vast media reach to expose Tesla, while Hearst recognized the potential for even more sensational stories that would keep his readers coming back for more.

As they plotted and schemed, Houdini did not fully grasp the magnitude of the genius he sought to discredit and instead of discrediting Tesla, Houdini inadvertently brought more attention and fame to him. This made no difference to Hearst as the result still had its desired effect, to sell newspapers. Hearst kept up a friendship with Tesla, even reaching out to him when he branched into filmmaking and wanted to know an effective way to show lightning on camera.

But Houdini remained furious with the failure of trying to discredit Tesla.

∞

New York City, Delmonico's - August 20, 1901

Amidst the glittering social circles Tesla frequented, no celebrity he met captivated him more than the enchanting French actress Sarah Bernhardt. Their paths had narrowly missed before, during Bernhardt's previous American visit, while Tesla toiled under Edison.

Bernhardt, seeking to preserve her voice and image for posterity, had visited Edison's laboratory, but a meeting with Tesla was not in the cards then. Tesla became a devout fan of the first superstar actress, attending Bernhardt's plays both in Paris and in New York. However, fate intervened on this night at Delmonico's.

The events, as they unraveled, were quickly noted in the press. But they were sanitized and altered, to protect both the restaurant for "leaking" such gossip, and Tesla's reputation as a lofty, eccentric genius with anything but sex on his mind. In today's terms, the fanciful report of what went down would be called "fake news." And Tesla himself often contributed to the confusion by providing conflicting details of events in his own interviews or published writings.

Supposedly, Sarah Bernhardt walked by Tesla and dropped her handkerchief at his feet; he returned it to her, not recognizing her. The reality was different! Tesla, engrossed in his notebook as his meal grew cold, was oblivious to the buzz that filled the restaurant as Bernhardt, a commanding presence even in her late fifties, made a grand entrance. The maitre d' hurried to her side as she surveyed the room with a practiced eye, her gaze alighting upon the oblivious Tesla.

"Who is that man over there?" she inquired in her accented French, knowing full well the answer.

"Nikola Tesla," the maitre d' replied, following her gaze.

"The mad scientist?" she asked, a hint of intrigue in her voice.

"Perhaps not so mad, Mademoiselle," the maitre d' objected politely. "He dines here often."

By now, the restaurant was abuzz with the recognition of the famed actress, their faces alight with excitement. Yet Tesla remained engrossed in his work.

"Can you seat me near him?" Bernhardt requested.

"Certainly," the maitre d' nodded, leading her past Tesla to the next table.

Tesla remained oblivious as Bernhardt was seated. After some time, he finally looked up and was startled to find Bernhardt gazing at him with a playful smile. A blush crept up Tesla's neck as he fumbled with his napkins.

"How do you do, sir?" she asked in a sultry voice.

"Mademoiselle Bernhardt," he stammered, bowing slightly, his heart pounding.

"You recognize me?" she replied with a girlish giggle.

"How could I not recognize The Divine Sarah? I have seen your performances in Paris many times. Cleopatra, Lady Macbeth, La Dame aux Camélias... that is my favorite. May I be so bold as to say that you are even more divine in person."

"You flatter me, Monsieur–"

"Tesla," he interjected, his cheeks burning.

"Ah, Nikola Tesla, the famous inventor," she purred.

Tesla nodded, a shy smile gracing his lips.

"Would you care to join me for dinner?" she asked, her eyes sparkling.

"I would be delighted," he replied, quickly gathering his things and joining her at her table. A waiter swiftly brought drinks and they raised a toast, their eyes locking over the rims of their glasses.

"You certainly possess an impressive mind," she commented, her voice laced with playful innuendo. "What excites you these days, besides older women?"

Tesla, still blushing, stammered, "Um... More research on photography of the inside of the body."

"You mean, like these?" she asked, delicately removing the scarf covering her chest and lightly trailing her fingers across her breasts.

"Uh, of the bones in the body. Like this." He pulled an x-ray image of his hand from his bag and showed it to her.

"You took this? I thought Madame Curie was working on this in Paris."

"Yes, but I perfected it," Tesla replied proudly. "It took two dozen patents to make this x-ray, some were mine."

"A noble project indeed." Bernhardt squeezed his hand, which was resting on his lap. Her hand probed around his lap. Tesla squirmed and she laughed.

"Well, now! I see exactly what excites you. And it isn't just your mind that's impressive." Her voice dropped to a whisper. "Would you like to continue our dinner in my suite?"

Tesla, caught off guard, could only manage a slight nod, his mind racing.

The surrounding diners had not missed the exchange, and whispers filled the air as Tesla and Bernhardt rose and left the restaurant together.

They barely made it through the hotel room door before Bernhardt shed her clothes, followed quickly by Tesla, their passion igniting a fiery encounter that defied reason.

Later, as they lay entwined on a bearskin rug before a roaring fire, Tesla finally found his voice.

"You are a remarkable woman," he breathed.

"And you," she replied, "are not so mad after all."

She kissed him and he watched as she skillfully led them into another passionate embrace. Then she used her scarf as a prop for what amounted to a sensual fan dance.

Tesla watched her erotic performance, transfixed as she trailed the scarf across her body, her breasts and her most intimate parts. When she finally dropped the scarf, he was as if putty in her hands.

For Tesla, this night was beyond his wildest dreams - the great lady of the theater, naked and a willing participant in a shared desire. He was a lucky man indeed...

The following morning, Tesla looked and felt both happy and worn. He dressed, paying little attention to the state of his clothes, and made his way to the door. He kissed Bernhardt's hand.

"Will I see you again?" he asked, a note of longing in his voice.

Bernhardt shook her head sadly. "I leave for Paris in two days."

"But please," he argued. "There is a dinner party tonight, with some friends. Could you join us at the restaurant just for that?"

She smiled at his hopeful expression. "Yes, of course. Who knows if our paths will cross again, darling. But at least we had this time together."

He nodded and kissed her hand again. To his surprise, she handed him her scarf. "For you, to remember me by."

"I will cherish it always," Tesla sighed. "Women are such a delightful distraction. I strive to focus on my work, but thank you, my dear Sarah. It was a night to remember."

And cherish it he did. Even though their paths did cross again, Tesla kept her scarf, unwashed, for the rest of his life.

Part Four

18

THE CORRECT FREQUENCY

Queens, New York — August 2024

John Watt fiddled with the Time Radio, attempting to call Tesla. He had tried to reconnect over the last week, with no success. Today Sara sat at his side, watching him with great interest.

"Manhattan Dove, are you there? This is the Queens Seagull."

After a long moment of silence, Tesla answered.

"I am here. Who is this speaking?"

"My name is John Watt. I'm calling you on your Time Radio, from the year 2024."

"I see. Apparently my project was successful."

"Oh, Mr. Tesla, it's strange that no one seems to have recorded you in your lifetime. But it's good to hear your voice now. "

"You too, John. How did you come to possess the radio?"

John smiled and turned to Sara, who gave his hand an encouraging squeeze.

"You gave it to my grandfather when he was very young, and he wanted it passed down to me. How can I be of help to you?"

Tesla replied, "It pleases me to learn that the Time Radio works correctly. This is one area of research that must be kept secret, John."

"I understand. But it's known that you were working on some kind of time machine."

"I need to understand which of my inventions were used for good and if any were used to hurt mankind."

"Every invention I know of has been an asset," John said. "But of course you had, what, close to 300 international patents? I need to research them all and get back to you on that."

"Yes, that is exactly what I want you to do." A sigh of relief was heard in Tesla's voice. "If any proved harmful I will cease work on them immediately. In that manner I can change history because they never will have existed."

"Wow!" John exclaimed.

"I want history to mostly follow its natural course. What we will endeavor to do is tune it for the benefit of mankind. The future, you see... belongs to me. To us! I can control the future from the past. But only with your help. Only your help, do you understand John?"

"Yes, sir, I do."

"Excellent."

"It's sort of like *Groundhog Day*."

"Groundhog day?"

"Never mind, Mr. Tesla, it's a movie. It won't be made for many decades after your time."

"And it is relevant... why?"

"It's comedy about a guy caught in a time loop, who has to keep reliving the same day over until he makes the right choices and becomes a decent human being."

"They find that amusing?" Tesla asked with surprise.

"Hilarious," chuckled John. "He gets to learn from his mistakes and can change the future."

"I see. Tell me, John, I feel we are close to war here. How does it end?"

"World War II?"

"Good God, they're numbering them!?"

"If you're talking about World War I, the Great War, it started in 1914 and I already did some research on that. I can tell you that the Austro-Hungarian Empire collapsed and Germany with it. The Russians became communist. Your homeland became more powerful and seized a part of Hungary. And the dude who started it all, Gavrilo Princip, a Serb by the way, went to jail."

"And dare I ask about this World War II?"

"That one was started by the Germans in 1939, actually by Adolph Hitler. Hey, come to think of it, Hitler is like my age now, I mean now in your time. If he should be hit by a train, right about now, some 75 million people would not die. Between the concentration camps, the military, the civilians... that's the estimate!"

"No, no! We mustn't even think of changing history's course like that!"

"With all due respect, Mr. Tesla, at least 75 million people would be saved if this little runt were to fall off a bridge. You have no idea the kind of torture that went on under Hitler's regime. We have newsreel footage that has survived. It's beyond belief what happened. What was allowed to happen and wasn't stopped in time by the good guys. Many movies have been made about it."

The silence on the other end was Tesla taking a moment to absorb this information. Finally, he responded.

"Right, then. Let me explain it to you this way. You must follow me on this now. If I were to murder this Hitler person before he can instigate World War Two, the action removes any reason for you to tell me about him, along with any knowledge the reason ever existed, thus removing any point in murdering this man.

"Certainly, someone else will be born that would not have otherwise been born had this Second World War not taken place. And this someone could be worse than this Hitler and influence or instigate an equally horrific event sometime later in the future."

"Okay, this is deep," replied John.

"What do you mean by deep?"

"I mean you're probably right."

Tesla hesitated then asked, "How about World War III?"

John shook his head. "Didn't happen yet, or maybe it's happening now but we don't fully realize it. Today's wars are different, not always shooting people. It's more about technological war, computer viruses, hacking into nations' files or emails or voting machines or personal bank accounts. Everything is going digital now, reading books, currencies, medical records, anything you can think of. In my lifetime I expect to see paper money possibly going away altogether. Things move so quickly now."

Tesla absorbed John's information and then asked, "Has all this made the world a better place?"

"I don't know, Mr. Tesla. In some ways, yes. In other ways, no. There have been plenty of other regular, smaller wars, terrible ones, all over the world in the last hundred years."

"I see that mankind's appetite for war has not wavered."

"Unfortunately, not. There's still a lot of hatred out there. In fact, Mr. Tesla, this is an election year. It's August 2024. And just last month one of the candidates was shot at by an assassin. At this point it's all very confusing as to what really happened, even how many shooters there were. It seems like you can never really understand history when it's happening right in front of you. But one thing for sure, had he not turned his head just before the bullet hit, his head would have exploded like JFK."

"JFK?"

"President Kennedy. John Kennedy."

"That name is not familiar to me."

"Are you still in 1913, Mr. Tesla?"

"Yes."

"Okay, so some years from now you will meet an investor named Joseph Kennedy. President Kennedy was his son. And after John was killed, his brother Robert was going to run for President and was also assassinated. Two brothers killed."

"You mustn't tell me information like this, John. If I am to meet someone directly related to someone in the future, this could be dangerous to their very existence in the future. My unintentional actions could alter that family's future. This becomes especially dangerous if that family influences the future of the country as you know it today. And not least of all, it would be an awkward meeting."

"That makes sense," said John.

"My hope has always been that the world could learn from its mistakes. Were they killed because of their politics?"

"I don't know. It seems they are still holding back information about that."

"Politics is not a subject I like to discuss," Tesla said in a firm voice, "as it seems often to be based more on emotional reaction than practical facts."

"I agree with you there," said John. "I was raised by my grandparents, and they advised me that there can be both right and wrong in political parties, and that sometimes the truth lies somewhere in the middle. You must judge for yourself and be willing to compromise if necessary so everyone can get along. They taught me to choose the person, not just the party."

"Those sound like wise words, my friend."

Part Five

19

A Gesture for the Ages

Pittsburgh, Pennsylvania – January 1891

In 1888, Tesla had sold some of his patents to his new mentor and benefactor, George Westinghouse. He also agreed to work for a year's time at Westinghouse's Pittsburgh offices, even though it meant clashing with the other engineers there over development of his main project at the moment – an induction motor.

The arguments were, as they had been with Edison's people, about whether motor engines should work on direct or alternating current. Westinghouse licensed the patent for Tesla's motor and paid him well for that year.

Tesla placed no blame on his boss for the development disagreements and delays regarding the optimum electric motor for vehicles. He was to be paid per motor royalties. As work continued to make it viable, Westinghouse paid Tesla a flat royalty fee of $15,000 a year on this groundbreaking motor.

Just over a year later, a financial panic and stock market crash hit, forcing Westinghouse Electric's investors to swiftly call in their loans. Westinghouse suddenly struggled to find a way not to lose control of his own company, as investors ordered him to cut all unnecessary costs. Tesla's yearly $15,000 now seemed excessive and frivolous to the money people, who obviously lacked insight into Tesla's genius.

∞

The enormous office of George Westinghouse was awash in the warm glow of half a dozen light bulbs and a desk lamp, casting long shadows across the rich mahogany furniture.

Outside, the streets of Pittsburgh hummed with the sound of a city on the cusp of a new era, an era that the two men inside this office had helped to usher in.

Tesla sat across from Westinghouse, his lean frame taut with tension. Between them on the desk lay a contract, its crisp pages at odds with the weight of its contents. Westinghouse's face was drawn, the usual twinkle in his eye dimmed by the gravity of their situation.

"Nikola," Westinghouse began, his voice hoarse with fatigue, "I hope you understand the position we're in. The Westinghouse company... it's on the brink."

Tesla nodded slowly, his piercing eyes never leaving Westinghouse's face. "I understand, George. Better than you might think."

Westinghouse leaned forward, his hands clasped tightly on the desk. "Then you know why I've asked you here. Your royalties... The company simply can't afford them. Not if we want to keep our own lights on, both figuratively and literally."

A heavy silence fell between them, broken only by the ticking of the grand clock in the corner. Tesla's mind raced, memories flashing before his eyes. He saw himself as a young immigrant, full of dreams and ideas. He remembered the countless nights of work, the failures, the triumphs. And he remembered the day George Westinghouse had looked him in the eye and said, "I believe in your invention, Mr. Tesla."

"George," Tesla said at last, his voice quiet but firm, "do you recall the day we first met?"

Westinghouse blinked, caught off guard by the question. "Of course. At your apartment. I was with Katharine Johnson."

Tesla smiled, a warm, genuine expression that transformed his usually serious face. "You were the only one who believed in me, in my vision. When others scoffed and called me a madman, you had already seen the potential in my dingy little apartment."

"I was right," Westinghouse said, a hint of his old vigor returning. "Look at what we've accomplished together, Nikola. We've lit up the world!"

"Indeed, we have, my friend," Tesla agreed. He stood suddenly, pacing the length of the office. "And that is precisely why I cannot allow our work to be undone."

Westinghouse watched him, confusion etched on his face. "What are you saying?"

Tesla stopped at the window, gazing out at the city below. "This company, our work... it's bigger than either of us, George. It's the future of humanity."

He turned back to face Westinghouse, his eyes blazing with an inner fire. "I once told you that I would give up my royalties if it would help you in your time of need. Do you remember?"

Westinghouse nodded slowly, hardly daring to hope. "I remember. But Nikola, I couldn't possibly ask you to—"

"You're not asking," Tesla interrupted, striding quickly back to the desk. "I'm offering."

With a swift motion, Tesla snatched up the contract. He held it to the desk lamp, examining the document that represented years of work, millions of dollars, possibly billions in future earnings.

"Nikola," Westinghouse said in a nervous voice, "think about what you're doing. This contract... it's your life's work."

Tesla shook his head, a serene smile on his face. "No, George. My life's work is out there," he gestured towards the window, towards the city lights powered by their invention. "This? This is just paper."

Tesla then took a better look at the paper, rubbing his thumbs on the smooth surface, and said, "Damn good paper, George. You must arrange for some to be delivered to my lab."

With that, Tesla gripped the contract firmly in both hands and, in one smooth motion, tore it in half.

The sound of ripping paper echoed through the office like a thunderclap. Westinghouse stood abruptly, his chair scraping against the wooden floor.

"Good God, Nikola!" he breathed, staring at the torn contract in disbelief. "What have you done?"

Tesla calmly tore the contract again, and again, until it was only confetti in his hands. "I've secured our future, George. Your company will survive, and with it, our vision for a brighter world."

Westinghouse rounded the desk, grasping Tesla by the shoulders. "But at what cost to you, my friend? The royalties... they would have made you a wealthy man."

Tesla laughed, a sound of pure joy that seemed to light up the room. "Wealth? What need have I for wealth when I have the whole world as my laboratory?" His eyes took on a distant look, as if seeing something beyond the confines of the office.

"There are greater inventions ahead, George. Greater discoveries waiting to be made. And now, thanks to this," he opened his hands, letting the shredded remains of the contract flutter to the floor, "we'll have the chance to make them."

Westinghouse stared at Tesla for a long moment. "You're a better man than I, Nikola Tesla," he said, his voice thick with emotion.

Tesla clasped Westinghouse's hand firmly. "We're partners, George. In this grand adventure of discovery. What good is my success if it comes at the cost of our shared dreams?"

Westinghouse nodded, wiping his eyes. "Partners," he agreed. "Now and always."

Tesla turned once more to the window, his eyes alight with visions of the future. "Come, George!" His voice was filled with excitement. "We have work to do. The world is waiting for us to light it up, but first, let's have lunch."

As they left the office together, stepping out into a future now secure, the torn contract lay forgotten on the floor — a small sacrifice on the altar of progress, a gesture that would echo through the annals of history.

Tesla's decision to waive his royalties on motor power for Westinghouse would prove to be the worst decision of his life. In hindsight, it cost him many millions of dollars in potential future income.

Six years later in June 1887, Westinghouse purchased Tesla's patent for a lump sum payment of $216,000 as part of a patent-sharing agreement signed with General Electric. Ironically, one owner of that company was none other than Thomas Edison.

∞

Colorado Springs, East Pike Peak's Avenue – June 1, 1899

The late afternoon sun painted his new laboratory in hues of orange and gold, a fitting backdrop for Tesla who bathed in its glow. His latest endeavor had brought him to this picturesque Coloradoan town, a temporary home for a grand experiment.

In direct contrast to Pittsburgh or hectic New York City, beautiful Colorado Springs sat at six thousand feet elevation above sea level, boasting vast fields and space, as well as clean, fresh, invigorating air to breathe. Additionally, the town agreed to provide him unlimited electricity for an experiment using a large Tesla Coil to be built there.

Tesla's latest move was an expensive venture, and to pull it off he enlisted the financial help of his friend John "Jack" Astor. The town welcomed Tesla's arrival with open arms, honoring him with a lavish welcome banquet.

In the coming weeks, his schedule was overfilled with important meetings and press interviews.

"Since my arrival in May," Tesla began, addressing a reporter with a voice that still held a hint of the Old World, "I've been immersed in wireless telegraphy. Sending signals from Pike's Peak to Paris, if you can believe it." He paused, a sly grin tugging at his lips. "And perhaps a bit further..."

The reporter, a seasoned journalist with a penchant for the extraordinary, scribbled furiously. "Further? You mean... to other countries?"

"Other planets," Tesla countered, his grin widening. "I've been receiving messages. A repeating signal, not of this world."

The reporter's eyebrows shot up. "Mars? Venus?"

"Perhaps," Tesla replied enigmatically. "More research is required, of course."

The reporter referred to his written notes. "I see you are also working on a wireless telephone?"

"Yes, but that is not my main focus of research here."

"And now," the reporter continued, eager to delve deeper into the mind of this enigmatic inventor, "you're creating artificial lightning?"

"Not artificial, but using the Earth's own potential. Observe those two hundred light bulbs outside, if you will."

The reporter followed his gaze. "They're not hooked up to any power source, just planted in the ground! You're saying you can wirelessly make them light up?"

"Indeed," Tesla confirmed. "A mere demonstration of the Earth's resonant frequency, you understand. Nothing too dramatic."

With a flourish, he pulled a huge lever with both hands.

A deafening crack echoed through the laboratory as a bolt of electricity, a hundred and thirty-five feet long, arced across the room, bathing everything in a harsh white light.

Screams erupted outside as the townsfolk scattered in the flickering light. The reporter, heart pounding, stepped outdoors and witnessed people hopping and yelping as sparks jumped between their feet and the ground.

And yes, all two hundred light bulbs lit up simultaneously! However, a few of them burst and extinguished.

Nearby, the lights in houses also blinked spontaneously, and horses pulling carriages reared in fright, their metal shoes sparking against the cobblestones.

Then a terrible groan echoed, and the city's power generator exploded, plunging the town into darkness. A stunned silence fell. Tesla, calm and unfazed, came outside and joined the bewildered reporter to observe the chaos.

"You see, my dear man," Tesla said, his voice almost inaudible over the continued frenzy, "Unlimited power. For this world... and beyond."

The reporter looked at Tesla in fear as if he were an evil sorcerer conjuring demons.

"Of course, there is still improvement to be made to keep the power steady and not surging over a period of time. But this is an impressive first step; I would definitely consider this experiment a success, wouldn't you?"

After this incident Tesla's welcome to this small Colorado town wore thin and there was even talk of arresting him for the considerable damage he had done to the town's direct current electrical infrastructure. Fortunately, and as always, Westinghouse was there to rescue Tesla from personal disaster and return him to the relative safety of New York City.

20

The Saga of J. P. Morgan

Tesla made his way towards the imposing headquarters of J. P. Morgan & Company at 23 Wall Street. His brilliant mind raced with anticipation. In his weathered leather briefcase, he carried the future — diagrams and calculations for a device that would revolutionize communication.

As he ascended the marble steps, the inventor's heart quickened, knowing that beyond these doors lay the key to realizing his grandest vision yet.

J. Pierpont Morgan, the titan of American finance, sat behind a massive mahogany desk. He was a large, imposing man with sharp, piercing eyes and a bulbous nose. He suffered from the medical condition rhinophyma, a result of a rosacea skin condition that made his nose look thick and almost purple. Though not a vain man, he insisted all photographs of him, including those published in the press, be retouched to cover his deformity.

Despite this very visible drawback, the financier had built an empire through savvy investments and aggressive consolidations, reshaping industries from steel to electricity.

Morgan's relationship with Tesla was complex. He had backed the inventor's alternating current system, which had triumphed over Thomas Edison's direct current in the "War of Currents." But Morgan was growing wary of Tesla's increasingly grandiose schemes, especially the Wardenclyffe

Tower project on New York's Long Island, which he never fully understood.

As Tesla entered the office, the scent of leather-bound books and Cuban cigars filled his nostrils. Morgan looked up from the stack of papers before him.

"Well, go on, Tesla," Morgan growled, his voice as rough as sandpaper. "Dazzle me with another one of your impossible dreams."

Tesla cleared his throat, his accent thicker than usual. "Mr. Morgan, I bring you a glimpse of the future — a device that will transform the way humanity communicates."

He spread his diagrams across Morgan's desk, pointing to intricate schematics and equations. "Behold, a wireless telephone that can not only transmit voice but also access real-time information through electromagnetic waves!"

Morgan's bushy eyebrows raised, a flicker of interest in his stern visage.

Tesla continued, his voice gaining confidence. "Imagine, sir, a device small enough to fit in your hand, yet powerful enough to connect you to the world. It utilizes a network of transmitters operating on carefully calibrated frequencies in the radio spectrum — between 3 kHz and 300 GHz."

The financier stroked his large mustache thoughtfully. "Intriguing. But tell me, Tesla, how do we measure usage?"

Tesla's excitement faltered. "Well, you see, Mr. Morgan, wireless transmissions don't emit impulses like traditional telegraphy. It's a continuous wave—"

Morgan's expression darkened. "No impulses? Then how do we charge for the service?"

Tesla, caught off-guard, fumbled for an answer. "I... I hadn't given much thought to the financial model. The technology itself is revolutionary! Imagine the possibilities—"

"Possibilities don't pay dividends, Tesla," Morgan growled. "Without a clear path to profit, this is nothing more than a fanciful toy."

Tesla's shoulders slumped but he pressed on. "But sir, the speed, and potential of wireless technology are unparalleled! In time, we could transmit entire newspapers directly into people's homes!"

Morgan scoffed, "Newspapers on a telephone? Preposterous! Who would ever want such a thing?"

Tesla's voice rose, desperation creeping in. "Mr. Morgan, please. This is the future of communication! The applications are limitless—"

"Enough!" Morgan thundered, slamming his meaty fist on the desk. "No impulses mean no profits. And no profits mean no investment. I've indulged your flights of fancy long enough, Tesla. It's time you brought me something practical."

Tesla stood frozen. He opened his mouth to argue further, but the steel in Morgan's gaze told him it was futile.

With trembling hands, Tesla gathered his papers. His voice almost a whisper, he made one last plea. "History will vindicate me, Mr. Morgan. The world will embrace wireless communication. I only ask for the chance to make it a reality, now rather then later."

Morgan had already turned his attention back to his ledgers. "Good day, Mr. Tesla. Don't waste my time with such nonsense again."

As Tesla stepped out into the bustling street, the weight of disappointment threatened to crush him. The city — the clatter of hooves, the shouts of vendors — seemed to mock his failure.

He clutched his briefcase close, the prototype inside now feeling like a lead weight. Tesla knew he was right, knew that one day the world would marvel at wireless communication. But as he walked away from the seat of financial power, he realized that vision alone was not enough. Without the backing of men like Morgan, his dreams would remain just that — dreams.

The inventor cast one last glance at the imposing façade of 23 Wall Street. Somewhere in that building, J. P. Morgan was already focused on his next profitable venture, Tesla's wireless telephone forgotten.

Little did Morgan know that seven decades later the world would see the first true mobile phone, developed using Tesla's patents. By then, both the visionary and the financier would be long gone, leaving future generations to wonder what might have been if Tesla's genius had been taken seriously seventy years earlier. Where would mobile phone technology be today?

At the time, though, Morgan was annoyed with Tesla, especially because of his perceived trickery. Originally Tesla had designed a certain size for Wardenclyffe and the idea was to eventually build duplicates around the planet. But when he learned that Marconi was ripping off his idea and intended to build a clone, Tesla insisted on building Wardenclyffe at twice the original proposed size. Morgan was not amused at the added expense.

It was George Westinghouse who had steered Tesla to collaborate with Morgan because he had abundant resources at his disposal. Tesla's loyalty to Westinghouse remained steadfast and so he obliged him. But Westinghouse had been branching out into other areas of innovation, such as steam engines, mining and shock absorbers for automobiles. His finances and health were suffering, and finally he had no choice but to resign from his company.

This left Tesla on his own to face increasing challenges in his partnership with the skeptical Morgan, whose main concern, like that of Edison, was profitability rather than recognizing Tesla's brilliance.

On another day, Tesla met with Morgan again. This time, Tesla was demonstrating another prototype he had invented.

"It's a wireless sonar controller for boats and ships," Tesla explained. "It emits pings into the water, and if it detects something solid, the ping bounces back."

Once again, Morgan was clearly uninterested.

"Why should we care what fish are doing under the vessel? Do we need a ping to alert us if there's a shark circling?"

"In inclement weather or fog, it could aid navigation. And during wartime, it could provide warning of nearby submarines."

Morgan looked at him with hostility.

"It's just a toy, Tesla. And an expensive one at that. There's no profit in it. Stop wasting my time and money. Come up with an idea that makes sense. One that brings dollars and cents."

He laughed, but Tesla did not find it amusing. He gathered his prototype and papers and walked out. Years later, the Titanic struck an iceberg, leading to its sinking and the tragic loss of some 1500 souls on board. However, if the Titanic had been equipped with Tesla's sonar, they could have averted the disaster.

∞

Another day, another Tesla invention. Across from Morgan stood Tesla, holding a wooden box.

"Well, show me something," Morgan growled.

Tesla reached into the box and produced a normal light bulb. "This is the current sixty-watt Edison model light bulb that costs sixteen cents to produce but sells to the public for one dollar. It lasts perhaps two hundred hours but often even less and it uses - nearly two kilowatts per day."

He swapped it for a different bulb, unable to hide his proud grin. "But my latest creation lasts thirty times longer, uses sixty percent less electricity, and cost only nine cents per unit more to produce."

Morgan's eyes narrowed to slits. "So it will put Edison's light bulb out of business."

"Well, I—"

"You are a dangerous enemy to have Tesla, I must remember that." Morgan stubbed out his cigar with unnecessary force. "The whole point is for those damned things to conk out so customers have to keep replacing them. More bulbs sold, more kilowatts used - it's all good for business!"

Tesla opened his mouth, closed it then opened it again with a sigh. "But surely a more efficient-"

"Useless!" Morgan interjected, spit flecking his desk. "Have you learned nothing from your time under that idiot Edison? As much as I would like to see him out of business, your light bulb would be bad for everyone's business, mine included. Next you'll be telling me you've invented the Snuzzle-Wuzzle Machine or some such balderdash."

Lips pressed tight, Tesla gave Morgan a nod and pivoted on his heel. "Very well, sir." He made his way to the door.

"And where do you think you're going?" Morgan called after him.

Tesla halted, back still turned. "My humble apologies. I didn't realize I'd wandered into the Flat Earth Society's annual meeting," he mumbled under his breath.

"What was that? Don't you mock me, mister! I am not nearly as forgiving as Westinghouse is!" Morgan's face purpled with rage.

Tesla turned with a slight smile. "Why, nothing at all, sir! I have another project that requires my attention..."

"Look here Tesla, I have been meaning to speak to you about all your crackpot ideas."

Morgan got up from his desk and approached Tesla in a confrontational stance. The men were standing face to face.

"I have repeatedly told you, I am not interested in providing free electricity to people across the globe! There is no end to the funds you require for your fool communication tower on Long Island?"

Tesla bristled. "Wardenclyffe is the future of wireless electrical distribution and wireless communication."

Furious now and eyes lit with anger, Morgan looked as if he might strike Tesla. "Listen to me carefully, mister! I agreed to that monstrosity of a tower because of corporate transatlantic communication and a favor I owed to Westinghouse, but this has now gone beyond reason. Just yesterday, I paid an invoice for eleven thousand dollars for it! For a genius, you are remarkably daft at times! Have you any idea how much money I have already sunk into that fiasco?"

"It is nearly completed," said Tesla.

"Yes, and how much more is it gonna cost me? That damned thing looks like a giant penis! You think people aren't snickering behind your back?"

Tesla started to explain why his Tesla Tower needed those particular dimensions, but Morgan cut him off with a snort.

"Don't wanna hear your excuses. If you ask me, maybe you built it that way to cover your own shortcomings. What kind of man brags that he lives like a monk out of choice?"

Tesla bristled, finally showing some anger. "I have no shortcomings—"

"Yah?" Morgan interrupted. "You know what's wrong with you, Tesla? You need to go out and get drunk. Stinking drunk. And fucked, multiple times. That'll loosen you up, stop that fantasizing about building huge peckers in the sky and drinking water at cocktail parties."

"With all due respect—" said Tesla sharply.

"No!... No electric automobiles. No free wireless telephones. No machines to listen to fish underwater, no forever light bulbs, no microwaving ovens, and I still don't know what the hell that is! And especially no free wireless electricity for the entire world. I am tearing down Wardenclyffe, it's a goddamn eyesore and an endless money pit.

"Edison warned me about you, and he was right! How Westinghouse put up with you I will never understand. I should have shut you down after your earthquake simulation experiment wrecked dozens of buildings and could have destroyed half of Manhattan. I am still sorting out the countless lawsuits."

"I disagree," Tesla argued. "Weather can be controlled, as I have proven, by creating earthquakes and artificial tidal waves. It's not always up to Mother Nature. And this should be known and understood because of the potential, in years to come, for those to manipulate weather for nefarious purposes."

"Wonderful, now you think you're playing God?" Morgan rolled his eyes. "Look here, man! I've entertained your lunacy long enough!"

Tesla snapped back: "It is difficult to explain to a layman what Wardenclyffe does but eventually they grasp it and appreciate it. But you, sir, you seem to be void of the most basic required intelligence to understand its potential."

As if looking for a physical altercation, he took a step closer to Morgan, standing nose to nose. Morgan stood his ground and locked his furious eyes with Tesla.

"The buck stops here, right now, mister!"

Unblinking, Tesla looked at Morgan much like he would a cornered cockroach before squashing it, but squash Morgan he did not. Instead, he shook his head in disgust and left the office without saying another word.

Their collaboration effectively ended that day, which also marked the end of Tesla's most ambitious project, the Wardenclyffe Tower. Had it been completed successfully and implemented, it would have provided wireless electricity directly from the air without the need for power lines, cables, or batteries, making electricity more accessible and affordable worldwide. This could have propelled technological development and elevated living standards, not just in America but around the world, especially in remote or underdeveloped regions.

Tesla tried in vain to find other investors willing to help finish funding Wardencylffe. To his shock and dismay, no one stepped forward. He was unaware that Morgan had contacted all major players and warned them against investing in Tesla's project — not out of spite but advising them that they would lose their money as he had. Perhaps Tesla did sense this blacklist stemmed from Morgan, as he reached out again and tried to rekindle a working relationship. But his letters to Morgan were in vain, even when he literally begged the man to finish the project. He eloquently admitted every sleepless night was spent with his tears soaking the pillow. Still, his heartfelt plea was to no avail.

The abandonment of Wardenclyffe was perhaps the most significant technological setback in mankind's history.

21

MILESTONE BIRTHDAY

In an effort to help Tesla organize and get his finances in order, some years back Westinghouse had appointed and paid George Scherff as Nikola Tesla's secretary and accountant. George had quickly settled into his new role with muted efficiency and worked loyally for Tesla for several years. Even when he eventually moved on to another job, they remained friends and George was there to help and even bail out Tesla financially when he needed money.

In later years, the roles reversed somewhat, and George appealed to Tesla for financial assistance when his wife fell ill. And still sometimes Tesla needed help and George made himself available to step in as needed. One such event was the occasion of Tesla's fiftieth birthday, which was to be celebrated with a memorable party.

∞

Delmonico's, New York City - July 10, 1906

The soft golden glow of Delmonico's chandeliers cast a warm light over the polished mahogany and crisp white linens of the restaurant's most exclusive dining room.

The air was alive with the gentle symphony of fine dining: the delicate clink of Baccarat crystal, the muted scrape of sterling silver against bone china, and the low, cultured murmur of New York's elite in conversation. Underlying it all was the rich aroma of expertly prepared cuisine, mingled with the subtle, smoky notes of fine Cuban cigars.

In a secluded alcove sat a gathering of some of the most influential minds of the age. The table was a veritable who's who of early twentieth century luminaries but all eyes were drawn to the man at its head: Nikola Tesla, the wizard of electricity, now celebrating his fiftieth year on this earth.

Tesla's thin frame was slightly hunched, a testament to the weight of his brilliant mind and the toll of his relentless pursuit of innovation. Yet his eyes, those piercing blue orbs that seemed to crackle with their own internal electricity, remained as bright and keen as ever.

"Nikola," George Westinghouse boomed, raising his glass, He was sitting to Tesla's left. "Fifty years young and still revolutionizing the world! To your bladeless turbine – may it spin us all into a brighter future!"

A chorus of "hear, hear!" rose from the table, accompanied by the crystalline chime of toasting glasses.

To Tesla's right, Katharine and Robert Johnson beamed with pride. They were the organizers of this gathering, with George Scherff's help. The carefully curated guest list read like a roll call of the era's greatest minds and talents.

"You've outdone yourselves," Tesla murmured to Katharine, his Serbian accent still thick despite years in America. "Though I confess, I feel some what... overwhelmed."

Katharine patted his hand. "Nonsense, Nikola. You deserve every bit of this celebration and more." Her voice dropped to a whisper. "Though I do wish poor Stanford could be here."

A shadow passed over Tesla's face at the mention of his friend, the brilliant architect Stanford White, whose life had been cut tragically short mere days ago. White had built many city landmarks, most famously the

Triumphal Arch at Washington Square. The memory of answering police questions about White's murder, entangled in some sordid love triangle with a famous actress of the time, still left a bitter taste in Tesla's mouth. It had shaken him deeply, forcing him to confront his own complex feelings for Katharine — feelings which, like his most revolutionary ideas, he kept carefully hidden from the world. But then again, it seems, Stanford did too.

A boisterous laugh from further down the table interrupted Tesla's thoughts. Mark Twain, his wild hair and mustache as iconic as ever, was regaling the group with one of his infamous tall tales. His eyes twinkled with mischief as he gestured animatedly and a chorus of laughter erupted from his immediate audience.

Particularly enjoying the absurdity of Twain's story was Francis Marion Crawford, an American author like Twain who authored many novels, most of them set in Italy. In person he was a serious-looking gentleman with a large drooping mustache that rivaled that of Mark Twain.

Crawford's works were classic, weird and fantastical stories that Tesla enjoyed so much, especially the novel about a genie that came to life. Crawford and Tesla had been friends for over ten years.

Crawford leaned forward, his face flushed with amusement.

"Mr. Clemens," Crawford interjected, using Twain's real name. "Surely you don't expect us to believe such a fantastical tale? Even for a writer of your imaginative caliber, this stretches credulity!"

Twain's bushy eyebrows shot up in mock indignation. "My dear friend, I have read your work and - what of its credulity!"

"Touché" Crawford replied with laughter, clinking Twain's glass with his own.

Twain continued, "Why, I've seen things that would make your head spin faster than one of our birthday boy's contraptions over there!" He nodded towards Tesla, who was listening to the exchange with growing amusement.

Rudyard Kipling, another great author of the time, perhaps best known for his beloved work *The Jungle Book*, had been listening intently and now chimed in.

"I dare say, Clemens, you've outdone yourself this time."

Crawford, grinning broadly, raised his glass in a toast again. "To Mr. Twain's space-faring frog! May its adventures inspire us all to reach for the stars – or at least the moon... as no doubt the first of us who will achieve this feat is our mutual dear friend honored tonight, Nikola Tesla!"

The assembled guests clinked their glasses together and Tesla found himself swept up in the happy moment. He marveled at the way Twain's outrageous story had brought levity to the table, uniting this diverse group of intellectuals and creatives in shared laughter and imagination.

The next guest to speak was John Jacob Astor IV. His accepting the invitation to join this celebration was a welcome surprise for Tesla. Back when Jack Astor gave Tesla $100,000, he expected the funds would produce a new lighting system. Instead, most of the funds had gone to Tesla's work in Colorado Springs. Aster was not impressed and had been somewhat estranged from Tesla after this. However, the two men had recently mended their differences; hence Tesla's joy at seeing Jack sitting at the table across from him tonight.

"Happy birthday, dear friend," smiled Astor.

"Thank you, Colonel Astor," Tesla happily replied.

Astor was the young man of the group, in his mid-forties, tall and handsome with the obligatory mustache but otherwise clean-shaven.

"My gift to you is not a tangible one but a problem your genius should enjoy helping to solve." Astor took a dramatic pause before speaking again, drawing everyone's attention.

"As you know, I frequently go abroad and travel at sea takes a week to make the journey one way. I have followed the work of flying machines with the Wright Brothers, but it seems their progress is slow. I would like to see the day that one could fly across the Atlantic in a day or less. Is that possible in the near future, do you think?"

Tesla nodded. "I have already drawn some designs of such an airship years ago in Paris. You're not talking of a flying balloon, but a self-propelled heavier-than-air reactive jet?"

"Yes," replied Astor. "The basic problem is this; an aeroplane would be too heavy to soar. Too many engines are needed for such a trip. Count von Zeppelin has designed a dirigible balloon, and his airship is more reliable and practical.

"To travel with many people in a metal flying machine across the ocean – or even across this nation, with necessary utilities and comfortable seating for several people, I fear technology is not quite there yet."

"But it can be done," Tesla said, smiling. "I had already determined that in Paris but unfortunately lacked the finances necessary to see the project through. Nothing is impossible, my friend."

Astor grinned back at him. "Then my gift to you is to order the building of such an aircraft, to help make long distance flight workable in something other than a balloon. I pledge to you finances shall not be a factor."

Applause erupted around the table at this announcement... along with a loud cheer from the far end of the table where, hidden by the haze of cigar smoke, sat the most surprising and powerful guest of all: Theodore Roosevelt, the 26th President of the United States!

His presence explained the unprecedented level of security surrounding the restaurant. Two dozen Secret Service agents were stationed in and around Delmonico's, with sharpshooters positioned on nearby rooftops and at street corners to ensure security.

Since the assassination of President William McKinley just five years earlier, the Secret Service took no chances and had an overkill policy in protecting the President.

"Mr. Tesla!" the President called out, his voice carrying easily over the ambient noise, "I must say, your latest invention – this air friction speedometer, it's simply spectacular! A testament to American ingenuity!"

Tesla inclined his head graciously. "You're too kind, Mr. President."

Roosevelt continued, "You, sir, are the very embodiment of the American dream! We are a nation of immigrants, after all."

He leaned forward, his spectacles glinting in the warm light of the chandeliers. His voice, usually booming and authoritative, softened with genuine admiration as he addressed Tesla directly.

"My dear Nikola," he began, his mustache twitching with a fond smile, "you know, when I speak of the American dream, it is you that often comes to mind. You arrived on these shores with little more than the clothes on your back and the brilliance in your mind. And look at you now!"

The President gestured expansively, taking in the opulent surroundings and the illustrious gathering. "You've lit up our cities, powered our industries, and sparked the imaginations of an entire generation. You, sir, are an example of what makes this nation great."

Roosevelt's eyes twinkled as he continued, his voice taking on a more personal tone. "Its men like you, Nikola, who remind us that the strength of America lies in the power of one's ideas and the strength of one's character."

He raised his glass in a toast. "To Nikola Tesla – scientist, inventor, and true American! May your next fifty years be as brilliant as the first!"

The table erupted in applause, glasses clinking as the assembled luminaries joined in the toast. Tesla, usually uncomfortable with such direct praise, found himself deeply moved by Roosevelt's words. He stood slowly, his tall frame straightening as he addressed the President and the gathered guests.

"Mr. President," Tesla began, his accent lending a musical quality to his words, "I am... profoundly touched by your kind words." He paused, collecting his thoughts. "When I first came to this country, I carried with me a dream – a vision of a world transformed by science and technology. America, with its boundless optimism and unparalleled opportunities, provided the fertile soil in which that dream could take root and flourish."

Tesla raised his own glass, his voice gaining strength and passion. "So let us toast not just to my achievements, but to the spirit of discovery that animates this great nation. To America, where dreams of a brighter future are born anew each day in laboratories, workshops, offices and yes, even in the imaginations of wild-haired outrageous writers and nonsensical romantic novelists!"

These comments drew chuckles from Twain and Crawford, and a broader laugh from the rest of the table.

"And to you, Mr. President," Tesla concluded, "for your leadership in fostering an environment where science and innovation can thrive. May we continue to light the way towards a future limited only by the boundaries of our collective imagination."

As Tesla retook his seat amidst enthusiastic applause, Roosevelt beamed with approval. The exchange had transformed the atmosphere of the gathering, infusing it with a palpable sense of shared purpose and possibility.

As the evening wore on, course after exquisite course was served: Oysters Rockefeller, turtle soup, filet mignon with béarnaise sauce, each accompanied by perfectly paired wines.

A magnificent dessert followed the meal — a decadent chocolate *gâteau* adorned with fifty delicate spun-sugar candles.

"Penny for your thoughts, old friend?"

It was George Scherff, Tesla's longtime assistant and confidant, who noticed the inventor seemingly lost in thought.

Tesla turned to him with a wistful smile. "I was just thinking, George... of all we've accomplished, and all that remains to be done. The world is changing so rapidly. I only hope my work will help shape it for the better."

Scherff nodded sagely. "If anyone can guide us towards a brighter future, Nikola, it's you. Now come, blow out your candles. I hear Katharine has arranged for Paderewski to play for us after."

While enjoying the dessert, the table banter was lighthearted and amusing. Tesla regaled his guests with a story about how Kipling had recently taken him out to dinner at a hotel restaurant in Hell's Kitchen and other culinary misadventures. After much laughter from the group, Tesla redirected his attention to the President,

"Speaking of food, I want to commend you, Mr. President, for the passing of the Pure Food and Drug Act. It was much needed."

Roosevelt agreed. "Two weeks ago! Congress passed the bill and politics aside, it was much needed. And now if we could do the same for social justice."

Ignacy Paderewski joined in the discussion. He was a Polish pianist, composer, and statesman, a favorite of concert audiences around the world. His stern features and wild mane of curly hair belied both his gentle nature and the powerful magic of his fingers on the piano keyboard.

"Social justice is a positive move," Paderewski said, and explained how he wanted to see his native Poland reach independence, and what he could do to further such goals.

Robert Johnson asked Paderewski, "Are you here in New York for long?"

Paderewski shook his head. "I finish this concert tour and then return home."

"That's a shame," said Katharine. "You are so popular here. Have you not thought of moving to New York, as Nikola did? This is a city of opportunity and welcomes great artists."

Paderewski chuckled. "My dear lady, the frantic nature of New York City is not for me. If I would ever retire to this great country, it would likely be to California, in a quiet area where I could own a vineyard and grow grapes to make excellent wine such as this." He raised his glass for a refill and continued. "But for now, I must help my people."

Roosevelt raised his glass and toasted Paderewski. "I salute you, my friend. I return to Washington tomorrow but let us arrange a meeting while you are stateside. If there is something I can do to help you and your cause, I will do so."

Tesla smiled happily at Paderewski and then at Roosevelt. He too raised his glass and unexpectedly yelled, "Bully for you, Mr. President!" Ignoring the dropped jaws of his friends at the table, he raised his arm and shouted even louder, "Charge!!"

The partygoers broke out in gales of laughter.

A short while later, Westinghouse cleared his throat, drawing the attention of the gathering. He reached into his jacket pocket and produced a small, exquisitely wrapped package.

"Nikola, my dear friend," Westinghouse began, his voice warm with affection. "Please, accept this small token of my appreciation."

Tesla carefully unwrapped the gift. As he opened the box, his eyes widened in surprise. Inside lay a beautifully crafted 24k gold cigarette case, complete with built-in lighter.

"George, I... I'm speechless," Tesla said, his voice thick with emotion. "This is magnificent."

Westinghouse smiled, placing a hand on Tesla's shoulder. "The world does not yet understand you as we do or appreciate the magnitude of your genius, but they will. This is a mere token of thanks for giving me the first opportunity to benefit monetarily from your genius but more importantly, for your friendship which has been one of the great joys of my life."

Katharine Johnson leaned forward, her eyes sparkling, and handed Tesla an elegantly wrapped book. "Nikola, this is from Bob and me; may it always give you pleasure and strength."

Tesla unwrapped the book. It was a flawlessly preserved first edition of Mark Twain's novel, *The Adventures of Tom Sawyer*.

"And I signed it for you," piped up Mark Twain.

Tesla was speechless and moved nearly to tears. He took a sip of water to wet his vocal cords in order to respond to Katharine and Robert.

"What to say?" Tesla's eyes misted.

Robert raised his glass. "To Nick, a man whose vision continues to illuminate our world, both figuratively and literally."

The group toasted, crystal glasses catching the warm glow of the chandeliers above.

And then George Scherff presented Tesla with a meticulously wrapped box that was long and narrow in shape. Tesla unwrapped it to reveal a beautiful fountain pen with gold trimmings and Tesla's initials on it.

"This is delightful, George! Thank you, I shall have much use of it."

George smiled and patted Tesla on the shoulder.

"My turn," said Mark Twain. "I have no new book for you. As you know, I've been writing my autobiography, but it's not complete. However, I am working on a new novel. I call it 'Number 44 – The Mysterious Stranger.' It deals with the duality of man's nature, something you and I have discussed many times. How man has his rational mind, and then his mind of dreams and aberrations, and the conflict between them. I trust you more than anyone else to understand it. Here is the manuscript, nearly half complete so far." He handed Tesla a large, wrapped envelope.

"I am honored, my friend," said Tesla, his eyes again misting. "I will read it with joy."

"Me next," said Kipling. "I know you love *The Jungle Book*—"

"*Rikki Tikki Tavi* is my favorite," Tesla said eagerly.

"Yes, but here is my new book, hot off the press. *Puck of Pook's Hill*. It's historical, it's a fantasy and yes, it's Shakespeare's Puck." Kipling autographed the book with a flourish and handed it over to Tesla. "I hope you will enjoy it."

"I most certainly will," said Tesla, forced now to wipe his tearful eyes. "Thank you, I am so grateful to receive this."

President Roosevelt stood up, handed Tesla a smallish box, and watched as he opened. "Cigars," the President grinned. "The best, from Cuba."

"I shall surely enjoy these," smiled Tesla. "Thank you, Mr. President."

And then, as if on cue, Crawford rose from his chair. With a grace that belied his gigantic frame, he stretched across the table, carefully balancing a wrapped package in his hands.

"Here's yet another book," Crawford said, his voice warm with affection as he handed the package to Tesla. "I hope it will illuminate your evenings. My new novel, *A Lady of Rome*. It's the very first copy off the press, signed especially for you."

Tesla set down the box of cigars and with reverence, reached for the book.

"Francis, you honor me beyond measure. Your words have always been a beacon of inspiration to me." He carefully unwrapped the book, running his fingers over the embossed title. "I find myself truly at a loss for words, a rarity for me, I assure you," he added with a self-deprecating chuckle.

Crawford smiled warmly. "Your brilliance lights up our world, Nikola. It's only fitting that we try to bring some light into yours."

And finally, Paderewski rose. "My dear friend, I have no proper gift for you but I hope you will accept these, and know I will choose some music to play in honor of you."

He handed Tesla two tickets for his upcoming Carnegie Hall recital. Tesla looked excited, gave a quick glance over to Katharine then caught himself, and returned his gaze to Paderewski.

"Thank you, thank you," he murmured. "A gift of your music... this means more to me than you know."

The party settled down again. As they sipped their wine and finished their dessert, Tesla laid the concert tickets, the cigars, the books and the fountain pen near to him on the table, and ran his fingers over the smooth, solid gold cigarette case.

"You know," Tesla said softly, looking around the table, "in all my years, I've pursued knowledge and innovation, often at the expense of personal connections. But at this moment, right now—" He paused... took a sip of water, cleared his throat then continued.

"My eyes have just now opened to the true power of human connections. And how important they are in life. Thank you all for your friendship and support. I am eternally grateful to have you all in my life. I am truly most fortunate."

Later in the evening, as the beautiful strains of Chopin filled the air, courtesy of Paderewski's skilled hands at the piano, Tesla sat back in his chair, a rare sense of contentment settling over him.

The future, with all its promise and peril, could wait. For this evening belonged to music, friendship, and Tesla simply becoming fifty.

22

THE UNSINKABLE SINKS

Atlantic Ocean - April 15, 1912

The night air was bitterly cold, biting through even the thickest of coats as the RMS *Titanic* listed dangerously to one side.

It was nearly 2 a.m. The proud ship, once deemed unsinkable now groaned and creaked like a wounded beast. Amid the chaos of screaming passengers and shouting crew members, one man stood still, an island of calm in a sea of panic.

John Jacob Astor IV, the wealthiest passenger aboard the Titanic, cut an imposing figure even now. His tailored suit, worth more than most men earned in a year, was soaked through with icy seawater. Yet he paid it no mind. His eyes, sharp and clear despite the late hour and dire circumstances, scanned the frenzied crowd around him.

In his pocket sat a checkbook that could have purchased this ill-fated vessel thirty times over. The Astor fortune was legendary, a vast empire of hotels aside from the Waldorf-Astoria, and real estate that stretched across the globe.

Here, on the tilting deck of a doomed ship, that fortune meant nothing.

A child's terrified wail cut through the din, catching Astor's attention. He turned to see two young siblings clinging to each other as the crowd surged around them. Their parents were nowhere in sight. Their wide eyes met his, a silent plea for help that tugged at his heart.

Without hesitation, Astor strode towards them. He scooped up the children, one in each arm, and pushed through the throng towards the nearest lifeboat. His pregnant wife Madeleine was waiting there, accompanied by her nurse and maid.

"Am I allowed to board with her?" Astor asked. "She is in a delicate condition."

The officer hesitated. "Actually, sir, right now it's still only women and children. But for you we can make an exception..."

Astor shook his head. "No need, I can take a later boat." He kissed his wife and watched as she was assisted onto the lifeboat.

For a moment, Astor paused.... The lifeboat before him represented safety, survival, and a chance to see his beloved wife again along with his third child, yet to be born. But the weight of the trembling children in his arms decided for him.

"No," he said firmly, his voice carrying over the chaos. "These little ones will take my place." Ignoring the officer's protests, Astor gently placed the children into the boat. He looked into their tear-stained faces and managed a reassuring smile. "Be brave," he told them softly. "Live long and happy lives."

He waved goodbye to his wife, whose anguished gaze silently begged him to join her. "No worries, darling," he called out to her. "Officer, what boat number is this?"

"Boat four."

"Alright then, I'll know how to find you later."

As the lifeboat was lowered away, Astor stepped back. He knew, with a certainty that should have terrified him, that he had just sealed his fate. Yet he stood tall and felt an odd sense of peace.

What Astor didn't consider in those moments of compassion and his noble sacrifice was that his death would have far-reaching consequences. In a laboratory in America, Tesla anxiously awaited news of his patron and friend.

With Astor's death, Tesla's dreams of revolutionizing the world with his inventions would face a setback from which Tesla felt he might never fully recover.

Tesla would now cease working on a hydrofoil jet engine for a flying machine. In the Harlem River, Astor had docked what the New York Times described as "an airship with a practical water craft." The two men worked privately together on this project, with the assumption that any flying test accidents using the hovercraft were unlikely to be fatal, since the aircraft could easily land back onto the river.

"For more than twelve months a mysterious craft lay in the Harlem River," noted the newspaper, in summing up Astor's estate.

"It seemed to embody some idea to combine an airship with a practical water craft.... Finally the boat disappeared."

Also mentioned in Astor's estate was this curious note: "500 shares of stock in the Nikola Tesla company. This stock was not carried on Col. Astor's books. It was purchased by Col. Astor under an agreement made with Mr. Tesla personally, of which his office had no information. The proceeds from the sales of the stock were used in certain experimental work which has not developed into a paying industry."

John Jacob Astor's decision to not save himself during the *Titanic* sinking was driven by his character, not his wealth.

∞

Central Park, New York City – 1913

Spring had settled over Central Park, painting it in a palette of tender greens and pastel blooms. A gentle breeze carried the sweet scent of newly opened flowers, mingling with the earthy aroma of damp soil awakening from winter's slumber. The sky above was a canvas of powder blue, punctuated by dreamy cotton-white clouds that drifted lazily across the sky.

Tesla, as always, impeccably dressed in a tailored black suit, moved with purpose through the park's winding paths. His eyes darted from tree to tree, as if searching for something only he could see, assessing each tree with the precision of a master engineer.

His mind raced with calculations and theories. In his right hand, he clutched a device of his own design — a marvel of scientific ingenuity that would have left his contemporaries slack-jawed in amazement.

The Chronometric Resonance Analyzer, or CRA as he had dubbed it, was a compact miracle of brass, copper, and crystalline structures. Its face bore a dizzying array of dials and meters, each calibrated to measure subtle variations in electromagnetic fields, quantum fluctuations, and temporal distortions.

As he walked, Tesla's free hand twitched at his side, itching to jot down the cascade of equations that flowed through his mind like an unstoppable current. The CRA hummed softly, its internal mechanisms whirring as it processed the invisible data that permeated the surrounding air.

The equation for quantum tunneling time flashed through Tesla's mind. He knew that to bridge the gap between present and future, to utilize a potential time machine, he would need to harness energies beyond the comprehension of current scientific understanding.

After hours of meticulous examination, Tesla's gaze finally settled upon a majestic oak tree that seemed to dominate its surroundings.

Its trunk, gnarled and massive, spoke of centuries past, while its vibrant canopy reached toward a future yet to come. The tree stood at least sixty feet tall, its sprawling branches creating a canopy that spanned nearly eighty feet in diameter.

A small smile played at the corners of Tesla's mouth as he approached the giant oak. His hand, calloused from years of work yet still sensitive to the subtlest vibrations, reached out to touch the rough bark.

"Yes," he murmured, his voice barely above a whisper, "You, my dear friend, will bear witness to the greatest experiment in human history."

The CRA's needles jumped erratically as Tesla pressed it against the tree's trunk. He quickly took EM (Electro-Magnetic) readings, his lips moving silently as he processed the data.

His eyes fell upon a simple wooden bench nestled among the oak's sprawling roots. Weathered but sturdy, it offered an unobtrusive vantage point from which to conduct his future communications.

He settled onto the bench, placing the CRA beside him as he pulled out his leather-bound notebook. With practiced precision, Tesla began to record his findings:

Latitude: 40° 46' 12.8" N

Longitude: 73° 58' 9.2" W

Ambient EM field strength: 0.5 mG

Quantum coherence factor: 0.9874

Temporal flux variance: 3.6 x 10-15s

His pen flew across the pages, filling them with a dizzying array of numbers and symbols that would be indecipherable to anyone but him. Complex equations sprawled across the paper.

"The resonant frequency of this location," Tesla muttered, "coupled with the natural conductivity of the oak and the EM properties of the surrounding soil.... Yes, this is perfect!"

He scribbled furiously, working through the calculations and then suddenly it occurred to him he had forgotten two important factors, the weather, and the human factor. It was impossible for him to accurately determine the exact day of contact because of certain limitations of his calculations.

A sudden cloud formation could interfere with the frequency thus causing contact failure; and then there was the possibility of someone other than him sitting on the bench, on the day and time of contact. At this time there was no way to solve either problem.

In his mind's eye, he could already see the invisible energy that would one day converge at this very spot, carrying a voice from the future that could faintly be heard from out of thin air in a small proximity of just twenty square feet around the giant oak.

As he made his final calculations, the park around him bustled with life. Children's laughter rang out from a nearby playground, couples strolled arm in arm along the sun-dappled paths, and a group of artists – reminding him of his sweet Anya – set up their easels to capture the beauty of the spring day.

None of them knew that they were witnessing a moment that would ripple across time itself. From this day on he would have to come to this precise spot every day, whenever possible, from morning to noon; and wait for the future to contact him via his Time Radio.

There was one slight drawback: in the present year of 1913, he did not have the technical means to build such a machine and in all probability, it would not be built for another twenty to thirty years.

Tesla's thoughts then turned to the *Titanic*, its tragic fate still fresh in the world's collective memory.

He had deliberately chosen the year 1913 to receive contact from the future, a year after the disaster, as so not to be able to prevent it from happening. The threads of time are delicate, he reminded himself. To save all those lives, including his benefactor John Jacob Astor, would be to unravel the very fabric of history.

Instead, he focused on the future he hoped to shape. By learning which of his inventions might be misused, he could then ensure not to create them, which would then preserve his legacy to that of progress, and not of destruction.

When the Time Radio is finally built, he thought, *be it in ten years or thirty years — and after it is hidden for — let's say, seventy years or so — then given to someone worthy of this monumental experiment — this will be the year, and this the very place where the signal carrying the user's voice from the future will converge.*

As the afternoon sun began its descent, casting long shadows across the park, Tesla rose from the bench. He placed his hand once more upon the oak's trunk, feeling the slow, steady pulse of life beneath its bark.

"Guard our secret well, old friend," he said softly. "For in your shadow, the past and future shall meet, and the course of human destiny may yet be altered. I hereby christen you the Oak of Eternity."

With a final nod to the tree, Nikola Tesla turned and walked away, his mind already racing with plans for the Time Radio that would bridge the gap between centuries.

Behind him, the tree stood silent and strong, its leaves rustling gently in the spring breeze. The oak tree, now with a purpose beyond its natural existence, stood as an unwitting sentinel.

∞

Mark Twain died in 1910, Jack Astor in 1912 and in 1914, Tesla suffered yet another loss of a beloved friend. His final dinner meeting with George Westinghouse was particularly heartbreaking for him.

Due to advanced age and declining health, Westinghouse was now confined to a wheelchair, appearing both old and frail.

Tesla was saddened to witness his close friend's decline, though he couldn't ignore the effects of aging on himself too. He found himself in late middle age, his hair now showing streaks of gray. In his mind, he was still the eager, sharp, and brilliant young inventor. He kept his body weight lean and exercised with long walks through the city.

But he could not deny that certain aches and pains went along with age, though he did his best to ignore them.

Westinghouse and Tesla dined together at their favorite restaurant, but the mood was subdued, and Tesla seemed somewhat depressed.

"Have another drink, Nikola," Westinghouse urged.

"Bad news?" Tesla asked.

"My accountant has gone over your finances, and you are in so much debt, the bottom line is that you are, on paper, penniless."

Tesla shrugged. "Finances have never interested me."

"All those court cases you've had over your patents being stolen by others. My God, you've made these men many billions of dollars, particularly that horse's ass Edison! And yet it is you who are broke."

"Any money I made went back into my inventions. I could dig ditches again, but I fear I am too old to do the job well."

"No one wants you to dig ditches, Nikola." Westinghouse cracked a weak smile.

Tesla's voice broke with emotion. "I couldn't pay the mortgage anymore on Wardenclyffe, George. Mr. Morgan refuses to help anymore and I fear the bank may foreclose on it. Once again, my life's work is destroyed."

Westinghouse sighed. "You are too trusting. I remember when Marconi worked as your assistant, he was there to study the Tesla coil and steal your thunder on the transatlantic voice call." Tesla nodded his agreement. "He used seventeen of my patents to make that transatlantic call work. Clearly he has achieved nothing by himself, and the courts will surely agree with me."

"But at what cost to your finances?" Westinghouse asked. "I'm a dying man, but I can never forget that you tore up your contract with me. So be reassured that your living and work expenses will be covered for as long as you live. Hopefully many more years."

Tesla's eyes were bright with tears. "I am proud to call you my friend, George. You have helped fight prejudice and money power. Humanity owes you an immense debt of gratitude and if they don't realize it now, they will one day."

When their meal finished, Westinghouse was surprised as Tesla stood up and uncharacteristically hugged him for a long moment.

∞

New York City, Met Life Tower, 1 Madison Avenue - 1911

Tesla's new cluttered office/laboratory in the South Tower was filled with strange contraptions and half-finished inventions littering every surface. George Scherff's tidy spirit rebelled at the chaos, but he bit his tongue.

He rapped softly on the door to Tesla's inner sanctum.

"Sir? A Professor Petrov from Moscow University is here to see you."

Tesla emerged, squinting against the dim light. His wild hair stood on end, crackling with static electricity. "Excellent, show him in."

He attempted to regain composure by smoothing his crumpled suit and grappling with his obstinate locks.

George admitted the visitor, a severe-looking Russian man of about sixty with a bristling mustache.

"Professor Petrov to see you, sir."

"Nikola Tesla! At last, the great mind and I meet."

Tesla's lips twitched in amusement. "Indeed. Though I fear my mind may be more eccentric than great."

Petrov waved away the attempted modesty. "Is no matter. Russians know true genius when we see it."

Tesla gestured to the sitting area. "Please, make yourself comfortable."

As the men took their seats, George reappeared with a tray of tea and biscuits; sustenance was required to power Tesla's brilliant brain. George poured and retreated to the corner, performing his usual vanishing act.

Between measured sips, Petrov outlined his proposal. It seemed the Tsar himself wished to invite Tesla, offering him unlimited resources and autonomy to pursue his research in Mother Russia. The Tsar was impressed with the possibilities of wireless electricity and wanted Tesla to help modernize his country.

Tesla listened impassively, making no comment until the professor finally fell silent.

"While I'm flattered by the generous offer," Tesla said at last, "I must respectfully decline."

Petrov was taken aback at Tesla's response. "But...why? Why you turn down such an opportunity?"

"Let's just say that my interests lie elsewhere at the moment." Tesla's tone remained light, but his gaze grew distant. "I aim to unlock technological marvels that could truly revolutionize the entire world — for the better."

The professor made a last appeal, but Tesla was unmoved.

He remained adamant in his dismissal of the offer. "My heart is set on America.... At least for now, my good man."

After several more minutes of attempted persuasion, the Russian conceded defeat. The conversation ended politely enough, but Petrov didn't bother to conceal his disappointment. He left soon afterward.

Tesla sat staring into the distance. Had he made a mistake? He second guessed himself. This was Russia who called on him.

The same Russia who rushed to Serbia's defense after the Austro-Hungarian Empire declared war on her. So many of her sons had given their lives in the defense of his homeland. It was a high cost that Russia paid. Had he not owed anything to this great empire? His beloved Anya was from there, and surely, she would be proud that he chose Russia.

He knew she always intended to return to Russia someday. They would have acknowledged his genius without suspicion and shown him the respect he deserved. Russia would remember him as its greatest genius, sing songs about him, and display his image on stamps. Perhaps one day, they might even establish a museum dedicated to him, showcasing his life's work.

None of this seemed likely to happen in America. So then, why stay in America? he asked himself. He did not have an answer.

Had he made a mistake?

He felt agitated, his heart pounding. A faintness came over him, or was it a feeling of déjà vu? He forced himself to calm his breathing and focus his thoughts.

Once again, his mind reverted to his friend Jack Astor and his tragic death at sea. Could he have prevented that? Could he now prevent unnecessary death and destruction in Russia, if he now agreed to work there? How to know what was best and how decisions would affect history played on his thoughts.

More and more, the necessity to develop his Time Radio was a certainty.

23

A Friend Returns

The crisp November air bit at Ernst Adler's face as he stood before the imposing façade of the great inventor Nikola Tesla's laboratory. The bustling streets of New York seemed a world away from the quiet determination that emanated from the building.

Adler took a deep breath, readying himself for the reunion thirty-plus years in the making.

Inside, Tesla's laboratory hummed with the promise of the future. Copper coils as tall as men stood sentinel in corners, while glass tubes filled with eerie, pulsating light cast dancing shadows across the walls.

Amid this well-orchestrated chaos, Tesla skillfully maneuvered what seemed to be a tiny turbine in his hands.

He was startled from his work as the sound of the knock reverberated loudly through the lab. He looked up, surprised, not accustomed to unexpected visitors. George was not with him, he was at the bank sorting out unpaid bills from months past.

With a sigh, Tesla set down his turbine and made his way to the door, opening it with a hint of impatience.

"Yes? Can I help you?" Tesla asked, his eyes taking a moment to focus on the man before him. There was something familiar about the weathered face, the broad shoulders, but it took a few seconds for recognition to dawn.

Adler stood there, a small, nervous smile playing on his lips. "Good evening, Tesla. It's... it's been a long time."

Tesla's eyes widened, his hand gripping the door frame for support. "Adler? Ernst Adler, is that really you?"

Adler nodded, his smile growing wider. "In the flesh, old friend. Though perhaps a bit worse for wear."

Tesla's initial shock gave way to a warm, genuine smile. He stepped back, gesturing for Adler to enter. "Please, come in! This is... this is quite a surprise. But a welcomed one."

As Adler stepped into the lab, the light fell across his face, revealing a thin but long scar on his left cheek and jaw. Tesla's eyes widened slightly, but he quickly composed himself.

"Adler, you must tell me everything," Tesla said, leading him deeper into the lab. "But first, please, sit. Can I offer you a drink? I have some excellent whiskey that a grateful patron gifted me."

Adler nodded gratefully. "That would be most welcome, Tesla. Thank you."

Tesla busied himself at a small cabinet, returning with two crystal tumblers and a bottle of amber liquid. He poured generous measures for both then offered Adler the gold cigarette case Westinghouse had given him for his fiftieth birthday.

"Please, help yourself. I find myself indulging more often than I should these days," Tesla said with a wry smile.

Adler accepted both the whiskey and a cigarette from the case with a nod of thanks. He took a slow sip of the whiskey, his eyes closing appreciatively.

"My word, Tesla. This is exquisite. Your patron has excellent taste."

Tesla chuckled, lighting his own cigarette. "One of the few perks of notoriety, I suppose. Now, Adler, please. Tell me where you've been all these years, what adventures have you had?"

Adler's face grew somber as he took a long drag from his cigarette. "Adventures, you say. I suppose that's one way to put it. Though I doubt they'd make for a pleasant dinner conversation."

Tesla leaned forward, his eyes fixed on Adler's face. "The scar... there is a story there, isn't there?"

Adler nodded slowly, his free hand unconsciously tracing the lines on his cheek. "Yes indeed. Shall we say a chapter in a book I never intended to write."

"Will you share that story with me, old friend?" Tesla asked softly.

Adler took another sip of whiskey while collecting his thoughts.

"After we parted ways, I found that America wasn't quite the land of opportunity for me as it was for you. I drifted for a while, taking odd jobs here and there. Eventually, I found work as a bouncer in some of the rougher establishments in New York."

Tesla winced slightly, but Adler continued.

"It wasn't glamorous work, but it got me by. As time went on, I developed a reputation. People began to seek me out for... specialized security work. Bodyguard work, mostly. Some for businessmen, others for people who preferred to keep their dealings out of the public eye, you know the sort."

"And the scar?" Tesla prompted gently.

Adler's hand went to his face again. "Occupational hazard, you might say. Complements from a rather persistent assassin in Chicago... 1902, I believe it was."

Tesla set down his glass, his face a mask of concern and guilt. "Adler, I had no idea. All these years, I've been wrapped up in my work."

Adler waved him off. "No need for guilt, Tesla. We each walked the path laid out for us. Yours led to greatness. Mine... well, mine led in circles mostly."

A heavy silence fell between them, broken only by the soft crackle of electricity from Tesla's machines.

"I've followed your career, you know," Adler said suddenly. "Every newspaper article, every mention of your name – I've read them all. Watched you for the past thirty years change the world from afar."

Tesla looked up, surprise evident on his face. "You have? I... I'm touched, Adler. Truly. And I must confess, I've often wondered about you over the years. Wondered what became of the man who saved my life on that ship so long ago."

Adler smiled, a hint of his old vigor shining through. "Ah, that night on the ship. Do you remember the poker game with those two grunts?"

"Yes, it was an event, was it not?"

"And how! It feels like another lifetime. Two young men, full of dreams, sailing towards the promise of America."

"And look at us now," Tesla said contently.

Adler chuckled. "Speak for yourself. I'm not nearly as accomplished as you. No great inventions to my name, no legacy to leave behind."

Tesla leaned forward, his eyes intense. "You're wrong, Adler. Your legacy sits before you. Everything I've created, everything I've achieved – it's all because of you. If you hadn't saved my life that night on the ship, none of this would exist."

Adler's eyes misted as Tesla continued, "You gave me a chance to do all that I have done. More than that, you showed me kindness when I needed it most. That has stayed with me all these years."

Adler fell silent, overwhelmed by emotion. He took another sip of whiskey, using the moment to compose himself.

"Tesla," he said at last, "I'm leaving America. Going back to Germany."

"Leaving? But why? And why now, with Europe at war?"

Adler sighed heavily. "That's precisely why. I am going to enlist, Tesla. I'm going to fight for my homeland. Put the only skills I have to some use."

The silence that followed was deafening. Tesla stood abruptly, pacing the length of his workbench.

"Have you gone mad? You know I'm Serbian by birth. Our countries are at war!"

Adler nodded solemnly. "I know. The irony isn't lost on me. Here we are, two immigrants who came to America on the same ship, and now..."

"And now the world has gone mad and you along with it," Tesla finished. He stopped pacing, turning to face Adler with a pained expression. "Is there nothing I can say to change your mind?"

Adler shook his head. "I'm afraid not, old friend. I've made my decision. America... it promised so much but delivered so little. At least in Germany, I'll have a purpose."

"How about family? Did you marry, do you have children? Will they go with you?"

"No, no, my dear friend, I am... just as you are, unmarried and without children."

Tesla walked to the large safe in the corner of his lab, opening it with practiced ease. He returned with a thick stack of bills, pressing them into Adler's hand.

"Then take this. Three thousand dollars. Ten times the amount you gave me all those years ago. Consider it... an investment in your future, whatever that may be."

Adler stared at the money, then back at Tesla. "No, I can't."

"You can, and you will," Tesla insisted. "Please, Ernst. Let me do this for you."

Adler nodded, carefully tucking the money away. "Thank you, Nikola. This means more than you know."

The two men stood in silence for a moment, the weight of their shared history and uncertain future hanging between them. Finally, Tesla spoke, his voice thick with emotion.

"Promise me you'll be careful. And if you ever need anything — anything at all — you know where to find me."

Adler clasped Tesla's hand in both of his own. "I promise. And thank you, for showing me that sometimes, the American dream does come true... even if it wasn't for me."

As Adler turned to leave, Tesla called out, "Adler! Those eight days on the ship... it was something!"

Adler paused at the door, a sad smile on his face. "Yes, it was, my dear friend. *Auf Wiedersehen*, Nikola Tesla."

"*Zbogom*, Ernst Adler," Tesla replied with the Serbian farewell.

As the door closed behind Adler, Tesla turned back to his lab, the hum of electricity suddenly seeming hollow in the wake of their parting. He picked up the whiskey bottle, pouring himself another measure. Raising the glass, he toasted the empty room. "To you, Ernst... survive."

Tesla placed the glass on the bench and picked up the tiny turbine he'd been working on earlier, but his mind was far away, on a ship crossing the Atlantic thirty-plus years ago, where an unlikely friendship was forged on a ship bound for America.

Despite his usual strong willpower, he had to push back tears that stung his eyes, and sobs that threatened to erupt and double him over with inexplicable grief. His hands shaking, he poured himself yet another drink. Took a few deep breaths and steeled himself to continue working. Satisfied that he'd regained his self-control, he picked up the tiny turbine again and forced himself to focus on it.

Outside, Ernst Adler walked away from Tesla's lab, the three thousand dollars a comforting weight in his pocket.

As he disappeared into the bustling New York streets, two men from different worlds, now on diverging paths, each carried with them a piece of their shared past — a reminder of the bonds that can transcend time, distance, and even the divisions of war.

∞

After George Westinghouse passed away in March 1914, Tesla faced a tumultuous period both emotionally and financially.

He drowned in despair as he struggled to cope with the loss of his dear friend and benefactor. The burden of unpaid bills loomed over him like a dark cloud.

The prestigious Waldorf-Astoria, once his sanctuary, turned its back on him, as he failed to keep up with his residence fees. His personal finances continued to be a crisis for him. He wandered from one hotel to another between 1915 and 1933, only to face the same fate as he did at the Waldorf-Astoria.

The cycle of eviction and displacement became a harsh reality. His friends, Robert and Katharine, knew nothing of these struggles. They understood Westinghouse left a private grant for Tesla to see him through to the end of his life. And though the monies paid to Tesla every month were most generous, they proved insufficient to maintain the lavish lifestyle to which Tesla had grown accustomed over the decades. His tastes were exorbitant, rivaling those of the most affluent socialites of New York's elite circles.

The Johnsons were busy with their own lives, much more than in previous years, and so Tesla's relationship with Katharine remained, one could say, dear friends with occasional benefits. She and Robert had raised two children. Their son Owen moved to Paris, so they increasingly made trips to Europe, particularly to Italy as, after World War I, Robert became the United States Ambassador to Italy under President Woodrow.

Yes, Tesla and Katharine loved each other and sent each other rather impassioned letters, all of which Tesla saved and would reread many times.

He was content with the fact that their paths in life had diverged. Such were the bruises and bumps of life, he felt, and the reality of being almost sixty now and having chosen to be married to his career. For all the lengthy life he would live, he was always driven by an urgent need to work quickly, to hurry as though time was his enemy. He feared there would not be enough time for him to get all the ideas in his head in working order, or at least diagrammed out and patented for the generations of geniuses to follow, who might find their world more receptive to his visions.

In interviews, Tesla was sometimes asked why he never married. He would later explain: "I have decided to dedicate my whole life to work and for that reason I gave up love and companionship of a good woman; and even more. I believe that a writer or a musician or an artist should marry. They gain inspiration that leads to finer achievement. But an inventor has so intense a nature, with so much in it of wild, passionate quality that, in giving himself to a woman, he would give up everything from his chosen domain. It is a pity, too; sometimes we feel so lonely."

It was a surprise to those members of the press who interviewed Tesla, to witness this stoic, normally unemotional man overcome with emotion, even breaking down in tears, when discussing the personal loneliness in his life.

The press had continued to fancy him as celibate, which seemed to make him even more attractive to women who sent him love letters or approached him in person, certain they could be the right woman to seduce him. It only added to his mystique and his stardom.

Despite his efforts to keep his mind solely on his work, there were times when Tesla inevitably indulged in wishing for the impossible. That he could reclaim the kind of deep love he knew he was capable of. That he had the emotional energy for and was even deserving of such devotion. That the emptiness in his heart, when he allowed himself to feel it, could be filled again with passion, tenderness and understanding. He privately longed for that day, but had little hope he would live to see it.

His friends acknowledged that he had suffered an emotional breakdown around the time his Wardenclyffe project was halted. Now they feared he was dangerously close to having another one.

24

WRONG PLACE, WRONG TIME

Central Park, New York - 1913

Walter Atwater, a man whose financial security was in serious jeopardy thanks to his newfound ability to lose money, trudged through Central Park. His shoulders slumped under the weight of impending unemployment, his mustache drooping in perfect sympathy with his spirits.

"Blasted stocks," he muttered, kicking a pebble and nearly taking out an unsuspecting squirrel.

Seeking solace, or perhaps just a bench to collapse on dramatically, Walter found himself before a majestic oak tree. Its branches reached skyward, as if trying to touch the clouds, completely indifferent to Walter's fiscal woes.

No sooner had Walter's posterior made contact with the bench than a veritable avian convention descended upon him. Pigeons, those feathered rats of the sky, swarmed at his feet, while a single white dove maneuvered beside him on the bench.

"Wonderful," Walter grumbled. "I've gone from the bulls and bears of Wall Street to a parliament of pigeons and a renegade dove. At least you lot don't expect me to increase your profits."

As if in response to this sterling wit, a strange static filled the air.

Walter's head whipped around, certain he was about to be accosted by an aggressive street performer. Instead, a voice emanated from... well, from nowhere in particular. As if from out of thin air.

"This is the Queens Seagull calling the Manhattan Dove. Come in, please..."

Walter blinked. He looked at the dove. The dove looked back, unimpressed.

"I don't suppose that was you?" he asked the bird.

"Queens Seagull to Manhattan Dove. Over..." the voice persisted. Walter jumped to his feet, sending pigeons scattering in a flurry of indignant coos. He circled the oak tree, half-expecting to find a vaudeville troupe hiding behind it.

"Hello?" he called out, feeling rather foolish. "Is this some sort of jest? Because I assure you, I am not in the mood for—"

"Yes, yes!" the disembodied voice crowed. "Mr. Tesla, can you hear me?"

Walter's mustache twitched in confusion. "Tesla? As in Nikola Tesla?"

"It's John Watt!" the voice continued, oblivious to Walter's bewilderment.

"I've lost my mind," Walter muttered to the dove. "The stress has finally broken me."

The voice carried on speaking of years and radios and other such nonsense, while Walter seriously considered whether the stress of impending financial ruin had finally caused him to take leave of his senses. A talking seagull from Queens was trying to communicate through him to a dove called Tesla.

He had heard stories about people who heard voices from invisible sources before going insane. And now, he feared, it was happening to him!

"Listen here, Seagull, or ahh — whoever you are," Walter finally interrupted. "I don't know what sort of tomfoolery this is, but I've had quite enough. Leave me alone!"

And with that, Walter abruptly got up from the bench and turned on his heel, ready to storm off when he nearly collided with none other than Nikola Tesla himself!

Walter recognized him immediately from the many photographs published over the years in the New York newspapers and magazines. He stood startled for a moment, for the inventor was taller and thinner than he expected, and his eyes had a commanding intensity to them.

"My good man," Tesla began, "Might I ask a favor of you?"

In a state of both confusion and exasperation, Walter straightened his posture and focused an intense gaze on Tesla.

"Look here, Mr. Tesla," he said, his voice dripping with forced politeness, "I don't know what manner of prank you're playing, but I assure you, it's in poor taste. Now, if you'll excuse me, I have a job and a wife to lose."

With that, Walter tipped his hat, pointedly ignored the chorus of cooing pigeons and the cool-headed dove staring at him. He strode away, leaving a perplexed Tesla in his wake.

Tesla wiped down the recently vacated bench with a handkerchief, took a seat on it, and exhaled a long sigh of relief. He pondered his good fortune that Walter had no further inquiries, though the gnawing realization that his Time Radio obviously worked — and he had missed the transmission — left him with a mixture of elation and frustration.

Tesla spent the remainder of the day on that bench, hoping the future might call again. But as the sun dipped below the city's skyline, Tesla was forced to concede defeat. The future, it seemed, had said its piece for the day.

As for Walter Atwater, his brush with the voice from the oak tree that claimed to be a seagull, the gang of pigeons, and the dove called Tesla, marked a turning point in his fortunes. In the weeks that followed, not only did he not lose his job, but he went on to become one of the most successful stockbrokers of his time. Perhaps it was the shock of hearing voices from trees, or maybe the universe cut him some slack, but Walter developed a natural ability to predict market trends.

When the great stock market crash of 1929 loomed on the horizon, Walter's instincts screamed danger. He liquidated his assets, secured a tidy nest egg for his wife and child, and weathered the financial storm with the serenity of a man who had once argued with a talking oak tree.

In his later years, Walter would tell this story to his son, a tale so strange it could only be true. It became a family legend, passed down from his child to his grandchildren. Walter's granddaughter Barbara, in particular, hung on every word, her young mind captivated by the mystery of the voice from the oak tree.

Her father even took her to the oak tree where it happened so many years ago, just as Walter had taken him, to the same place several times, but the voice was never heard again.

Years later, that same granddaughter would join the FBI, unaware that her grandfather's tale contained the very information the agency had long sought. For in the dusty archives of the FBI, a file existed — a secret file detailing rumors of a device that could pierce the veil of time itself.

And so the wheels of fate began to turn. The very invention that Nikola Tesla had labored to protect, the secret he had gone to such lengths to conceal, now teetered on the brink of discovery.

All because of a chance encounter between a desperate stockbroker, a parliament of pigeons, a renegade dove, and an oak tree that spoke from the future.

25

LIFELINE

Nikola Tesla paced the plush burgundy carpet of his hotel suite, wringing his hands.

His brilliant mind whirred with equations and calculations as always, but his heart raced with hope he dared not voice. Could it be true? After all this time?

A sharp rap at the door nearly made him jump out of his skin. He smoothed his vest, took a steadying breath, and made his way across the ornate Persian rug to the entrance. His trembling hand grasped the brass knob. This was it.

He pulled open the door and there she stood, a vision in emerald green traveling clothes. Anya. His Anya. Suitcase in hand, tendrils of dark blonde hair escaping her hat, regarding him with those sparkling hazel eyes he could drown in.

Anya, radiant and alive, a small suitcase clutched in her delicate hand. Her lips curved into that familiar smile that had haunted his dreams and waking moments.

Tesla blinked once, twice, certain his mind was playing a cruel trick on him. He stood frozen, unable to comprehend the sight before him. Was this a hallucination born of grief and desperation? Had he finally succumbed to the madness that had always lurked at the edges of his brilliant mind?

"Niko?" Anya's voice, soft and melodious, cut through the fog of his disbelief. "May I come in?"

Wordlessly, Tesla reached out and took the suitcase from her hand, setting it down with trembling fingers. Then, as if pulled by an irresistible force, he drew her into his arms.

"My love," he sobbed, his entire body shaking with the force of his emotion. "You have come at last."

He held her close, breathing in the familiar scent of her hair, feeling the warmth of her body against his. If this was insanity, he decided, then he would gladly surrender to it.

"I am in disbelief to see you here," Tesla whispered, his voice thick with emotion. "Like an angel come to my rescue. Can this truly be real?"

Anya's arms tightened around him, her voice soothing as she murmured, "Darling, I shall never be apart from you again. I'm here, I'm real."

Tesla pulled back, his eyes searching her face, drinking in every detail.

"Last night, I dreamed of you," he confessed. "It felt just as it does now, so vivid, so real."

A soft smile played on Anya's lips. "Dreams do come true, my love."

"Am I dreaming now?"

In response, Anya leaned in and kissed him lightly. The touch of her lips against his sent a jolt through Tesla's body, awakening sensations he had feared lost forever. The kiss deepened, growing more urgent, more passionate.

"Is this real enough for you?" Anya murmured as they finally parted, both breathless. "I wanted to surprise you, to see the joy in your eyes when I appeared."

25

LIFELINE

Nikola Tesla paced the plush burgundy carpet of his hotel suite, wringing his hands.

His brilliant mind whirred with equations and calculations as always, but his heart raced with hope he dared not voice. Could it be true? After all this time?

A sharp rap at the door nearly made him jump out of his skin. He smoothed his vest, took a steadying breath, and made his way across the ornate Persian rug to the entrance. His trembling hand grasped the brass knob. This was it.

He pulled open the door and there she stood, a vision in emerald green traveling clothes. Anya. His Anya. Suitcase in hand, tendrils of dark blonde hair escaping her hat, regarding him with those sparkling hazel eyes he could drown in.

Anya, radiant and alive, a small suitcase clutched in her delicate hand. Her lips curved into that familiar smile that had haunted his dreams and waking moments.

Tesla blinked once, twice, certain his mind was playing a cruel trick on him. He stood frozen, unable to comprehend the sight before him. Was this a hallucination born of grief and desperation? Had he finally succumbed to the madness that had always lurked at the edges of his brilliant mind?

"Niko?" Anya's voice, soft and melodious, cut through the fog of his disbelief. "May I come in?"

Wordlessly, Tesla reached out and took the suitcase from her hand, setting it down with trembling fingers. Then, as if pulled by an irresistible force, he drew her into his arms.

"My love," he sobbed, his entire body shaking with the force of his emotion. "You have come at last."

He held her close, breathing in the familiar scent of her hair, feeling the warmth of her body against his. If this was insanity, he decided, then he would gladly surrender to it.

"I am in disbelief to see you here," Tesla whispered, his voice thick with emotion. "Like an angel come to my rescue. Can this truly be real?"

Anya's arms tightened around him, her voice soothing as she murmured, "Darling, I shall never be apart from you again. I'm here, I'm real."

Tesla pulled back, his eyes searching her face, drinking in every detail.

"Last night, I dreamed of you," he confessed. "It felt just as it does now, so vivid, so real."

A soft smile played on Anya's lips. "Dreams do come true, my love."

"Am I dreaming now?"

In response, Anya leaned in and kissed him lightly. The touch of her lips against his sent a jolt through Tesla's body, awakening sensations he had feared lost forever. The kiss deepened, growing more urgent, more passionate.

"Is this real enough for you?" Anya murmured as they finally parted, both breathless. "I wanted to surprise you, to see the joy in your eyes when I appeared."

Tesla shook his head, still bewildered. "I have lost everything," he said softly, "and yet gained everything by your presence."

He cradled her face in his calloused palms and her eyes fluttered closed as their lips met again in a deep, hungry kiss after years apart. Tesla poured every ounce of longing into that embrace, salty tears spilling down his cheeks. She was home.

When finally, they broke apart, he gazed at her with naked adoration. "My brilliant, beautiful Anya."

She smoothed back his unruly shock of gray hair. "You know I'm a woman of my word, my love. When I promised to find you again, I meant it." Her eyes shone with a sudden sheen of tears. "No more parting from me, do you understand? We've wasted too much time already."

"Never again," he vowed fervently, kissing her hand. "These years without you have been unbearable. I'm just...I'm so thankful you're here, alive and safe." He cupped her face again, searching her eyes. "Are you well? You're looking a bit peaky."

Anya waved a dismissive hand. "The crossing from Liverpool was a choppy nightmare, that's all. Now that I've arrived and breathed the American air, I'll be right as rain."

Fear gripped him suddenly — fear that if he let go, she would vanish like a mirage. With a desperation born of that fear, Tesla pulled Anya with him into the bedroom. They fell onto the bed together, a tangle of limbs and emotions.

For a long while, they simply lay there, Tesla holding Anya close, content to feel the rise and fall of her chest, to listen to the steady beat of her heart. But as the reality of her presence sank in, other needs began to assert themselves.

Tesla's hands began to explore, reacquainting themselves with the curves and contours of Anya's body. Their lips met again, and again, each kiss more passionate than the last. Clothes were shed, barriers both physical and emotional crumbling away.

In the aftermath, as they lay entwined in the soft glow of the setting sun, Tesla felt a peace he had thought forever lost to him.

"You will stay here with me," he murmured. "I'll never let you go." Anya's response was a soft kiss pressed to his chest, right above his heart.

Tesla drifted off to sleep only to awake with a start. He was relieved to find Anya still lying next to him. Actually, she was propped up on her elbow, smiling impishly at him.

"Straight talk, if you please, mister," she chuckled, "Now that I'm here, what's so blasted important that you couldn't be satisfied keeping me lounging on the Adriatic for our twilight years?"

He leaned in, eyes sparkling with excitement. "Something spectacular, my love. Something to change the world. Imagine if we could transmit electricity wirelessly, with no unsightly cable or towers to mar the landscape. Energy beamed through the very air and ground, powering every home, vehicle, factory!"

"You're of a mind to set the world on fire," she laughed, "Should I be concerned?"

"Hardly!" He sprang up, pacing again as he launched into the pitch that had been rattling in his brain for years. "By harnessing the electrical charge within the planet's telecommunication circuit layers, we can create a unified omnipresent electromagnetic field capable of transmitting any frequency across any terrain!"

He paused, searching her face with the tiniest flicker of doubt. "You're not buying a word of it, are you?"

"I'm enraptured as always by your technical prattle, darling." She grinned and blew him a kiss. "Though I admit, your inventions always did sound like lunatic ravings until I saw them in action."

A knock sounded at the door. Anya looked up curiously as Tesla strode over and pulled it open to admit a hotel server bearing a tray with a fine china tea set.

"You had them bring up tea already?" she said, touched by the simple gesture.

"I wanted everything to be perfect for your arrival," he said, showing the server to the sitting room and tipping him generously. "My love deserves only the very best."

As the door closed, he poured the steaming amber liquid, doctoring each cup with precise measurements of cream and sugar, just as she liked.

When he handed her the cup and saucer, their fingers brushed, sending electric tingles up his arm. He caught her gaze, open and vulnerable in that moment.

His heart jumped, for he knew what they would be doing again very soon, what he had dreamed of doing with her — whether he was awake or asleep — for so very long. Yes, he could contain his need and luxuriate in the slow foreplay of the inevitable. It was worth the wait because he had all the time in the world now to realize his fantasies.

"Thank you," Anya murmured, sipping slowly. "It's wonderful to be home."

He beamed, settling onto the divan and toasting her cup with his own. "To us, my darling. The future awaits."

26

Love and Pain

The most impassioned relationships can lose their spark with time. Like couples who have weathered many storms together, their once aligned interests can drift apart, the strong efforts required to keep their bond intact becoming increasingly difficult.

Over the years, the cruelest blow of all for Tesla was watching the brilliant, vivacious Anya slowly deteriorate into an invalid, rarely venturing out socially by his side.

He had seen right away upon her arrival that she was unwell.

A slow, lingering malaise increasingly sapped her strength and her interest in life outside their hotel suite.

She accepted her role of tending to his needs at home while his work consumed him. Anya even turned a reluctant blind eye to his flirtations and indiscretions with others, realizing the legendary inventor needed more intimacy and variety than her fragile condition could provide. But they had never spoken of this painful new reality straining their relationship.

Tesla continued his affair with Katharine whenever she and Robert were in town. As the years had passed, he had occasionally wondered whether he should finally squelch the rumors of his "celibacy" and reveal that yes, he was capable of having a physical relationship with a woman. But to come forward would hurt Katharine's reputation rather than his own.

Polite society did not reveal married women stepping out on their husbands. And so nothing was said, although gossip still abounded, especially from those who saw Tesla and Katharine in public together.

Despite her enduring, all-consuming love for Tesla, Katharine faced one daunting obstacle - she had no private place for their intimate time together, and Tesla could not take her home, as Anya was always there and seldom left the hotel. After agonizing over the dilemma, he finally secured a separate secret room in another hotel nearby, allowing them to consummate their passion for privacy.

One sultry summer night, well past midnight, Tesla staggered home, reeking of wine, his unkempt appearance making it obvious he had not been working. The other shoe had finally dropped. He had known a confrontation was inevitable...

Anya awoke as Tesla clumsily disrobed and changed into his bedclothes. "You're just getting home now?" she said coldly, causing him to jump.

"I'm sorry, Anya," he mumbled guiltily, perching on the edge of the bed, avoiding her accusatory glare.

Anya slowly pulled herself upright, her penetrating stare piercing his soul. "You've been with another woman."

It was not a question. Tesla swallowed hard and nodded. "I can't lie to you, yes."

"Katharine?"

Tesla nodded. Anya seemed devoid of emotion as she searched for the right words. "Why? Don't you love me anymore?"

"You know I do," he replied softly. "But you understand, a man has needs..."

She looked away, staring down at her trembling hands. "Do you want me to go away?"

"No!" Tesla's response was immediate and visceral. "You must never leave me."

A flicker of relief passed over Anya's face. "If that is your wish. But promise me never to bring another woman here, to our home. Find another place for that, do you promise?"

"Yes, I have done that," he assured her.

Pain and sorrow creased Anya's delicate features. "I gave up everything to be here with you - my life, my art - because I believe in you and your work. But I should have married you when you asked me. That was a terrible mistake. I'm so sorry, Niko."

Tesla's anguished expression crumpled as he fell onto the bed, racked with heaving sobs. Anya cradled his head in her arms, gently kissing away his tears before tenderly kissing his lips. He recoiled, shaking his head in disgust.

"The fault is all mine. It's you who should forgive me because I can never forgive myself."

Anya ignored his words, continued to caress and kiss him. Despite his emotional torment, desire stirred within Tesla.

He caught himself and looked at her questioningly. When she smiled seductively and nodded, he still hesitated.

"Are you sure, my darling? Are you feeling able enough?"

Anya silenced him by pressing her finger to his lips. "Shhh..." She pulled him close, and they made love with a tenderness borne of their enduring bond and the forgiveness only deep love can provide.

While Tesla and Anya understood his straying, Katharine's life descended into a waking nightmare. She fell into an increasingly deep depression over what she considered the failure of her marriage.

She blamed her husband for her loneliness and isolation, but the root cause was her passionate love affair with the man who had awakened her sexual nature, a man who was not her husband.

She felt trapped, and as her despair mounted, the only light left in her life was her infrequent meetings with Tesla. As always, their time together was limited by necessity and discretion, but their feelings for each other were genuine and intense.

The affair was always suspected among her circle of friends, but her husband remained in denial, not wanting to accept that the man he had known and befriended was sleeping with his wife.

Or maybe he knows and doesn't care, Tesla speculated. After all, wasn't it deemed acceptable for those with wealth and in high society to have lovers on the side?

Perhaps Robert had his own attachments elsewhere, but whatever the circumstances, the subject remained unspoken between the two men.

∞

In 1920, the Johnsons moved to Italy. Robert's appointment as U.S. Ambassador resulted from his success in heading up massive relief efforts there, after the devastation of World War I.

Tesla had a sense of foreboding about their move, as the previous year Katharine fell seriously ill in the midst of a worldwide influenza pandemic.

Tesla had worried at Katharine's slow recovery and hastened to assist her by changing her diet, seeing she ate certain healing foods and his favorite vegetable concoctions he insisted be put together for her. Whether his nutritional program did the trick, or she thrived on Tesla's concerned hands-on ministering to her, Katharine finally regained her strength to a great degree.

Tesla's friends and Robert Johnson, in particular, were puzzled at his extreme fear and attentiveness during Katharine's illness. At times he was almost hysterical with stress. They had never witnessed him so upset, dramatically rearranging his life to all but nurse a close friend, and were at a loss to understand his out-of-character behavior.

The Johnsons lived in Italy for four years. Many letters were exchanged between them, which helped to keep them involved in each other's lives. On a personal level, Katharine wrote Tesla of her great loneliness at being away from him. Tesla's friends, meanwhile, noted he was more socially withdrawn in her absence.

When the Johnsons returned to America, it was evident Katharine's health was again on a fast decline. She died on the last day of 1924 — New Year's Eve. Robert was at her side; Tesla was not.

He was too heartbroken to see her on her deathbed; and it only added to his grief when Robert advised him that Katharine's last words were her wish that her husband keep in close touch with Tesla.

As midnight approached, and the traditional ball was dropped to celebrate the New Year, 1925, the cheers could be heard in the streets of Manhattan, a roar of celebration rising among the crowds.

Tesla, however, took to his bed, weary from his overwhelming grief. Anya did not comfort him with words, as she knew that would be useless. Instead, she held him close in an understanding embrace, a silent anchor point of love which allowed him to cry until there were no more tears, and to finally fall into a restless sleep.

As a final poignant note to Katharine's life, her memorial plaque on the family's graveyard plot paid tribute to her strong feminist identity by naming her in bold letters as "Kate Agnes McMahon" with her formal name "Katharine" written underneath in small type, along with "Wife of Robert Underwood Johnson."

Katharine's birthday was in April, and Robert held a family birthday party in her memory. He insisted Tesla attend and it was catered to Tesla's liking, even to the choice of music played.

Soon after that, Robert fell in love with a teenaged actress, Marguerite Churchill. Tesla wasn't privy to how long the relationship lasted. But it had ended by the time Churchill went to Hollywood, had a middling film career and married a handsome young actor.

Tesla did not begrudge his old friend finding happiness so soon after Katharine's death; his own life had presented itself with unexpected twists and turns. Who was he to judge how and when a man could fall in love.

27

THE CELEBRITY PARADE

Over the years, George Scherff became accustomed to the revolving door of celebrities and investors who made it their business to visit Tesla, always with some agenda in mind.

On one such day, George heard a sharp rap on the door. He rose to admit the visitor, only to find Tesla had beaten him to the entrance. Tesla swung the door open.

"Yes, what is it?" he said, annoyed. He was mid resolving a work problem and not in the mood to be social.

"Good afternoon, Mr. Tesla." A tall, thin man in a bowler hat and overcoat stood on the doorstep, carrying a briefcase. "My name is Hiram S. Rowland. I'm a lawyer representing the Western Union patent division. Would you have a few minutes to spare for a chat?"

Tesla regarded him suspiciously. "About what?"

The lawyer cleared his throat. "About a recent patent filing."

"Very well, you'd better come in." Tesla stepped back to allow the visitor to enter then shut the door.

George trailed the pair to the sitting area and served the new guest. As Mr. Rowland adjusted his spectacles, George caught a glimpse of a peculiar scar under his left eye. Odd for a lawyer, he thought, to have a scar like that. It seemed like a knife may have caused it.

George tensed, something felt off.

He left the men and, although he was out of their line of sight, he could see them from the reflection in the window. George had not been hired to be just an assistant and an accountant, but what few people knew was that George was also Tesla's capable muscle should the need arise.

Tesla took the seat opposite the visitor. "What do you want?"

The lawyer set his briefcase on the floor and folded his hands, assuming an official air. "To be honest, your patents are creating a bit of a stir."

"Yes, my patents do that," Tesla replied with a certain smugness. "Some people believe they might represent a grave threat."

The lawyer's eyes narrowed and his voice grew colder. "A threat we cannot allow," he stated firmly.

The two men stared each other down for a long moment. Then Tesla spoke, his words measured and deliberate.

"Is the Western Union Company threatening me... or is it just you threatening me?"

The lawyer's lip twitched. "It's quite the opposite. In fact, it is your patents that are threatening my employer and hence the purpose of my visit today. The Western Union Company is prepared to purchase these troublesome patents." The lawyer took some paperwork out of his briefcase.

"And if I don't wish to sell them?"

"That would be most unfortunate," replied the lawyer in a sharp, threatening voice.

George abruptly appeared before the seated men. The lawyer diverted his attention to George, locking eyes with him.

"May I be of any further assistance, sir?" George asked Tesla, his glare not leaving the lawyer's eyes.

"Am I to assume you are not interested in selling Patent PCX–1.889.7 43?" The lawyer asked politely enough yet in a threatening tone.

"Yes, that would be an accurate assumption. The telegram's days ... well, you might say are numbered," Tesla answered sharply.

The lawyer stood abruptly, breaking his stare down with George then brushed invisible dust from his suit.

"Thank you for your time, Mr. Tesla. Have a good day." He spun on his heel and strode briskly out.

George locked the door behind him.

"George," Tesla called. "Would you mind bringing me a glass of water? And don't forget the ice."

"Certainly, sir," George replied and made his way to the kitchen.

"And George, no more visitors today."

"Of course," George answered before disappearing into the kitchen.

Tesla's patents threatened to make the telegraph obsolete within fifteen years. The Western Union Company, after being unsuccessful in purchasing these patents from Tesla, was forced to diversify and ventured into finance. But happily for them, this new venture proved even more successful than their core business of telegrams.

∞

Among the many projects Tesla worked on, there was one George privately questioned as to its feasibility. He was used to Tesla's eccentricity, but this particular invention seemed to stretch all credibility.

Tesla named it his Teslascope and its goal was to wirelessly transmit communications to planets other than Earth. He had been working on it, on and off, for several decades; in fact, since his time in Colorado Springs.

He advised George he had successfully already contacted Mars and had created a disturbance in outer space, having ruled out the sun, the moon, and the planet Venus.

For years Tesla declined to speak publicly about this project. Nor did he provide George with details. Yet circuits, coils, conductors, and schematics formed a congregation spread out on his workbench.

George observed this work on the Teslascope but declined to ask questions, knowing Tesla would provide no enlightening information about it.

One reason Tesla refused to discuss the Teslascope was that he knew he would not live long enough to experience an age of space travel.

Automobiles had come a long way since the earliest models of Henry Ford; airplanes were improving their functionality hoping coast-to-coast travel could someday be achieved non-stop. But progress in the various forms of travel was too slow for Tesla.

Already his work on electric cars that needed no gasoline had been vetoed by industry and society, for the most part. He knew his day would come, but when?

He tried to convince himself that work on the Teslascope was idle tinkering. But what if he could create such a device, and it worked? What of the cosmic dangers in meddling with time and space? Did he think this through enough? And if successful, could he tell anyone? No! It was crucial no one knew. The dangers were immense, and he likely revealed too much to Anya already.

He had no idea whether there was life on Mars, but in Colorado Springs he had sent a signal and received one back, so obviously, communication was possible. He knew the planet was Mars because it was closest to Earth.

And so among all his other inventions, he continued to work on the Teslascope.

It would not be until his 75th birthday that he dared to explain the theory of this to *Time* magazine, stating with certainty he had conceived "a means that will make it possible for man to transmit energy in large amounts, thousands of horsepower, from one planet to another, absolutely regardless of distance. I think nothing can be more important than interplanetary communication. It will certainly come someday and the certitude that there are other human beings in the universe, working, suffering, struggling, like ourselves, will produce a magic effect on mankind and will form the foundation of a universal brotherhood that will last as long as humanity itself."

∞

Along with his work in contacting outer space from Earth, Tesla also began work on an invention that would fire from above and create an impact on Earth.

It was soon after the Great War, or World War I as it was later called. With improved and faster travel, and improved weapons, Tesla had no doubt that the wave of the future would include deadlier wars.

And so he arranged a meeting with a man he greatly respected, one who had improved the functionality and speed of another transportation mode: trains. The invention of the steam engine had again made the world smaller, making cross-country travel an easier reality.

"Sir?" The gentle rap of knuckles on the laboratory's door broke Tesla's contemplations. "Your visitor has arrived."

George ushered in the stately Elijah McCoy, an elderly African American inventor. He was a kindly-looking man although his much of his handsome face was hidden behind a heavy beard and mustache.

"The real McCoy himself," Tesla beamed, striding forward with an outstretched hand. "It is a massive honor to receive one of engineering's stellar stars in my terrestrial workspace."

McCoy's eyes crinkled behind his spectacles as he returned the firm handshake.

"The sentiments are mutual, though I suspect my humble neutron star pales in the incandescent brilliance to your potential to cause supernovas in the core of our galaxy."

Both men laughed and sat down. George brought drinks and food to them, and they finally settled in for a serious talk.

"And now Mr. Tesla," said McCoy. "You wanted to discuss your latest project. How can I help you?"

"It's in the very beginning stages," Tesla admitted. "In concept what I'm developing is similar to what sonar does under water. It can locate and defend against an airborne enemy. A self-powered projectile that launches from a carrier in the sky. It can launch from the ground presently, but I hope to find a solution so that it may launch from the sky."

"A weapon?" asked McCoy.

"No, not at all. A defensive counter measure against airborne weapons."

"Why do you feel the need for it?"

"I fear in time, the airplane will advance technologically and be used as a terrible weapon against man, and there must be something to counter it."

McCoy looked thoughtfully at Tesla before he spoke.

"This century is still young and yet it seems man has no limits to our barbaric desires for destruction."

"That is true," agreed Tesla. "When complete I will divide the plans for the Teleforce, that is what I am calling it, into seven sections and offer it to seven nations. No one part will work alone; in order for the Teleforce to be realized all seven parts of the plan must come together. All seven nations must work together to develop the Teleforce."

"A wise strategy, my friend. However, unrealistic. I don't believe you will get seven nations to agree to share the same idea for the defense of the skies."

Tesla nodded. "I suspect as much for now. But the future is my hope." He glanced away from McCoy and suddenly looked vulnerable and insecure.

"Sir, you have lived a long and productive life. Do you ever regret that which you have not developed quickly enough? For example, if only Morgan hadn't shut me down and I had finished perfecting the sonar earlier, those lost souls on *Titanic* would have been warned about the iceberg a mile before they hit it. I could have saved all those lives, including my good friend, my sponsor, Jack Astor." Tesla's eyes welled up with tears.

"We all have regrets in our past," McCoy said gently. "But better to focus on the present." He smiled at Tesla and added, "It would be my honor to lend whatever help I can to safeguard the future."

Tesla's demeanor returned to his normal, professional self. "I'm pleased to hear that. Here is my problem. The system I envisioned is currently a ground-to-air defense system, however it would be far more effective if it were an air-to-air defense system. But sustaining indefinite flight is the dilemma."

"There is only one feasible solution," said McCoy.

"Continuous orbital flight," both said at the same time.

Tesla continued, "Navigating it remotely once it's in orbit will not present much of a problem. I have nearly perfected that aspect."

McCoy nodded. "Getting it into orbit and in one piece, then detaching it from its transport vessel is the challenge then."

"Indeed," agreed Tesla.

McCoy looked over at Tesla's cluttered work bench where he was building the Time Radio. "What's all that?" he asked.

"It's a radio."

"Nasty business that, with Marconi."

Tesla shrugged and then continued, "This is no ordinary radio. It would take no less than thirty patents, all of which would be mine, to make it work. But I am not registering this one."

McCoy frowned. "Is that wise?"

"The world shall not know of this radio. It's far too dangerous."

"Then I shall ask no more questions of it, and let's return to the problem of getting your air defense system into orbit."

Part Six

28

WIRELESS ELECTRICITY

Queens, New York — August 2024

"Mr. Tesla, what really happened with Wardenclyffe Tower?"

John Watt was mid discussion with Tesla via the Time Radio. He had spent much time pouring through books and websites about Tesla's life and had made a list of questions to ask him.

"The world, my boy, was not ready for progress," Tesla replied sadly. "At least not in my time. There were those who feared change, who clung to the old ways. They saw my vision as a threat, a disruption to their power and control, to their profits."

Tesla continued, his voice growing animated. "Imagine ships at sea, powered wirelessly from across the ocean, and automobiles, trains, buses and even aircraft moving man from destination to destination silently. Factories humming with energy, without the need for costly and inefficient power lines. Clean and plentiful energy would light up the man's home. All this drawn from the very Earth itself!"

"You mean wireless electricity? No need to plug a device in with a cord?"

"Exactly. It's not a matter of me inventing anything, I just discovered what was already there."

"And Wardenclyffe Tower could have provided that for New York?"

"That is what I was working on."

"But Mr. Tesla, there had to be others who supported your work?"

"Yes, John, there were. But their voices were drowned out by the chorus of opposition. The forces against me were much too strong, and in the end, they prevailed."

"Well, not entirely, sir. Wireless electricity is common in 2024, but it's only for small devices and short distances. The idea of transmitting power wirelessly on a global scale is incredible."

A heavy sigh filtered through the Time Radio. "It saddens me to hear that my greatest invention has been reduced to powering mere trinkets so far in the future."

John's mind reeled at the possibilities. The idea of transmitting power wirelessly on a global scale was unimaginable. Why was mankind restricting itself from this great benefit?

"But how, Mr. Tesla?" John asked, while thinking to himself: *Why Google this when you can ask the great Nikola Tesla himself?* His voice was filled with wonder. "How can electricity travel without wires?"

"The Earth herself is the conductor, my boy." Tesla's voice took on a professor's patient tone. "Just as sound waves travel through air, electrical waves can course through our planet. Wardenclyffe Tower would have acted as a transmitter, sending these waves across the globe to be captured by receivers. These receivers would then convert the waves back into usable electricity, powering the world."

"Would we not feel this electricity run through our bodies?"

"No, not at all. The electromagnetic fields typically operate at frequencies not perceptible to human senses. We can't see, hear, or feel them directly."

"Amazing!"

"In fact, I have been pondering the idea of medical devices to use targeted electromagnetic fields to stimulate nerves, which can be felt, it's all a matter of frequencies, you see. This would be a deliberate increase in frequency that can be used for therapeutic purposes."

"I think you have already done that, sir. Ah ... or, will do that. I remember reading something about electromagnetic fields to stimulate nerves, there are machines that do this now and even clinics that specialize in this therapy."

"I am pleased to hear this."

"So let me see if I understand this. In an ideal world today, I could go to Best Buy, it's a store that sells computers and electronics, or do a wireless order on Amazon, and purchase a mini-Wardenclyffe. It would come in different sizes. I could get a tiny one to power a house or a farm, especially if I lived out in a rural area. Or larger ones could be purchased to provide electricity for a city."

"Yes, that's correct."

"We do have wireless transmissions today across the planet, it's called the Internet. But it's not free, you have to purchase a plan, usually comes with a wireless phone, and provides you wireless access for as long as you pay. "

Tesla's voice hardened. "From your words, John, it seems the same problems persist. Yes, one must purchase the device, but the power itself should be free. And those in charge still resist this concept, just as they did in my time."

"That's exactly how it is, Mr. Tesla. But let me ask you, is it possible to send electrical energy to the moon?"

"Certainly. The moon, like the Earth, is a conductor. Electrical waves can travel through the vacuum of space, just as they can travel through the Earth. A transmitter on Earth could send those waves to a receiver on the moon, which could then convert them into usable energy."

"But what about the distance? The moon is over 200,000 miles away."

"Distance is not an insurmountable obstacle, John. The strength of the signal would decrease with distance, of course, but this could be overcome by using a powerful transmitter and a large receiver with booster stations in-between. Additionally, the use of resonant frequencies could help to increase the efficiency of energy transfer over long distances."

"Resonant frequencies?"

"Yes. Resonance is a phenomenon that occurs when two objects vibrate at the same frequency. In wireless power transfer, resonance can be used to increase the efficiency of energy transfer. By tuning the transmitter and receiver to the same resonant frequency, we can ensure the energy is transferred with minimal loss."

"I see," John said, his mind racing with the possibilities. "We could build a colony on the moon and power it from earth."

"Indeed, John."

"That is super cool!" John gushed. "But there is one good thing going on here on Earth you should know. There's an electric car company named after you. The Tesla car has all the latest high tech in it; I got to test drive it. If I had the money, I would happily buy one. Elon Musk, the man who founded the company is kind of an eccentric genius."

"I am sorry, John, what do you mean by car?"

"An automobile."

"Of course, an abbreviation for the word carriage."

"To be honest, we've all been calling them cars forever—"

John was startled by a sudden loud pounding on the apartment door. He froze, uncertain what to do.

"Mr. Tesla," he whispered, "there's someone at the door. I have to go. I'll call you again later."

He quickly shut off the Time Radio, plunging the room into silence. Who could be knocking at this hour? Had someone discovered his communication across time? The consequences of such a discovery raced through his mind — government agents, scientific institutions, powerful corporations that might want to suppress Tesla's knowledge yet again.

John sat motionless, barely breathing, straining to hear any movement outside his door. Minutes crawled by. No second knock came, but the tension remained, coiling in his stomach like a spring. Finally, gathering his courage, he crept to the door, each floorboard creak sounding thunderous in the quiet apartment.

With slightly trembling fingers, he eased the door open just a crack, prepared to slam it shut at the first sign of danger. Instead, he found only a brown Amazon package sitting innocently on his welcome mat. The relief that flooded through him was almost dizzying.

He snatched up the package, retreated inside and threw all three locks. As his racing heart began to slow, John realized how careless he'd been. In his excitement over speaking with Tesla, he'd forgotten the gravity of what he was doing. This wasn't just some fascinating historical discussion — he was communicating across time with one of history's most controversial inventors, potentially altering history.

With renewed determination, he gathered his notes and questions, each one now feeling more precious and dangerous than before. He switched the Time Radio back on, ready to resume his conversation with Tesla. John couldn't shake the feeling that he was part of something much bigger than himself — something that powerful people might do anything to get hold of.

Part Seven

29

MOBSTERS AND MONSTERS

Tesla never imagined becoming friends with a gangster, despite meeting countless intriguing individuals. Yet it happened in 1923, and theirs was an interesting friendship and partnership.

Charles Lucky Luciano contacted him, actually interested in investing in some of Tesla's inventions. They met and there was much discussion between the two. Tesla hadn't known what to expect but in person, Luciano was a good-looking man even though his bushy eyebrows and hooded eyes could make him look scary when he wasn't smiling.

It was some five years later when Luciano arranged for a dinner meeting with Tesla and another associate of his, a gentleman always looking for good investments. They met at Delmonico's Restaurant and ate at a table for four.

Before Tesla's arrival, Luciano greeted his associate Joseph P. Kennedy, a handsome, charismatic fellow in his mid-thirties, and Kennedy's date, the young, sultry film star Gloria Swanson. Luciano's thugs sat nearby, ever watchful.

Kennedy seemed annoyed, as Tesla was late for their dinner. He removed his round glasses, wiped them down then put them back on, staring toward the restaurant entrance as if this would hasten Tesla's arrival. Surprisingly,

Luciano didn't care. He explained how they could profit big time from Tesla's work. Luciano was now talking a major investment.

"Joe, I'm telling you, we'll make a fortune with this guy's inventions," Luciano said enthusiastically. "He comes off like a real nut job, but these microwaves he's talking about, I think it's gonna be big."

Just then, Tesla hurried over and joined the group. "Mr. Luciano, I apologize for being late."

"No problem, Nikky, glad you could join us. This here's Mr. Joseph Kennedy and Ms. Gloria Swanson, the film star. Mr. Nikola Tesla."

Tesla greeted them with a smile and a lingering look at Swanson. "Miss Swanson, an honor. I am indeed a fan of your motion pictures. Mr. Kennedy."

Joseph Kennedy stood up to shake Tesla's hand, but Luciano stopped him. "Mr. Tesla doesn't shake hands."

Kennedy withdrew his hand. "Oh, I see."

Tesla and Kennedy exchanged looks and took their seats. Luciano grinned and now addressed Tesla.

"Joe is interested in maybe buying some of your patents."

"Which ones?" Tesla asked.

"How about we get some drinks first."

Tesla gave Luciano a slight nod and a smile. It was an intriguing scene - the brilliant inventor, the ruthless mobster kingpin, the shrewd businessman, and the silver screen siren gathered around the table at the prestigious restaurant.

As the waiter arrived to take their drink orders, the candid conversation continued to unfold. Tesla, ever the polite gentleman, gestured for petite, dark-haired Gloria Swanson to order first. She flashed a coy smile and requested a glass of champagne.

Joseph Kennedy, not one to be outdone, ordered a fine scotch on the rocks. When it was Tesla's turn, he surprised the group by requesting a simple glass of water. Luciano chuckled and shook his head. "Nikky, you gotta live a little! Get the man a glass of the good stuff," he instructed the waiter, who promptly noted down an order for Tesla's preferred beverage. Once the drinks were served, the topic of conversation swiftly shifted to business matters.

Kennedy leaned forward, his eyes sharp and calculating. "So Mr. Tesla, Lucky seems to think you've got some game-changing inventions up your sleeve. Care to enlighten us?"

Tesla took a sip of his whiskey, his gaze unwavering. "Indeed, Mr. Kennedy. I have been working on a technology that could revolutionize the way food is cooked — a system that uses electromagnetic energy that the food absorbs, causing friction between the molecules, generating heat. In theory, this energy could cook meats of three to four pounds in mere minutes rather than over an hour, as with conventional cooking ovens now."

Swanson's eyes widened with intrigue, while Luciano nodded appreciatively.

Kennedy said dryly, "Sounds like something out of a science fiction novel, Tesla."

"This is the future of cooking," Tesla insisted, "a technology that will render conventional ovens obsolete."

Luciano was impressed while Kennedy was still skeptical. Gloria Swanson, however, seemed captivated by Tesla.

"How does it actually work?" she inquired, her voice laced with curiosity.

Tesla's eyes lit up at the opportunity to explain his groundbreaking invention. "The food absorbs the microwaves which cause water molecules in food to vibrate rapidly. This vibration creates friction between the molecules, generating heat which cooks the food from the inside out. Unlike conventional ovens that cook the food from outside in, microwaves penetrate food and heat it directly, which is why they cook much faster."

As Tesla spoke, the atmosphere around the table shifted, the initial skepticism giving way to a sense of awe and intrigue. Even Kennedy, ever the pragmatist, leaned in, his mind grappling with the potential implications of Tesla's work.

Luciano broke the spell and, true to his opportunistic nature, wasted no time. "So Nikky, what do you say? You got a deal for us?" he asked, his voice laced with anticipation.

Tesla's gaze shifted from Gloria Swanson to Joseph Kennedy. "Gentlemen, I believe we have the opportunity to change the world," he said, his tone resolute. "But first, let us discuss the finer details over another round of drinks, shall we."

As the waiter returned to take their orders, the candid conversation continued, with each participant weighing the risks and rewards of this unprecedented partnership. The future had never seemed more electrifying.

∞

The 1920s was an interesting decade. On the one hand, Prohibition suppressed the legitimate sale of alcoholic beverages. The result of this was that gangsters and bootleggers had a whole new industry to profit from. Case in point was the friendship between Joseph Kennedy and Charles "Lucky" Luciano. Kennedy was a bootlegger and Luciano was repeatedly hijacking his trucks. Kennedy, being a smart businessman, suggested to Luciano that instead of hijacking, why not just give him a cut? This arrangement worked well for them, and they went on to more legitimate investments together.

On the other hand, the 1920s was an era of freedom for women, as they broke away from the restraints of Victorian styles and morals. They could now vote, wear short haircuts and short skirts. They could openly smoke, drink, drive an automobile and take on important jobs in markets that had once excluded them.

Such trends were encouraged by the movie industry. As the 1930s began, sound films were now the rage. The Hays censorship code had not yet kicked in, so the early "talkies" featured stories about charismatic gangsters that you loved to hate. In 1931, two such blockbusters were *Little Caesar* with Edward G. Robinson and *The Public Enemy*, in which James Cagney famously shoved a half grapefruit into Mae Clarke's face.

It was perhaps inevitable that Tesla had his Hollywood moment. That same year, Carl Laemmle, founder of Universal Studios, contacted Tesla and requested a meeting at the studio's New York office.

Tesla was as excited as any movie fan would be. Whereas normally he would have insisted Laemmle visit him, Tesla eagerly accepted the invitation to meet the studio head on his own turf.

Upon entering the Universal office, Laemmle came to the front desk and welcomed Tesla himself. To his surprise, Tesla experienced a moment of dizziness, an overwhelming feeling of déjà vu. He felt had done this already, as if his life was replaying itself.

He used to experience these feelings occasionally, but now they occurred almost daily. Could this have something to do with the Time Radio he was building? Had he been successful in creating it and were these feelings of déjà vu an unavoidable side effect? Certainly it was a subject to carefully ponder when he was alone.

Laemmle was a short, slight gentleman with kind eyes and a sincere smile. As they walked back to his office, Tesla admired the framed posters hanging on the hallway walls.

"*All Quiet on the Western Front*!" he exclaimed, stopping to view that poster. "A masterpiece indeed and such a poignant movie. I confess I wept during it, especially at the ending."

Laemmele nodded, smiling at Tesla. They moved on to the next poster. Tesla stopped short and studied it, his smile fading.

"*Dracula*," he muttered.

"Did you see it?" asked Laemmele. "I had not thought chillers could be so successful, but it has turned out to be our biggest hit this year. A profit of $700,000 is nothing to sneer at, which is why our next major picture is going to be another horror story. Did you not like it?"

Tesla sighed. "I confess I did see it and Mr. Lugosi was a fine actor in the role. The problem is, my birthplace is very near Transylvania, and you cannot imagine how many people have approached me over the years, particularly after this picture's release, asking me if I am a real vampire, perhaps like Vlad Dracula from history, and do I drink human blood. They are serious in their questions, and I must confess, it is quite distressing."

"I'm sorry to hear that," sympathized Laemmle, "But know that my asking you here today was not to demean you in any fashion, but to honor you and request your help."

"How do you mean?" asked Tesla, immediately cheering up.

They had reached Laemmle's office. The studio mogul ushered Tesla inside, offered him a chair, then sat at his desk and poured drinks for both of them.

"Tesla, I have followed your career, especially your struggles with Thomas Edison. I must say I have admired your bravery over the years. You may recall that I had my own run-ins with Edison."

"Yes, I am familiar with that," said Tesla. "Edison wanted a monopoly on patents for motion pictures and tried to stop you and everyone from forward progress."

"Which is why I went to Europe to succeed with my patents. Edison still tried to stop me with endless legal actions, but they didn't hold and that's how my studio was founded. He couldn't stop me."

"You are a genius," Tesla declared. "Perhaps if I had known you then, you could have helped me avoid much deceit and heartache."

"Can't fix the past but I can help you now," smiled Laemmle.

"Here's my proposition. My son Junior produced *All Quiet* and *Dracula*. He's very young, Tesla, but very smart at what he does. He is producing our next project, *Frankenstein*. You have read the Mary Shelley novel, of course."

"Yes, I have."

"We have a marvelous British actor to portray the monster, Boris Karloff. He's been in many pictures up till now and you've no doubt seen him on screen. He's a character actor but this picture will make him a star. There's a particular scene and we had in mind – actually, I have two gentlemen I'd like you to meet. They will explain our request for the picture."

Tesla sat patiently, watching as the studio mogul made a call on his intercom. A couple minutes later, two men entered the room. Tesla rose to meet them. Junior stepped forward, a handsome fellow in his early twenties.

"This is my son, Carl Junior," said Laemmle.

"A pleasure to meet you," Tesla replied, smiling.

"The honor is mine, Mr. Tesla. I'd like you to meet my special effects associate, Kenneth Strickfaden."

Tesla greeted Strickfaden too, a man in his mid-thirties with a shock of unruly hair not unlike Tesla's own.

Junior continued, "Ken will be Karloff's stunt double and also our set designer. The climatic scene in our script is when Dr. Frankenstein brings the monster to life. And for that, we need the Doctor to have an amazing laboratory that can work magic."

"Mr. Tesla, it's a great honor to meet you," interrupted Strickfaden. "I have followed your work for years. What I envision is this: in the novel, it is the electricity from lightning that animates the monster. But in a motion picture, it must be more dramatic. We would like your permission to use a large Tesla Coil as the main instrument with enough power to bring the monster to life."

"That is not such a farfetched idea," chuckled Tesla. "I can't vouch for monsters, but for men and women, shocking the chest with high voltage electricity can surely restore a heartbeat. It has been medically proven."

"Exactly!" said Strickfaden. "The magnificence of your coil will do the trick. In the script, we see the monster's fingers begin to move and Dr. Frankenstein cries out 'It's alive! It's alive!' The audience will be both thrilled and scared."

"So you are agreeable to this, Mr. Tesla?" asked Junior.

"Yes. I have never seen one of my inventions on the big screen, so this will be a treat indeed."

Carl Laemmle Senior shot Tesla a warm smile. "We feel this motion picture will do as well, if not better, at the box office than *Dracula*. This means your Tesla Coil will be seen around the world and possibly for many years to come."

"Gentlemen, that pleases me more than you will ever know," said Tesla happily. "I will have a Tesla Coil ready for you when production starts. You can count on me."

∞

The summer of 1931 descended upon New York City with a vengeance, its oppressive heat clinging to the metropolis like a damp wool coat. But within the confines of Tesla's laboratory on this day, a different world awaited. Gone was the suffocating heat of the streets, replaced by a crisp, invigorating coolness that seemed to defy the very laws of nature.

Tesla had recently installed one of the few commercial air conditioning systems in New York — a marvel of engineering that cost more than an average New Yorker's annual salary. The price had been exorbitant, but for the eccentric inventor, it was a necessary expense. His brilliant mind required a comfortable environment to function at its peak, unburdened by the distractions of physical discomfort.

"Yes, yes," he muttered, his accented voice just above a whisper. "The resonance must be perfect. Adjust the frequency... just so." His long, nimble fingers manipulated delicate components with the precision of a surgeon. Tesla worked with a feverish intensity, oblivious to the world beyond his sanctuary of science. Outside, the city sweltered and suffered. But here, in this oasis of innovation, the future was taking shape — one careful adjustment at a time.

And then the door swung open. Two men stepped into the laboratory, their suits impeccably tailored, their eyes cold and calculating.

They moved with the practiced ease of predators, their hands hovering near their holsters, ready to unleash the deadly weapons concealed beneath their jackets.

Tesla, sensing the sudden shift in atmosphere, got up from his workbench to face the intruders.

"Gentlemen," Tesla greeted them. He knew these men, still his voice tinged with a hint of caution. "To what do I owe the pleasure of this unexpected visit?"

The men did not reply, instead their eyes surveyed the laboratory. One man silently gestured to the other who then retreated from the laboratory and returned a moment later with a third man, Charles Lucky Luciano.

"Nikky!" Luciano's raspy voice filled the room. "I hope I'm not disturbing you. I have a little something here for you."

Tesla's eyes twinkled with curiosity. "Always a pleasure, my dear friend."

"You think I'd forget your birthday?" The mobster placed a meticulously wrapped box on Tesla's worn worktable.

Tesla raised an eyebrow, intrigued. "What is it?"

"Open it and see," Luciano said, his smile widening.

With a flourish, Tesla unwrapped the gift, revealing a magnificent crystal whiskey decanter filled with amber liquid and a set of six matching glasses. The decanter was intricately etched with geometric patterns, and the glasses were hefty and adorned Tesla's initials.

Tesla's eyes widened in admiration. "Charles, this is exquisite! But why such extravagance?"

Luciano chuckled, "A gift for a genius. I made more money investing in your patents this year, than all my other enterprises put together. And we Sicilians know a thing or two about good whiskey and good friends."

Tesla raised an eyebrow, a playful smile forming on his lips. "Shall we toast to my genius then."

He poured two glasses of whiskey from the crystal decanter, handing one to Luciano. "To friendship," Tesla toasted, raising his glass.

"To genius," Luciano replied, clinking his glass against Tesla's.

The two men savored the whiskey, their conversation flowing effortlessly. They spoke of science, innovation, women, and the future of humanity. As the evening wore on, new visitors to the lab were turned away by Luciano's muscle. The crystal decanter emptied, but the bond between the two men deepened.

Tesla, the visionary scientist, and Luciano, the pragmatic and ruthless mobster, found common ground in their shared appreciation for beauty, intellect, and pursuing excellence.

The crystal whiskey decanter set remained a cherished possession of Tesla's, a symbol of an unlikely friendship forged in the heart of New York City during a time of both technological and social upheaval. It was a reminder that even the most unlikely paths could intersect, creating unexpected alliances and lasting friendships.

∞

Detective Sergeant Richard Mallory stood at the edge of the Hudson River. The rain pounded on his fedora, the brim sagging under the weight of the downpour. The dim glow of the DC streetlamps struggled to penetrate the fog that had rolled in from the water, casting an eerie sheen over the river's bank.

Mallory turned up his coat collar against the chilly November night, not that it made much difference since his trench coat was drenched.

"What've we got, O'Brien?" Mallory's breath fogged in front of him as he spoke, his voice gruff from lack of sleep and too many cigarettes.

Officer O'Brien lifted the edge of the canvas covering the body. "Female, mid-forties. Pulled her out a couple of hours ago. It's not pretty, sir."

Mallory crouched down; his weathered face set in a grim expression as he examined the victim. Her skin was ghastly pale, tinged blue from the icy river water, and her once-vibrant red hair was matted with blood and river weeds. The gash across her throat was deep and jagged, a silent scream frozen on her lifeless face.

"Jesus," Mallory muttered. "Look at her fingers." The fingers were a mangled mess, bones snapped in several places.

O'Brien nodded solemnly. "Broken, sir. Looks like she put up one hell of a fight."

Mallory's keen eyes moved to the victim's wrists, noting the dark bruises that encircled them like macabre bracelets. "She was restrained. This wasn't just a murder. She was tortured."

A gust of wind carried the mournful wail of a distant ship's foghorn. Mallory shivered, though not from the cold. "Any identification on her?"

"Nothing, sir. But one of our guys thinks he may have seen her working at Luciano's restaurant not too far from here."

Mallory's eyes narrowed. "As in Lucky Luciano?"

"That's the one, Sergeant."

Mallory scoffed, shaking his head. "Luciano didn't do this."

"How can you be so sure, sir?"

"If it were Luciano," Mallory explained, "We wouldn't have found her body." A wave of frustration washed over him. "Where the hell is the coroner?"

"Tied up on another call, sir. Double homicide over in Central Park."

"Damn it. Was the body photographed?"

"Yes, sir. Just before you got here."

Mallory nodded. "Good. Get her out of the rain."

"And put her where?"

Mallory's voice was harsh, edged with the exhaustion of a man pushed to his limits. "I don't care, O'Brien. Your car, the back of a paddy wagon...just get this woman out of the damn rain."

O'Brien, sensing his superior's mounting anger, didn't hesitate. He motioned to two officers standing nearby, and together they carefully lifted the canvas-wrapped body, their faces grim as they carried it away from the river's edge.

Mallory watched them go, his gaze lingering. A murder in the city was hardly news, but this...this felt different.

There was a certain darkness to this one, a cruelty that hinted at something far more sinister than just murder for the usual reasons.

The following evening found Mallory and his occasional partner, Detective William Byrne, standing outside Tesla's hotel.

"You sure about this, Rick?" Byrne asked, his voice low. "Questioning Nikola Tesla? He's practically royalty in this town."

Mallory nodded, his jaw set. "Don't care who he is. He's not above the law."

"But I've met him before," argued Byrne. "He's an old guy. He's milquetoast, doesn't look like he could get it up if he tried, much less murder someone."

"Sometimes that's the worst kind," retorted Mallory.

"Alright, it's your badge. You're running point on this. Just don't forget, he's tight with the mayor."

They entered the hotel, identified themselves at the check-in counter, and inquired about the floor and suite Tesla was on. A few moments later, they were in the hallway outside of Tesla's door. Mallory rapped sharply and the door opened almost instantly. Obviously, Tesla was expecting them. The front desk had already telephoned him.

"Mr. Tesla," Mallory said, flashing his badge. "I'm Detective Sergeant Mallory, this is Detective Byrne. We'd like to ask you a few questions about a murder."

Tesla's eyebrows raised, his voice thick with surprise. "Murder? My goodness. Please come in, gentlemen."

The detectives entered the suite. Tesla gestured for them to sit, his movements elegant despite his obvious agitation.

"Mr. Tesla," Byrne began, "do you recognize this woman?" He produced a photograph of the victim, taken before her untimely vile demise.

Tesla's face paled as he took the picture with trembling hands. "Yes of course," he whispered. "Mary... Mary Adams. She works at a restaurant I frequent."

"Worked," Mallory corrected. He leaned forward, his eyes locking onto Tesla's eyes. "And what exactly was the nature of your relationship with Miss Adams?"

Tesla's eyes flashed with indignation. "I beg your pardon, Detective? Are you implying something untoward?"

Byrne interjected, "We have witnesses who say that you and the late Miss Adams were quite... shall we say, friendly?"

Tesla stood abruptly, pacing the room. "This is preposterous! Yes, Mary and I engaged in playful banter. She was a bright woman with a keen interest in science. But to suggest anything more is an insult to her memory and my fine reputation!"

Mallory remained seated, his voice calm but firm. "Where were you two nights ago, Mr. Tesla?"

"I was here. I rarely leave my suite at night."

"Can anyone corroborate that?" Byrne asked.

Tesla's shoulders slumped. "No," he admitted quietly.

Mallory stood, moving closer to Tesla. "Mr. Tesla, Mary Adams was found in the Hudson River last night. Her throat was cut, her fingers broken, and her wrists showed signs of restraint. It was a brutal, calculated murder. If you know anything — anything at all — that might help us find who did this, now's the time to speak up."

Tesla stumbled back as if struck, collapsing into a nearby chair. His face turned numb, his breathing ragged. "Good God," he murmured. "Poor Mary. Who could do such a thing?"

"That's what we're trying to figure out, Mr. Tesla. Did Mary ever mention any problems? Anyone who might wish to harm her?" asked Byrne.

Tesla shook his head, his eyes distant. "No, never. She was always smiling, always.... Have you notified her daughter? I believe she lives in Los Angeles."

"Yes, we sent a telegram this morning," Mallory replied while carefully eyeing Tesla's hands. They showed no scratches or cuts that might show he was the perpetrator.

"Perhaps her daughter may have some insight on that matter," Tesla offered.

Byrne fixed Tesla with a hard stare, his eyes narrowing. "Mr. Tesla, are you aware of the identity of the proprietor of the restaurant that Mary worked at and you frequented?"

"I believe it's Charles Luciano," Tesla replied, his voice carefully neutral.

"And do you know what kind of man Luciano is?" Byrne pressed, his tone accusatory.

A flicker of annoyance crossed Tesla's face. "Detective Byrne, I don't concern myself with newspaper gossip. I am a scientist, a man of facts." As if the facts of a man's life could ever be confined to mere newsprint.

Byrne leaned forward again, his eyes boring into Tesla's. "Is it not a fact that from time-to-time Luciano invests in your work?"

Tesla held his ground, his gaze unwavering. "It is," he conceded. "But then again, Mr. Luciano also invested in our mayor's recent reelection campaign."

The implication hung heavy in the air — a man like Luciano spread his influence far and wide.

Tesla's mind, however, was racing. Could Luciano truly be involved in Mary's hideous murder? The thought was both chilling and absurd. Luciano was his friend. He never feared him or thought him to be a killer without cause. Mary would give no cause to Luciano or anyone else to kill her.

Yet this was New York, where fortunes were made and lost from careless whispers. And Luciano would often conduct business meetings in the restaurant. Anything was possible.

After a few more minutes of questioning, Mallory knew they would get nothing useful from Tesla. He motioned to Byrne they were done, and the two detectives got up, thanked Tesla for his time, and left.

The murder of Mary Adams was never solved. The only suspect ever considered was Charles Luciano, despite the lack of motive. Tesla's only connection to the grisly murder was by association to the victim and the suspect.

The press gave little attention to the case of Mary Adams, and Detective Sergeant Mallory kept Tesla's name out of the press, probably because he favored keeping his job for a few more years.

30

THE PLAN

Bronx, New York – March 1936

The tires of a sleek, black Cadillac whispered against the manicured drive of a sprawling mansion. A man in a crisp suit stepped out, opening the rear door for Tesla.

Tesla emerged, eyes sweeping over the opulent structure. Several years had passed, and yet this was the first time he had been invited to Luciano's home. He wondered what the reason was.

The mansion was a testament to wealth and power, with its twenty-plus rooms bathed in the warm glow of exterior lights, a grand fountain casting dancing shadows on the meticulously kept lawn.

"This way, sir," the chauffeur gestured towards the mansion's entrance.

Inside the foyer was a symphony of Italian marble and shimmering crystal. A half-ton chandelier hung from the ceiling, casting a thousand points of light onto the scene below.

"Wait here, please," the chauffeur murmured, disappearing into one of the adjoining rooms.

Left alone, Tesla's gaze drifted across the priceless artwork adorning the walls. He questioned himself: Why am I here? Is it still about the Mary Adams murder after all this time? Did Charles have her killed? Does he intend to kill me?

Moments later, Frank Costello emerged, a wide smile splitting his face. Costello was Luciano's partner and one of the very few big-time mobsters who actually managed to spend most of his life outside of prison. A hefty Italian-born New Yorker, Costello was ruthless and would become the big boss after Luciano was gone.

"Tesla! Long time no sees! Charlie's in the study wrapping things up with his lawyer."

"Yes, unfortunate," Tesla replied. "I've read about Mr. Luciano's legal troubles."

Costello scoffed. "Troubles? What troubles? It's all gonna get sorted out."

"I'm pleased to hear that," Tesla said politely.

"They can't keep Charlie locked up if they want us to stop those Nazi bastards from sneaking into the country."

"That is indeed good news," Tesla replied.

"Truth is," Costello's tone shifted, "Charlie called you here to give you a heads-up about some trouble heading your way."

Tesla frowned. "I don't understand."

"Charlie will explain. Shouldn't be long now."

Costello entered a different room, leaving Tesla to wait. Just then, the study doors opened. Luciano walked his lawyer, Moses Polakoff, to the front door.

"Mr. Tesla," Polakoff nodded in acknowledgement.

"Mr. Polakoff," Tesla replied, slightly clearing his throat.

Luciano addressed the lawyer. "Get it done, and forget about Dewey. When Bugsy comes in, I'll send him to you." Then he turned to Tesla just as Costello came out of the other room and joined them.

"Hiya, Nikky, sorry to keep you waiting," said Luciano with what appeared to be a genuine smile. "Let's go into the study."

Tesla and Costello followed Luciano into a room that resembled a luxurious library. Inside the study, another familiar gangster face, Meyer Lansky, sat nursing a double whiskey on one of the sofas. Russian-born Meyer, who was raised on Manhattan's Lower East Side, stood to greet Tesla.

"A pleasure as always, Tesla."

"Mr. Lansky." Tesla acknowledged.

Luciano gestured Tesla towards a seat. By now, Tesla felt both nervous and perplexed.

"Whiskey, Tesla?" Costello offered.

"Yes, thank you."

Costello poured two glasses, handing one to Tesla. A heavy silence fell over the room. Tesla glanced at Luciano, who was now seated behind a massive oak desk.

Finally, Lansky broke the silence. "Tesla, this isn't what it looks like. Quite the opposite, in fact."

Luciano nodded. "Nikky, we've learned your life's in danger."

"How so?"

"Adolph Hitler," Luciano grimaced.

"A madman," Tesla replied.

Lansky said, "Some guy already contacted you about going to Germany, right?"

Tesla nodded. "Yes. I told him I was not interested."

Lansky continued, "That's the problem. Seems like Hitler wants you there, willingly or not. And that guy is bad news."

Costello, drumming his thick fingers on the arm of his chair, cut in. "But we ain't gonna let that happen, see? You're our egghead, and we like ya just fine where ya are."

Tesla adjusted his collar nervously. "I... appreciate your concern, gentlemen. But I must ask, how did you come by this rather alarming information?"

Luciano, his eyes sharp as a hawk's, smirked. "We own the docks, genius. And them docks, they got loose lips. But only for the right ears, *capisce*?"

"Yeah," Costello interjected, puffing out his chest. "Our ears."

Luciano continued, "It's why Uncle Sam's gonna be keen on makin' nice with us.... Anyhow, a couple days back, some guys slipped in on a freighter. Claimed they was Sicilian."

"But our boys ain't no chumps," Costello added, tapping his nose. "These mutts was too blonde to be Sicilian."

Luciano nodded, a dangerous glint in his eye. "So we had us a little chat with the captain. Turns out, them fellas was Hitler's own spooks. And if there's one thing we don't like, it's spies."

Tesla, his mustache twitching slightly, responded. "Well, this is quite... disconcerting news."

The room erupted in laughter. Luciano slapped his knee, nearly doubling over. "I swear, this guy's a riot! 'Disconcerting,' he says. That's Tesla-talk for 'holy shit,' boys!"

As the laughter died down, Lansky leaned in, his tone serious. "Don't you worry about them, we'll round them up before they get anywhere near you. In the meantime, we've lined up some protection for you."

"You won't even know they're there," Luciano assured him, winking. "Unless you need 'em, of course."

Suddenly, the door burst open and in strode Benjamin "Bugsy" Siegel, decked out in a suit that cost more than a family holiday to Florida. He was a handsome man and a childhood friend of Meyer Lansky, both of them mischief makers together at an early age.

The room fell silent, tension thick enough to cut with a knife, and Lansky's eyes narrowed. "Well, well, look who finally decided to show up."

Costello grunted, not bothering to hide his annoyance. "What's the matter, Bugsy? Couldn't tear yourself away from the mirror?"

Bugsy, unfazed by the cold reception, flashed his movie-star smile. "Fellas," he nodded to his less-than-pleased partners. "Sorry I'm late. Had a little... situation with a dame. You know how it is." He turned his attention to Tesla, giving him a once-over. "Tesla, guess the guys told you Hitler wants to snatch your skinny ass and bring it back to Germany."

Tesla nodded.

Luciano, his patience thin, cut in. "Why are you always late? While you were out playin' Romeo, Polakoff was here half a day waiting for you and getting on my nerves. He left an hour ago just as Nikky arrived. Now you're gonna go to his place and finish your end."

Bugsy rolled his eyes and snapped back, "Well, ain't that a kick in the head, that's an hour drive." And then he diverted his attention to Tesla. "Hey Tesla, you're looking thinner every time I see you. "Who the fuck told you it was a good idea to eat like a rabbit. You ain't got 100 pounds, do ya?" Bugsy grinned, a half-smoked cigar dangling precariously from his lips.

As was often the case regarding Bugsy speaking to him, Tesla was at a loss for words.

"Knock it off, Bugsy!" Luciano barked.

"What...? I'm concerned. Forget about the Nazis, a fucking stiff wind could blow him away."

Lansky interrupted. "Tesla, forgive our friend's disrespect. He's going through something."

And then Costello chimed in, "And the hell if we know what."

Tesla cleared his throat, finally finding his voice. "I assure you, gentlemen, my diet is quite sufficient—"

"Sure, sure," Bugsy cut him off, taking a seat in one of the comfortable armchairs. He winked at Tesla. "It looks real sufficient. As for these Nazi fucks, don't you worry your big brain about a thing, we got you covered. Any Kraut dumb enough to come after you is gonna have to go through us first."

Luciano, Costello, and Lansky nodded.

"Thank you," Tesla said and paused, suddenly feeling lightheaded as if that feeling of déjà vu had returned. There was something to what these men were telling him. He sensed Hitler was far more dangerous than anyone really understood, and maybe the madman was indeed scheming to utilize him in his pursuit of evil. Tesla had a sudden realization about what the future might hold – another terrible war.

A few deep breaths, and Tesla regained his equilibrium. He looked around at the men watching him and then spoke.

"And if I may, I'd like to ask a favor of you gentlemen."

"Like what?" asked Luciano.

"It's regarding my end."

"What end?"

"My death... and not at the hands of those Nazis," Tesla clarified, taking a sip of his whiskey. "As you know, I've devoted my life to technologies that could benefit humanity. But there's always the risk they could be misused after I'm gone." He saw the mobsters' faces grew serious and continued:

"I'd ask that when my time comes, you ensure my final working papers, schematics, prototypes – anything related to my most powerful inventions – are secured and taken to Yugoslavia."

"Why Yugoslavia?" asked Luciano.

"Serbia is part of it now. I have already made arrangements as to who should receive it. I'll have instructions prepared for you when the time comes. I cannot risk that knowledge falling into the wrong hands."

Luciano nodded slowly. "You have my word, Nikky. Your life's work won't be twisted by punks and warmongers after you're gone."

"We'll make sure of it," Lansky echoed.

A sense of relief washed over Tesla. "I cannot sufficiently express my gratitude with words, my friends, so I would like to pay whatever it costs for you to complete this service for me. I have not used any of my funds allocated for medical emergencies, nor do I expect to. Those funds I can transfer to you gentleman."

"Or... you could use those funds for a lot of pussy and go out with a bang," Bugsy said, taking a puff on his cigar.

Lansky interjected, "Forgive Bugsy's crudity. What he meant to say, Tesla, is that your money is not required for this service."

"That's right," Luciano agreed, and Costello made it unanimous with a nod.

"Just one question." Bugsy raised a hand as if he were in grade school. "What if our end happens before his end does?"

"Then we'll have a contingency," said Lansky.

"What the fuck does that mean?" Bugsy asked.

Costello cut in: "A second plan, Casanova."

Luciano couldn't tell if Bugsy was being serious and was that stupid or he was pissing around again. In fact, in all the years Luciano knew Bugsy, he could never quite figure him out.

"See, nothing to worry about," said Bugsy to Tesla.

∞

Hours later, Tesla and his gangster friends were served a meal worthy of New York's finest restaurants. But dinner talk was surprisingly serious.

"We hear they're building a labor camp for political prisoners, opening this summer near Berlin," said Lansky, his gaze steadily on Tesla.

"Political prisoners, my ass." Luciano rolled his eyes. "It's mostly for your people, Meyer, you and Bugsy. Hitler hates Jews; hell, he hates most everyone. You two, you're honorary Sicilians... but what Hitler's doin' over there, it ain't right!"

"I fear it may come to war again," said Tesla.

Costello nodded in agreement. "No one here's doing anything to prevent it."

After dinner, they all retired to the living room, to share smokes, drinks, and more conversation. Costello tried to lighten the mood by changing the subject. He leaned forward in his plush leather armchair, curiosity gleaming in his eyes.

"Say, Tesla," he said, a hint of admiration in his voice. "I heard you can speak seven languages. That true?"

Tesla gave a modest smile. "Actually, my good man, it's eight."

Costello let out a low whistle, genuinely amazed. He shifted to the edge of his seat, elbows resting on his knees. "I know you speak Italian — what're the other ones?"

"He speaks pussy. The old geezer may look all shy but I bet he's still getting it," said Bugsy with a wide grin.

Tesla straightened his already impeccable posture. "Well, Italian, as you've mentioned; Serbo-Croatian, which is my native language; Czech; French; German; Hungarian and Latin, the language of scholars; and of course, English."

"Well, ain't that something," Costello mused, nodding appreciatively.

Luciano, who had been quietly nursing a glass of scotch, set his drink down with a sharp clink. His eyes hardened, then fixed on Tesla. "Hey, Nikky, one more thing," he said in a calm voice.

"Yes?"

"If that scum prosecutor, Thomas Dewey, brings you in for questioning 'bout me, you know nothing 'bout nothing. *Capisce?*"

Tesla blinked rapidly. "Yes, of course."

Luciano continued, "And if he leans on you — if he so much as looks at you funny — you tell him you wanna call your lawyer. Then you call us, see?" At Tesla's nod, he added with a wolfish grin, "We'll have five of our best pencil pushers down there faster than you can say 'microwave oven.' They'll push a pencil so far up his ass, it'll come out of his mouth."

Tesla, despite his discomfort with the crude imagery, nodded solemnly. "I understand, gentlemen. Your... protection is most appreciated."

Costello, his eyes twinkling, leaned back in his chair and loosened his silk tie.

Lansky, as he frequently did, remained silent and observed the conversation like a hawk, attentively raising his glass to favorable remarks and comments.

"Say, Nikky," Costello began, a hint of a smile playing on his lips. "How come all these years you was never scared of us."

The directness of the question surprised Tesla. After a moment's consideration, he straightened in his chair.

"Fear, Mr. Costello, is often born of ignorance. I am not an ignorant man. While I am certainly aware of your... reputation, and what you do, I am also aware that our worlds do not intertwine. Therefore, I am of no consequence to your primary interests and no threat. It would serve no point to be in fear of you. I might also add I consider each of you my friend."

Lansky finally broke his silence and spoke in a muted yet authoritative tone. "We've invested nearly a million in your various inventions over the years, and we've made back almost twice that... but what if we had lost twice that... would you have had fear then?"

Tesla met Lansky's gaze unflinchingly. "I understand you are men of ambition and intelligence, and you understand and appreciate risk and the consequences of risk but above all... you are men of honor, not unlike myself.

"While our methods of what we do differ, we are similar in nature so if you had lost your money on your first investment there would not be a second investment. But I would still be here, as I see no sense for you to remove me from being... over a risk that you chose to take."

Luciano chuckled, "This is why we love you, Nikky," and he lifted his glass to Tesla from behind his desk. Lansky, however, stood up and strode to Tesla as did Costello and even Bugsy; and they all clinked glasses with him.

For the rest of the evening, the conversation remained light. Costello regaled them with tales of his and Luciano's rise from the slums of East Harlem and how they met the two childhood friends, Lansky and Bugsy. Bugsy wanted to know how many women Tesla had bedded.

Tesla declared that throughout his life, his work consumed him so much he did not have the time for the pleasures of female companionship. Bugsy didn't believe it for a moment, but didn't press Tesla further.

As the night progressed, Tesla strangely warmed to these dangerous men. He had always had a close relationship with Luciano and only met the other three occasionally and briefly. Their world was far removed from his laboratories and lecture halls, but tonight Tesla was one of the guys.

He even ventured to share some of his more fantastical ideas, which would sound far-fetched and nonsense to many of his peers. He had never shared such information with any of them before. And to his surprise and delight, instead of mockery, he was met with genuine interest.

What Tesla didn't know about his mob friends is that they had been shadowing him since 1923. Tesla was an investment for them and his wellbeing was paramount to them. The mob assigned Bugsy the job of ensuring Tesla's safety, with 24-7 protection but low profile and complete secrecy. Bugsy knew every man and woman Tesla encountered both publicly and privately, which explained his fascination with Tesla's intimate life with women.

As the grandfather clock in the corner chimed midnight, Tesla rose to take his leave. Costello and Luciano escorted him to the door, as Bugsy had left earlier to meet with the lawyer Polakoff. Two burly men flanked Tesla and would serve as his new shadows, this time with Tesla's complete knowledge.

"Remember, Nikky," Luciano said, clapping him on the shoulder. "Anything you need, any trouble comes your way — you come to us first."

Tesla nodded, a mixture of gratitude and trepidation washing over him. As he stepped out into the cool night air, he felt a strange sense of security.

Tesla left the mansion that night, knowing his legacy was in safe hands.

31

FACING MORTALITY

New York City — Fall 1937

Tesla emerged from the New Yorker Hotel. He had moved there in 1934 and it remained his residence until his death.

He enjoyed living there, as the ambiance reminded him of his happiest days living at the old Waldorf-Astoria. That hotel was torn down 1929 and the site replaced with the new Empire State Building, which Tesla could see from his living room window. Also in his magnificent view across town was the new Chrysler Building.

Tesla also began the winding down of his career, at least in the quantity of new inventions. His life became more about receiving tributes to him and his achievements, granting interviews, writing up his own history as he felt it should be told, or commenting on the world at large with its successes and errors in the advancement of technology.

While he had received many honors and awards over the years, there was one he turned down. That was the Nobel Prize, the greatest honor for a scientist. In 1915, newspapers reported that he and Thomas Edison were to share the prize for Physics. That point alone upset Tesla. He further assumed his award was for his recent patent on what amounted to today's smart phone, a hand-held device offering the potential of both audio and video phone calls internationally, by use of Wi-Fi. Tesla considered himself a serious inventor, whereas he felt Edison remained more of a businessman.

To add insult to injury, Tesla resented that Marconi had already received a Nobel Prize for invention of the radio, when the Nobel Prize Foundation was fully aware that Tesla was in the middle of a lawsuit with Marconi, to prove Marconi stole his ideas and that his invention pre-dated Marconi.

When Tesla refused his award, both he and Edison's names were discarded and two other men were announced as the official prize-winners.

In 1936, newspapers began announcing that Tesla was once again up for consideration for the Nobel Prize. The following year he was nominated again for Physics but did not win. Perhaps he would have accepted now at this late date, but his stubborn nature likely killed the deal, to the regret of his family and friends. A Nobel Prize not only brought great prestige but would have certainly helped his future finances.

In the end, Tesla simply moved on with his life. He was eighty-one years old now and felt no need to prove himself to the world anymore.

As was his peculiar habit, one day in October he set off towards Central Park, no doubt to commune with his friends of the feathered variety.

It had been a difficult month; Robert Johnson had just passed away and Tesla felt his inner circle of close friends was nearly depleted. He was inclined more and more to withdraw from society and to keep to himself, especially since the press was made aware that despite his great scientific accomplishments, financially Tesla was continually floundering.

Crossing the street against the light, Tesla stepped out in front of a bright yellow cab. The driver, engrossed in some sort of heated argument with his passenger, didn't even see Tesla at first.

"Look out—!" the cabbie exclaimed as he slammed on the brakes, but it was too late. Tesla's slender frame connected with the front fender with a sickening crunch before being launched skyward like a rag doll fired from a cannon.

He sailed thirty feet before gravity intervened, introducing him to the unforgiving concrete in a burst of pain and profanity unbecoming of a gentleman. Pedestrians gawked and recoiled as if witnessing a human sacrifice, hands covering mouths as screams pierced the cold morning air.

Two husky cops shoved their way through the gathering throng, sizing up the crumpled figure on the concrete.

"Well, I'll be damned," one muttered under his burly mustache, "Ain't that the Tesla fella?"

To everyone's amazement, the battered inventor's eyes fluttered open. Grimacing, he lifted his head and arched his back, preparing to lift himself on his feet.

"Not so fast there, Gramps," the other officer cautioned, placing a restraining hand on Tesla's shoulder. "Just stay still and let the meat wagon take a look at you."

Tesla squinted up at him, his face a mask of bewilderment. "Meat.. .wagon?" he wheezed, and then coughed. "I think not, my good man."

He waved away their concerns with an imperious gesture, like a prince dismissing the court jester.

Groaning, the old inventor tilted his neck from side to side until it emitted a crunch, then staggered upright despite the officers' protests.

"You need to get to a hospital and get checked for broken bones," the police officer said, eyeing Tesla's twisted form.

Tesla grimaced as he tried to walk. "No hospital..." He took a few agonizing steps forward, his face contorting with each movement. "I greatly appreciate your concern, officer, but acute care facilities and I do not match up well."

The cop's brow furrowed. "Unless you can walk away from here on your own, you don't get to say no to a hospital, mister genius!"

Tesla nodded and pointed across the street to the New Yorker Hotel. "That's where I need to go. If you gentleman could just assist me to the hotel, I would be most grateful."

With the help of the officers, Tesla hobbled to the hotel entrance. George Riley, the hotel manager, immediately came rushing over, his face aghast. "Mr. Tesla! What happened?"

"He got schmuck'd by a tin Lizzie. Doesn't want to go to the hospital," the officer said with a roll of his eyes.

Riley looped Tesla's free arm over his narrow shoulders, taking some of the inventor's weight. "We'll get you sorted out right away, sir."

Tesla offered a pained smile. "There's no need to fret, my good man..."

Once they reached the elevator, the police officer broke away and departed, leaving Riley to wrestle Tesla's dead weight. Anya rose from the divan when they entered the suite, her book falling unnoticed to the floor.

"Darling! What's happened?" Her eyes widened at his battered appearance.

"A minor vehicular altercation, my sweet." Tesla slumped into a chair with Riley's help, already waving off her concern. "No need to make a fuss."

Riley looked around, concerned, then he and Anya stared at the motley array of contusions covering Tesla's thin frame. "Those don't look minor!" argued Riley. "We need a doctor, immediately."

"No," Tesla insisted. He tried weakly to stand but in agony, sucked in a sharp breath.

Riley and Anya seemed to exchange worried glances as they eased Tesla's coat and vest off, revealing the full extent of his injuries. Angry purple welts and blossoming bruises painted nearly his entire torso. Tesla looked up at Anya, who bit her trembling lip, fighting back tears.

With Riley's help, Tesla twisted in front of the full-length mirror, gently probing each rib in his battered chest. "One... two...three definite fractures. Possibly..." He drew a ragged breath. "Possibly four."

He turned back to the hotel manager. "A roll of gauze and adhesive tape from the corner pharmacy, if you would be so kind? I can bind the area myself."

Anya's chin snapped up. "And a bottle of whiskey," she said, her voice low. "For the pain."

"Yes, whisky," Tesla agreed.

Riley bobbed his head in assent. "Got it ... be back in a few minutes, Mr. Tesla!"

As Riley hurried off, Anya guided Tesla to the bedroom and helped him ease back onto the bed. She perched beside him, studying his grimace of discomfort. "How bad is it, really?"

One side of Tesla's mouth quirked upward in a pained half-smile. "The searing bolts of pain in every breath suggest...quite bad. But I shall persevere, my love."

Riley soon returned, a bottle of scotch in one hand and a pharmacy parcel in the other. Tesla snatched the liquor first, draining a few healthy swallows with a relieved sigh despite the burn in his ravaged chest. Then he removed his shirt with Riley's aid, the two of them working in silence to wrap his injured ribs.

"Thank you, Mr. Riley," Tesla said once they'd finished. He reached for Anya's hand, giving it a reassuring squeeze.

"That should suffice for now."

32

THE DREAM OF ELECTRIC MOTION

New York City, Tesla's Laboratory — 1939

Tesla sat in his dimly lit workshop, his weathered hands resting on the cool metal of one of his previous inventions he was upgrading. The gentle hum of electricity flowing through different devices filled the air, providing a soothing melody for the elderly inventor.

Over the last decade, Tesla had focused on enhancing and refining existing inventions rather than creating new ones. His mind remained sharp, but his body couldn't keep pace. Long gone were the days Tesla would work 19-20 hours per day.

He closed his eyes. Memories washed over him like waves, carrying him back through time to the genesis of his most cherished dreams.

From his earliest days as a curious child in Smiljan, Tesla's mind had teemed with visions of the future - a future where humanity's ingenuity would conquer the limitations of the natural world.

Of all his inventions, two held a special place in his heart, not just for their potential to revolutionize the world, but for the sheer joy they brought him. These were his passion projects.

The first was his flying machine. In 1873, at age seventeen, he built his first "prototype", using a wooden box to test air pressure. Tesla could see it clearly in his mind; a silent aircraft would soar through the air, carrying passengers across continents in a matter of hours. He imagined a world where distance was no obstacle, where the skies were as busy as the streets below.

By 1882, he began designing his "flying machine" and upon first arrival in New York two years later, began speaking publicly about it, describing the features of his envisioned airplane in an effort to get funding.

He later admitted, "I believed that I would be the first man to fly; that I was on the track of accomplishing what no one else was anywhere near reaching. I was working entirely in electricity then and did not realize that the gasoline engine was approaching a perfection that was going to make the aeroplane feasible."

But alas, his vision was too far ahead of its time. His early work on airplanes was overshadowed by the Wright brothers stealing his thunder in 1903 when they made their historic flight at Kitty Hawk.

This disappointment did not daunt Tesla for long. His motto was that he could always build a bigger and more effective model. By 1908, he alerted his friend John Astor, that he was ready to take an order for a self-propelled airplane.

Tesla had faced challenges in obtaining the necessary funding to realize his aerial ambitions. When he finally did secure funding from John Astor IV, it was tragically lost when Astor perished on the *Titanic*.

Even then, Tesla didn't give up. Long before the outbreak of World War I, he eerily predicted that "Aerial vessels of war will be used to the exclusion of ships." In 1921, he obtained a patent for his "flivver plane." Flivver was a slang word of the time for a cheap automobile; and his model was part plane and part helicopter, so could fly both horizontally as well as vertically.

For the next seven years, he worked on the Flivver plane, obtaining more patents but never obtaining the funding need to build one. He additionally worked on "flying machines" that more resembled rockets than planes, with no wings, and predicted that automobiles would eventually have the capability to fly as well in years to come, even if not in his lifetime.

Tesla's second passion project, however, was a different story. The electric automobile, a concept that had captivated Tesla's imagination since the early 1890s, slowly but surely became a reality.

In 1892, Tesla described his vision for automobiles: "Imagine a world where our streets are no longer choked by horse-drawn carriages and the air is no longer filled with the foul stench of horse manure. A world where horseless carriages glide silently, powered by an invisible energy that surrounds us, wireless electricity.

"This energy will power the world's machineries, including horseless carriages, or as the great Karl Benz refers to them, automobiles. They would have no need for coal, oil, or petroleum.

"I'm going to create an automobile that runs on invisible electricity alone."

In the years that followed, Tesla threw himself with vigor into his work on both wireless electricity and electric automobiles.

By 1901, he had registered a new patent for utilizing cosmic energy, what he called the "power of the universe." This, he believed, would be the key to powering his electric vehicle.

As the world entered the tumultuous period of World War I, Tesla continued his work. In 1918, he achieved a significant milestone with the creation of the first air friction speedometer. Initially used in luxury automobiles, it would soon become a standard feature in vehicles across the world.

But Tesla's true triumph came as an open-air prototype of a "motor carriage" that could seat two people. It was a far cry from the sleek, silent vehicle of his dreams, but it was a start.

Three years later, in 1921, Tesla had refined his prototype. On a sunny afternoon, he unveiled his creation to Anya, who by then had joined him to live together in New York. They were enjoying their customary afternoon tea when Tesla broached the subject.

"You know," he began, a hint of frustration coloring his voice, "it's absurd to say that Ford automobiles have motors."

Anya looked up from her scone, a quizzical expression on her face. "What do you mean, dear?"

Tesla leaned forward, his eyes intense. "They are outfitted with engines! Engines use petroleum, while motors are exclusively powered by electricity. They don't even utilize the correct terminology!"

Anya chuckled softly, recognizing the familiar fire in Tesla's eyes. "I love your enthusiasm, dear. You're like an excited child with a new toy!"

Tesla's face softened into a smile. "That I am," he admitted. Then, with a glint in his eye, he added, "You being my good luck charm, will you venture out with me for a test drive?"

He saw Anya tense slightly, uncertainty flickering across her face. Anya had never quite recovered from the severe illness she contracted in Paris. Quickly, he sought to reassure her.

"Don't worry, my love," he said gently, reaching across the table to take her hand. "It will do you good to be outside and breathe fresh air. We can take a short spin near Central Park. There won't be many people about at this hour. I assure you, you will enjoy the outing."

Anya hesitated for a moment, then nodded, her trust in Tesla overcoming her anxiety. "Very well, Nikola. Let's see this marvelous invention of yours."

The late afternoon sun cast long shadows across the street, and a cool breeze carried the scent of approaching autumn. They made their way to where the vehicle was parked. Tesla explained the intricacies of his creation and explained the presence of four engineers waiting for him by the vehicle.

"You see, Anya," Tesla said, his voice brimming with excitement, "This motor carriage runs entirely on electrical power. No petroleum, no steam, just pure, clean energy. It's the future of transportation, I'm certain of it."

As he was explaining this to her, three of the four engineers were pushing the vehicle while the fourth was behind the wheel steering it.

Anya looked amused at the sight, and then it struck Tesla what she must be thinking. He let out a chuckle.

"My dearest, I assure you this is not the standardized operating procedure of this vehicle, it's just that the mini wireless electric generating tower has a limited reach of four hundred yards and we are well out of that reach right now. So the engineers need to push the vehicle a short distance before it can become operational."

"I see," Anya replied with a soft laugh.

As they followed the engineers pushing the vehicle, Tesla continued explaining how the wireless electricity from the mini tower worked. It was a scaled-down version of the Wardenclyffe Tower that J. P. Morgan tore down years ago, and emitted wireless electricity in the air for up to 400 yards. Tesla detailed for her how the vehicle converted it to energy to propel it forward.

"It's all based on my original Tesla Coil. The goal has always been to harness available electricity, in whatever sized frame is built. That was the basis for my work in Colorado Springs, which obviously was successful."

"A little too successful perhaps," Anya smiled.

Tesla chuckled. "It affected a small area whereas Wardenclyffe was a much larger project."

"And created a manmade earthquake across the city! What next, my love?"

"When I can secure the funding, we turn again to the sky, both for travel and to control weapons from afar. But today, we have a mini-Wardenclyffe to power this automobile."

"So all the prototypes are based on your Tesla Coil and wireless electricity," Anya commented. "You will utilize electricity both in the sky and the ground?"

"Yes, the potential is everywhere around us. If you sat in a chair in your stockings and rubbed your feet on a rug, you would create static electricity. And few locks of your lovely hair might fly all around your head!"

"Oh horrors, we can't have that!" she laughed. "But I understand now."

Tesla joined in her laughter. "Well, dearest, you have to admit that in my research discoveries, I am a hundred years ahead of the world!"

At last, they arrived at the 400-yard marker, the point where the vehicle could obtain the electricity to start moving. Tesla assisted Anya as she got into the passenger seat, while he positioned himself in the driver's seat.

"Is the electricity in the air now?" asked Anya with some trepidation.

"Indeed, my love. It is flowing through your body now, can you feel it?"

"No!" exclaimed Anya, alarmed.

"Excellent, then that means everything is in order."

With a few switches flipped on the dashboard, Tesla effortlessly brought the vehicle's motor to life, its soft hum almost inaudible. As the vehicle jerked forward, Anya felt her heart race and swallowed hard, clutching the sides of her seat.

After a few moments of smooth driving, Anya's fear subsided, and was even forgotten, replaced with a thrilling sensation of excitement. The wind whipped across her face, bringing a healthy flush to her cheeks. For the first time in years, she laughed with pure, unbridled joy.

"Oh, Niko!" she exclaimed, her eyes shining. "It's wonderful! So smooth, so quiet. And look how fast we're going!"

Tesla beamed with pride, both at his creation and at the happiness it had brought to his beloved Anya. "This is just the beginning, my dear," he said, raising his voice enough to be heard over the rush of wind. "Imagine a world where every street is filled with vehicles like this. No more noise, no more pollution. Just clean, efficient transportation for all."

Over the next decade, Tesla continued to refine and improve his electric automobile. In 1931, he achieved what he considered his magnum opus in electric transportation. Taking a Pierce-Arrow automobile, he completely refitted it, removing the traditional engine and replacing it with an electrical "power receiver" of his own design.

This new system featured twelve radio tubes and a large vertical antenna. But what made it truly revolutionary was its power source - or rather, the lack thereof.

This amazing vehicle, like the first prototype years earlier, worked with no external power source except what was in the air itself, wireless electricity.

On a crisp autumn morning in 1931, Tesla took his creation out for a test drive. As he pressed down on the accelerator, he felt a surge of exhilaration.

The automobile responded instantly, accelerating smoothly and silently. To his amazement and delight, he found it could attain speeds of up to 90 miles per hour!

But Tesla wasn't content to stop there. Always the innovator, he added extra features that pleased his inventive spirit. Among these was the ability to have a flashing left or right turn signal - a feature that eventually became standard in all automobiles.

As news of Tesla's electric vehicle began to spread, his dream of a clean, efficient future of transportation was finally within reach. Many automobile manufacturers asked about the technology, seeing its potential to revolutionize the industry. All except one notable holdout: Henry Ford of the Ford Motor Company.

"Petroleum is the future," Ford had declared at an industry gathering, his voice booming with confidence. "Electric automobiles are a passing fancy, mark my words."

Despite Ford's skepticism, other manufacturers explored the possibilities of electric vehicles. Tesla's invention had sparked a wave of innovation and excitement throughout the industry.

However, the inventor soon faced an obstacle far more formidable than any technical challenge he had encountered: the entrenched interests of the fossil fuel industry.

The Rockefeller family, whose vast fortune was built on oil, saw Tesla's invention as a direct threat to their empire. They understood that if electric automobiles became widespread, the demand for petroleum would plummet. This was a risk they were not willing to take.

Behind closed doors, representatives of the Rockefeller interests approached the major automobile manufacturers — Ford, Chrysler, and General Motors. The message was clear: if these companies pursued electric vehicle technology, they would find themselves cut off from the steel they needed to build their automobiles. It was a masterful play of economic leverage. The Rockefellers controlled not just oil, but also significant interests in the steel industry of Pittsburgh. By threatening to withhold this essential material, they effectively held the entire American auto industry hostage.

In a smoky boardroom, executives from the major automobile companies gathered to discuss their options. The air was thick with tension and the acrid smell of cigar smoke.

"Gentlemen," began the CEO of General Motors, his voice grave, "we find ourselves in an impossible situation. The Rockefellers have made their position clear. If we continue to pursue electric vehicle technology, we'll be cut off from our steel supply."

The room erupted in a cacophony of voices, each executive trying to make themselves heard. Finally, the Ford representative spoke up, a hint of smugness in his tone.

"Mr. Ford told you all that petroleum was the future. Now do you see?"

The Chrysler executive slammed his fist on the table, causing coffee cups to rattle. "That's not the point! We're being strong-armed into abandoning a potentially revolutionary technology. There has to be another way."

But in the end, faced with the prospect of losing access to their primary building material, the auto manufacturers had little choice but to comply.

One by one, Chrysler being the last, they all reluctantly agreed to shelve their plans for electric vehicles. Research into the technology was all but abandoned, and the dream of an electric automobile future seemed to fade away.

Tesla, unaware of these backroom dealings, continued to push for the mass production of his electric vehicle. He approached investors and manufacturers with enthusiasm, certain that once they saw the potential of his invention, they would be eager to bring it to market.

But time and again, he was met with polite refusals and vague excuses. The true reason for their reluctance — the iron grip of the fossil fuel interests - remained hidden from him until one day his friend, Charles Luciano, told him why he was getting all the refusals and excuses.

"Nikky, I'm going to spill the beans to you since it seems no one else has the guts to do it."

"I'm sorry, Charles, could you please clarify — beans?"

Luciano grinned at Tesla's naiveté, not being well-versed in the idiomatic expressions of the time. "The Rockefeller family, see," he patiently explained. "They are strong arming everyone to stay away from your electric automobile idea."

"Good God! Why?"

"'Cause there's no money in it for them. Their fortune is mainly based on petroleum."

"And so mankind's progress will be held hostage because of one family's greed for monetary gain?"

"Well, yeah... But with a couple of family head adjustments, I think they can be persuaded to appreciate the future you see."

"By head adjustments... You don't mean-"

"You know any other way Nikky? We can't pay them off." At Tesla's dismayed reaction, Luciano reassured him, "Just joking, buddy!"

As the years passed, Tesla's dream of an electric automobile future slowly faded. The streets remained filled with petroleum-guzzling vehicles, their engines belching smoke and noise. The clean, silent world he had envisioned seemed further away than ever.

Yet even in the face of this setback, Tesla's spirit remained unbroken. Even though he knew he wouldn't live to see it, his vision of electric vehicles eventually became reality, decades after his time.

In the early 21st century, another visionary and entrepreneur would resurrect his dream. Elon Musk would pick up the torch that Tesla had been forced to set down.

Musk, like Tesla before him, saw the potential of electric vehicles to revolutionize transportation. With innovative technology, sleek design, and sheer determination, Musk's company, Tesla Motors, named in honor of Nikola Tesla, began producing electric vehicles that captured the world's imagination. Although not wireless electric vehicles like Tesla's original design, they were electric, powered by batteries.

Where Tesla had faced insurmountable opposition from entrenched interests, Musk found a world more ready for change. Concerns about pollution and climate change had made consumers more receptive to alternative energy vehicles. Advances in battery technology had made electric cars more practical for everyday use.

As Tesla-branded vehicles began appearing on roads around the world, Nikola Tesla's long-deferred dream was finally becoming a reality. The quiet hum of electric motors are incrementally replacing the roaring of petroleum engines.

In a poetic twist of fate, the very company that had once led petroleum-powered vehicles, Ford Motor Company, now found itself racing to catch up in the electric vehicle market. The future that Henry Ford had once dismissed as a "passing fancy" had arrived, vindicating Tesla's vision nearly a century after his death.

As electric vehicles become more common, people are discovering the story of Nikola Tesla and his pioneering work. His name, once relegated to the footnotes of history, is now spoken with reverence as the true father of the electric car revolution.

Tesla's dream had not died — it had simply been waiting for the right moment, and the right person, to bring it to life.

And as the world embraces this cleaner, quieter future of transportation, one could almost imagine the ghost of Nikola Tesla looking on with a satisfied smile, his vision finally realized.

33

THE GATHERING STORM

Tesla sat hunched over his workbench. A familiar hum filled the air. True to his word, he had recovered from his broken ribs without medical intervention and was back at work, his body a testament to the resilience of his brilliant mind.

The only concession he made to his automobile accident was using a cane when he went out to social events. And even then, he waved it about like a status symbol accessory, as would any dapper older gentleman in society.

Tesla may have basically retired but he still had one last invention to perfect. And that was his Time Radio. The device was a marvel of theoretical physics. At its heart lay an impossibly complex array of electrodes suspended in a chamber of super-heated plasma.

As he made a final adjustment to the frequency modulator, he paused and took a deep breath...

"Anya, my dear," he called out, his voice fainter these days. "I'm afraid I shall have to forsake my beloved coffee and tea."

Anya poked her head into the laboratory. "But why, dearest? Surely a little indulgence won't harm you."

He waved a dismissive hand. "My heart is not what it once was, my love. I must take precautions." A sly smile tugged at his lips. "Though for you, I shall make an exception for our nightly order."

As Anya nodded and retreated, Tesla's gaze returned to the Time Radio, his only project these past few years. He had labored over the device tirelessly, but today, a weariness settled into his bones.

Feeling his mortality keenly, he allowed himself a moment's rest, sinking into the worn chair beside his desk. Thankfully, after a short power nap, he awoke somewhat refreshed and returned to work.

∞

By mid-1941, Tesla was no longer venturing out of the New Yorker Hotel. He received invitations to hundreds of VIP events but rarely attended them. The hotel took care of all his needs.

A press buzz started that Tesla was dying and that was the reason given as to why no one saw him anymore.

The source of this rumor was William Randolph Hearst, who decades earlier had especially liked to focus on Tesla's failures rather than his successes. By 1941, the Hearst newspaper syndicate owned about 40% of all media in America.

Tesla did not find this gossip amusing, nor had he forgotten that Hearst and Edison were allies back in the day. Thus, when Tesla received a VIP invitation to a screening of a new movie, *Citizen Kane*, he made an exception and attended.

The film was to open on May 1st at the RKO Palace Theater in New York City. The word was out that Orson Welles, the producer, star, director and co-writer, was portraying the thinly disguised life of Hearst himself. Because of this, Hearst and his gossip column maven, Louella Parsons, launched into a full-out attack of the film; threatening lawsuits, exposure of Welles' current affair with the still-married actress Dolores Del Rio, and temporarily blacklisting any reviews of RKO films in their press. An offer even came from studio moguls led by MGM's Louis B. Mayer, upwards of $800,000, to destroy all prints of the film and destroy the negative!

The film premiered as scheduled with all the controversy.

The press was cautious and reviews were mixed, as many in the profession did not want to antagonize Hearst any further and possibly hurt their own jobs. But audiences loved it, as did Tesla. "This might be my favorite movie," he stated, and he saw it several more times.

He was highly impressed with Orson Welles and the entire cast and production. And was also delighted to figuratively shove it to Hearst and his yellow journalism by showing himself as evidence he, Nikola Tesla, was still very much alive!

Citizen Kane eventually was voted the greatest movie of all time in many polls. Ironically, in 1980, Orson Welles played J.P. Morgan in a film about Tesla's life. Tesla no doubt would have been pleased with this choice of actor.

∞

After his adventures with *Citizen Kane,* Tesla remained homebound in the New Yorker Hotel. He turned down most visitors but there was one he welcomed in 1942, and that was Serbian-born King Peter II of Yugoslavia. Not yet twenty years old, the young King was sent into exile when his country was overrun by the Nazis. He fled to London and set up a government-in-exile there for a time before coming to the United States.

His attempts to wield help from both Winston Churchill and President Franklin Roosevelt proved less than successful. However, First Lady Eleanor Roosevelt showed her support by attending a party in King Peter's honor. And after that, the King arranged a meeting between Tesla and himself, hoping that perhaps Tesla, still the most famous and revered Serbian hero, could make a difference.

Tesla was a long time and proud American citizen, but he was also a Serbian citizen. No one knows what he and the young king discussed in private for nearly six hours. Although during a television interview years later, Alice Monahan – the maid who had served Tesla and the King that day – disclosed that she heard Tesla and the King discussing various monasteries in Serbia.

∞

New York City - December 20, 1942

Tesla's eyes landed on the Christmas cards strewn across his desk, a reminder of the well-wishes that were pouring in.

One, in particular, caught his attention — a message from none other than the famous theoretical physicist Albert Einstein himself. Tesla chuckled, running a finger over the familiar handwriting. For all their serious professional disagreements, he couldn't help but admire the man's relentless pursuit of knowledge.

A thought sparked, and before he could second-guess himself, Tesla reached for the telephone. "Albert, my dear friend," he said as the line crackled to life. "Thank you for the holiday wishes."

Einstein's warm laughter filled his ear. "Not at all, Nikola. How are you feeling?"

"Much improved." Tesla settled into the conversation like an old friend. "I found that changing to a vegetarian diet helped my recovery. I recommend you try it."

"Perhaps so. I have always eaten meat with a somewhat guilty conscience and in recent months I have done much research on the spiritual and the physical universes which seem to operate off different laws," said Einstein. "There seems to be many truths in Buddhism, for example."

"Indeed, it is a cosmic religion that transcends a personal God. That harmony is needed in our modern world. I have studied it myself for that very reason."

"Nikola, what have you been up to these past few years?"

"In fact, you may be interested in—" He caught himself, remembering the need for secrecy even though the Time Radio was now safely in the hands of Henry Watt. With a practiced ease, Tesla abruptly changed the subject.

"Mostly refining my past work. I'm afraid the years have finally caught up to me, dear friend. I haven't the energy I once had. And how about you? I heard you have withdrawn from the Manhattan Project—" He hesitated, treading carefully into sensitive territory.

A weighty silence stretched between them, punctuated only by the crackle of static. Finally, Einstein spoke, his voice heavy with the burden of his conscience.

"I am not a part of that; as you know, I am a pacifist," Einstein began, each word measured. "But I am also a Jew, and what Hitler is doing must be stopped. One cannot stand by anymore and do nothing. They asked me to write to President Roosevelt, to offer my research and I did .... Now I'm not so sure that I should have."

Tesla's grip tightened on the receiver. "And now you have regrets?"

Einstein's sigh seemed to carry the weight of worlds. "Yes, it's madness. I don't know how I will bear the guilt if Oppenheimer succeeds, and I fear the rascal will succeed. He is a brilliant mind." There was a pause then Einstein continued, his voice dropping to a near-whisper.

"The argument is that the Nazis are building their own nuclear bomb. If they should succeed where Oppenheimer fails, America will be their test target, and the fault will be mine."

"I understand your moral dilemma," Tesla said, his voice compassionate. "That is the very reason I gave up work on the particle beam. The destruction it was capable of... it sickened me to my very core."

"You made the wise decision to not share your research," Einstein replied, a note of wistfulness in his tone. "I wish I had only done the same. Then perhaps I could sleep at nights."

"You mustn't think like that, Albert. Oppenheimer would have eventually figured it out himself. He is a good man at heart, I believe, and will come to feel the same terrible remorse that we have suffered."

A weighted silence stretched between them, hanging heavy in the ether. At last, Einstein spoke, his curiosity getting the better of him.

"What are you really working on now? I don't believe you are only refining your previous inventions. No doubt whatever it is it will shake the scientific world to its core?"

"I am looking to the future, Albert, and how I can take responsibility for humanity and the safety of our planet. These are tense times but I have a plan." His voice dropped to a conspiratorial whisper. "Unfortunately, I can say no more about it."

Einstein chuckled. "I knew it! I am sure whatever it is, it will yet again be the talk of the world. Your AC current already powers civilization; perhaps you have now found a way to harness the energy of the stars themselves?"

"Not this time, Albert," Tesla said, his tone suddenly somber. "This one, no one shall know about. At least, not for a very long time."

There was a pause as Einstein processed this uncharacteristic secrecy from his usually boastful colleague. "Well then," he said at last, "may it succeed like so many of your previous inventions. And may you enjoy good health for many more years; the world would not fare well in your absence."

"Thank you, Albert," Tesla whispered, gently ending the call.

34

A Last Hurrah

New York City – December 27, 1942

It was still Christmas week. In a stark departure from its usual lively atmosphere, the lobby was quiet, devoid of the usual activity of guests and staff. At the front desk, a solitary clerk was lost in a gripping novel. And not too far away, Luciano's men, who were assigned to protect Tesla, were peacefully asleep on the plush lobby sofas.

With a whoosh, the glass doors parted to reveal a sudden burst of brisk winter air, and a mysterious figure materialized as if out of thin air.

There was no reaction whatsoever from Luciano's men, not a single twitch between the two men, both still sound asleep.

An elderly man, his frame slightly stooped but still carrying an air of dignity, shuffled into the lobby. He wore a cream-colored raincoat and a dark fedora pulled low over his forehead, casting his face in a shadow.

He seemed weak and limp, obviously hurt and in pain. One hand was in his pocket, the other loose at his side. As he made his way to the front desk, he left a trail of small blood droplets behind him.

The clerk looked up startled, his novel forgotten. "Sir? Can I help you?"

The man's eyes bore into the clerk's, icy and unwavering, as he spoke with a sense of urgency, yet a careful restraint.

"Ring Nikola Tesla."

"Sir, it's nearly 3 am. Mister Tesla is..."

The man cut him off in mid-sentence and said, "Ring him!" with a threatening voice and piercing look.

The reaction from the clerk was as if he had been slapped in the face.

"Might I ask your name sir, to announce you."

"Adler. Tell him it's Ernst Adler."

"Very good, sir."

The clerk picked up the phone to call Tesla. Just then, Adler took a shuddering breath and leaned on the counter in pain. The clerk's eyes followed Adler's arm as he clutched his chest. Despite not yet noticing the droplets of blood trailing behind Adler or the puddle forming under his raincoat, a sense of danger crept over the clerk as he spoke into the phone.

"Mr. Tesla, there is a Mr. Adler in the lobby to see you .... Yes, Ernst Adler... Very good, sir."

He hung up the phone and focused his attention back on Adler, who by now was in much more visible pain.

"Mr. Adler," he began cautiously, "Are you alright?"

Adler drew in a sharp breath, straightening his posture with a painful effort. "I'm... perfectly fine," he managed to say, each word spoken in a tight knot of agony.

The clerk wasn't convinced. His eyes widened with unease, then morphed into a haunting fear that made his fingers twitch relentlessly on the countertop. Adler noticed this and grabbed the clerk's wrist, locking it tight in his grip.

"If you don't mind young man," Adler said, his voice taking on a hard edge, "I suggest you mind your own business."

The clerk flinched, then swallowed hard and nodded.

Adler narrowed his eyes. "Do-you-understand?" he asked again, slowly and deliberately.

"Yes, sir. I do. I do, Mr. Adler."

Adler leaned forward, took his blood-stained hand out of his pocket and put it onto the polished wood counter. The clerk's eyes widened, his breath hitching in his throat.

"Now, if you would be so kind as to hand me the telephone."

The clerk, hands trembling, retrieved the phone from beneath the counter and placed it before Adler. With a swift, practiced motion, Adler yanked the cord from the phone, rendering it useless.

He set the broken phone down with an almost gentle touch, his eyes locking with the now terrified clerk.

"Don't worry," Adler said, his voice a low, chilling whisper. "I'll be gone soon enough. Now where is Tesla?"

"Mr. Tesla is expecting you on the 33rd floor, suite 3327," the clerk said, struggling to keep his voice from shaking.

With a final, piercing look at the desk clerk, Adler nodded and strode across the lobby, leaving behind a trail of blood droplets on his journey to the elevators.

The clerk now could not help but see the blood trail to the front desk and then to the elevator. As soon as Adler stepped into the elevator, he dashed into the office, leaving the front desk behind.

Tesla, meanwhile, was dressing by the bed. "Stay here, my love. Do not leave this room until I call you."

Anya gracefully draped the bed sheet around her and sat up on the bed. Her face was awash with concern and alarm.

Tesla left the bedroom, closing the door behind him. A flurry of thoughts rushed through his mind as he made his way to the door, his anticipation growing with each step. He reached the door then waited. Not a few seconds later, he heard the elevator arrive at the floor.

Tesla braced himself, took a deep breath, and with a steady hand, turned the knob and swung open the door. With many years since their last encounter, Tesla and Adler finally locked eyes in a moment that felt electric.

Adler staggered to the door and Tesla caught him in his arms before he could collapse. He gently ushered Adler into the suite, shutting the door with the back of his foot.

"My good man, you're bleeding."

"Yes, it appears I am, old friend."

Tesla sat Adler on the sofa. "You need a doctor, at once!"

"No! No doctors. We need to talk."

"Yes, in good time, but first we must get you looked after." Tesla peeked inside Adler's coat to examine the source of his bleeding. "Good God man! You've been shot!" he exclaimed. "More than once!"

Adler winced. "That's inconsequential. What you must know is that Hitler wants to get his hands on you in the most vile way. He handpicked me and a team of highly skilled operatives to abduct you."

Tesla's eyes widened in disbelief, for it was not the words but the man uttering them that left him utterly stunned. "Yes .... Well, I am somewhat aware of this plot. But I would never have imagined that you would be part of it."

"I'm not really, after I learned you were the target. I accepted the mission only so I could assure its failure."

Just then, Anya emerged from the bedroom, tying her bathrobe sash. She stopped, standing fully hidden in the shadows, and looked at Adler, horrified.

"Nikola, who is this man?"

"Don't fret, my love. Adler saved my life onboard that horrid ship when I first came to America. Remember, I told you about it."

Adler's head swam as he struggled to stay lucid, his eyes darting about in confusion. Struggling to catch his breath, his head drooped with exhaustion.

Tesla inspected his friend's wound more thoroughly.

"Who are you talking to?" Adler muttered.

Tesla ignored his question. "You most certainly need a doctor, even two doctors and quick!"

Adler lifted his head a bit. "I won't make it." He tightly grasped Tesla's arm.

"Nonsense!" Tesla roared.

"It's not over," Adler whispered. "Otto Skorzeny is still out there. I missed him." He gazed sadly at Tesla for a moment, his eyes filled with both pain and regret. "He is loyal to Hitler and will stop at nothing to complete the mission. The plan was to extract you, bring you to Berlin. Failing that, we were to eliminate you."

"Is that the man who shot you?"

"Yes."

"Then I shall prevent him from doing this again."

"Are you not understanding what I am telling you? There is no again! He will kill you. And I won't be here to stop him."

Adler reached into his pocket and produced an automatic gun, placing it firmly in Tesla's grip.

"Take this," Adler ordered Tesla.

"Good God, whatever for!" Tesla exclaimed.

"If you're counting on those two thugs in the lobby to protect you then, my dear friend, you're already a dead man."

"Dear God, have you—"

With a sharp interruption, Adler exclaimed: "Didn't have to, they're asleep like a couple of babies. Do not hesitate when you see him. Point and shoot until it will shoot no more."

Adler struggled to his feet and embraced Tesla, sobbing and coughing blood.

"My dear friend, I am sorry that I failed."

"I can change this outcome...." Tesla argued.

Adler let out a painful laugh. "Had any other man said that I would think him mad but you, somehow I believe you can do just that."

Adler struggled to catch his last breath. And with that, he died in Tesla's arms.

Tesla held him close for a long moment then eased the dead man back into the chair. Softly, he whispered, "This is not how it ends."

The front door erupted with a thunderous knock that shook the entire suite, punctuated by the clamor of urgent voices.

"Mr. Tesla, open the door!"

It was Luciano's men from the lobby. Tesla placed the gun into Adler's coat pocket and then looked at Anya who was fear-riddled and frozen in place. Tesla gestured to Anya to return to the bedroom and then hurriedly made his way to the door, fearing it would be broken down.

Luciano's men rushed in, quickly sized up the situation, and within a very few minutes, Adler's body was removed and the room was cleaned up, as if Adler had never been there.

35

TESLA IS DEAD

New York City - January 8, 1943

A convoy of Plymouth sedans and NYPD cruisers with sirens wailing and lights flashing, shattered the quiet of the night as they slid to a halt in front of the New Yorker Hotel.

A small army of well-dressed FBI agents and uniformed police officers poured out into the snowless winter night.

Inside the hotel, an air of apprehension hung heavy in the lobby. The front desk staff, their faces a mixture of worry, confusion, and sorrow, had gathered around the other late-night employees. One woman, her eyes red and swollen, dabbed at her tears with a handkerchief.

Agent James Miller, a tall, imposing figure with a no-nonsense demeanor, strode towards the desk. His agents and the police officer filled the entire lobby.

"Who's the manager?" he barked.

Calvin Rutherford, a middle-aged man with graying temples, stepped forward. "That would be me, sir. Calvin Rutherford."

Miller nodded curtly. "How many know?"

"Just us and Alice."

Miller's eyes narrowed. "This stays quiet. No one else is to know. Is that clear?"

"Yes, sir. But there will be questions..."

"Tell them whatever you want," Miller interrupted. "Just don't mention Tesla. And who is Alice?"

Ronald Wilson stepped forward. "That's the maid, Alice Monahan. She found him."

"And who are you?"

"Ronald Wilson, the assistant manager, sir."

Rutherford interrupted, "Wait, the bellboy! Henry Watt knows too."

"Where is he?" barked Miller.

"Henry's already left," Wilson replied.

"Who's taking us up?"

Rutherford hesitated then reluctantly agreed to lead the way.

Miller turned to the hotel staff. "The rest of you stay put. And I want to speak to this Alice. Also, someone find this Watt fella and have him come back to the hotel."

Miller turned to Agent Landers, his number two. "If they don't get him back within the hour, get his address and have someone pick him up." Then he whispered: "The Jersey office agents should be here soon. When they get here, secure the outside parameter, no one leaves the hotel or comes in, understood?"

"Yes, sir."

"Let's go, Rutherford," Miller ordered. And so Miller, Rutherford, two uniformed officers, and a half dozen agents piled into the elevator and rode it to the 33rd floor.

Miller's eyes swept the hallway as they exited. "I want this floor locked down." He then turned to Rutherford. "Are there stairs at both ends of this hall?"

Rutherford nodded. Miller waved the police officers to both ends of the hall as Rutherford led the way to room 3327. Rutherford's hand trembled as he unlocked the door.

Miller barked one final order before entering Tesla's suite. "No one leaves their rooms on this floor until they've been interviewed and their identities verified."

Rutherford opened the door, took a breath and stepped aside. "What should I tell the guests?" he asked.

"Whatever is in your protocol," replied Miller.

"We don't have a protocol for this sort of thing."

"Then make one up," Miller snapped, entering the room. His agents followed him. Agent Miller sized up the suite and said, "We need more lights."

Donahue sprang into action, swiftly moving from one corner of the room to the other, diligently flipping the switches of every light and lamp, illuminating the entire suite.

"Summers!" Miller called out.

Agent Paul Summers, a younger man, stepped forward.

"Yes, sir," said Summers nervously.

"Find out who was on switchboard duty tonight and if she's not here, find her and bring her here. And no more incoming or outgoing calls from this hotel unless they're for or from this room."

Agent Summers nodded in relief at his assigned task and left the suite. Meanwhile, Miller made his way to the bed where Tesla's body lay. Donahue joined him.

The men stood and gazed at the sight before them. Tesla, so terribly emaciated and wearing only a pair of men's stockings, was partially covered by a blanket, his eyes closed. He looked at peace.

Miller carefully examined the body without touching it. There were no visible signs of foul play. "Do you smell it?" He asked Donahue.

"Yes, sir!"

"Some sort of perfume or cologne?"

"I don't think so."

"Some sort of chemical element then?"

"Yes, I believe so."

Miller scanned the bed, the pillows, then moved his face closer to the bed and Tesla's body to trace the faint smell but could not find the source.

"Sir, its hanging ... in the air," said Donahue, frowning.

Miller bobbed his head up and took a deep whiff. Yes, the smell was more pronounced in the air over the bed.

"Interesting how it lingers," said Donahue.

Miller then scanned the suite again; everything was tidy. No signs of any sort of struggle. The safe on the other side of the room caught his eye and he made his way over to it.

Miller kneeled to examine the surprisingly open and empty safe. He inspected the door for forced entry, but none was evident, nothing suspicious about it.

"Donahue," he called out, "Who else has been in this room since his body was found?"

"Rutherford said at least three men were already here, and they left with some papers and photographs."

"What papers?"

"I don't know. Maybe they knew the combination and cleaned out the safe."

"What papers? What men?" said Miller, each word deliberate.

"Don't know," replied Donahue, his words clipped and tentative.

Miller's eyes narrowed. "Find him, take his statement and get an ID on these men." He paused, fixing Donahue with a steel-cold stare. "I want details."

"Yes, sir." Donahue's spine straightened automatically, his shoulders squaring as he stood at rigid attention.

"This isn't the marines, Donahue." Miller sighed, rubbing his temple. "No need to wait for me to dismiss you."

A flush crept up Donahue's neck. "Of course, I'll get right on it, sir." He turned, his movements still carrying that military precision. He made his way to the door, and as he was about to step outside the suite Miller's voice stopped him cold.

"And Donahue." Miller's tone had changed — darker now, carrying a warning. "If his story suddenly changes, arrest him."

With one foot already in the hallway, Donahue turned around and looked at Miller with focus. "On what charge, sir?"

Miller's lip curled slightly, his expression hardening. "Obstruction of a federal investigation."

Donahue nodded once, sharp and quick. He started to leave but Miller called him back.

"Check if the towels in the bathroom are damp," he ordered, and Donahue obligingly walked into the bathroom.

Just then, the phone rang, the shrill of the ring cutting through the silence. All eyes in the suite were now on the phone. Miller answered it, his voice low and urgent.

"Agent Miller here... Yes, Mr. Hoover. He's dead, apparently in his sleep... No immediate signs, but the safe is open and empty... No sir... I understand... We're containing the situation... Understood, sir."

As Miller hung up the phone, Donahue emerged from the bathroom. "Everything's bone dry in there, sir. It's... odd."

Miller nodded, his suspicions growing. "When's the last time you went to bed without washing up, Donahue?"

"Never, sir. Unless I'm in the field with no facilities."

Miller did not reply; once again, he was scanning the room. His eyes fell on a table by the window, set for tea for two.

"Someone else was here with him."

∞

The door opened and Agent Summers entered with Alice Monahan. Summers announced her.

"Sir, the room service maid."

Agent Miller locked eyes with Alice. "Please have a seat."

Summers escorted Alice to the sofa farthest from the bed. She still looked unnerved, and her reddened eyes revealed she had been crying.

Before Miller could get started with Alice, the door opened, and Foster popped in.

"There's a development downstairs," he reported. "A reporter from *The Telegraph*."

"Keep him isolated from the hotel staff. Do the same if any more come."

"Yes, sir."

"And Foster, apparently someone from the staff is talking, get a lid on it."

Foster nodded and disappeared.

Miller looked at Alice again, and his voice softened.

"I'm Agent Miller. May I call you Alice?"

She nodded, dabbing her eyes with her handkerchief.

"Do you remember the exact time you discovered Mr. Tesla?"

"I do. It was just a couple hours ago."

"Do you normally service Mr. Tesla's room at that time?"

"Oh, heavens no. Usually I take the tea tray down before eight."

"Why were you late?"

"I wasn't. I had come to collect the tray on time as I always do but Mr. Tesla had the do not disturb sign on the door handle."

"Does he usually put the sign up?"

"No, he's never used it before."

Miller absorbed Alice's answer with a slight frown then continued questioning her. "Did you hear anything inside?"

Alice appeared hesitant to answer.

"Alice?"

"Well no," she said slowly. "Not last night. But I often hear Mr. Tesla in conversation, it's the strangest thing. I know he's alone but still I can hear him speaking. You understand, of course, I wasn't eavesdropping or anything like that, it's just when I pass the room I can hear him."

"Just him or were there other voices?"

"Just him usually, but I could swear sometimes I hear a lady's voice too."

"How do you know he is alone?"

Alice gave a slight smile. "I work this floor, and I always pay attention to guests coming or leaving, if I don't, I miss my tip sometimes. And I have never seen a woman come or leave from Mr. Tesla's room but I always bring him tea for two."

"What time do you normally bring the tea?"

"Always at six. And I collect the tray a little after eight."

Miller was quiet for a moment, then continued. "After you saw the sign you didn't knock on the door?"

"Heavens, no! I wouldn't disturb Mr. Tesla."

"But yet you did a couple of hours later."

"I was concerned."

"When you entered the room was there anything out of the ordinary?"

"Dear Lord, all I truly remember is Mr. Tesla lying in bed and I knew right then that something was terribly wrong."

"I'd like you to take a look around the room and tell me if anything is out of the ordinary. No need to get up."

Alice nodded, wiped her eyes again, and studied the room carefully. She abruptly sat up straight.

"The chair!"

"What chair?"

Alice pointed to a chair at the table. "That one, it's usually by the window. Mr. Tesla would sit near the window and stare out it."

"How did Mr. Tesla look to you when you brought the tea?"

"Like he always did. Maybe a little more tired than usual."

"Is that safe normally open like that?"

Alice followed his gaze to the safe across the room. "Oh, dear Lord. No, no, I've never seen it open. I didn't even notice it."

Foster popped in again and motioned to Miller. "Sir? The Mayor is here."

Miller stood up, excused himself to Alice, and addressed Agent Foster. "Keep him away from this floor and the reporters."

Foster protested, "He's the Mayor!"

"I don't care. Have someone take the maid home and put someone on her."

Foster nodded and Miller returned to Alice.

"Agent Foster will arrange for someone to take you home now. It's important that you not speak to reporters until we've had an opportunity to investigate properly."

"Of course, sir." And with that Alice got up, took one sad last look at Tesla and followed Foster out, passing the coroner and an FBI photographer coming in.

"He's on the bed. There's a slight odor. I'd like your thoughts on it," Miller said to the coroner, who nodded and proceeded to the bed and Tesla's body.

Miller went to the chair Alice pointed out and studied the carpet near the chair for anything unusual but found nothing suspicious.

He then took the chair near the window and sat in it just as Tesla would have done. He stared through the window and saw nothing unusual, just the New York skyline with a wonderful view of two city landmarks: the Chrysler and Empire State Buildings.

The coroner called out, "Agent Miller?"

Miller got up from the chair and joined the coroner while the FBI photographer finished photographing Tesla.

Miller addressed the photographer. "I want you to photograph the entire room and everything in it and put that chair back where it was." Miller then returned his attention to the coroner, who spoke with some concern.

"I cannot be certain, you understand. At least not until I have done an autopsy, but I think the odor is chloroform, masked with some sort of mild citrus."

"Could he have consumed it in the tea?"

"No. It would have a horrid taste, he would certainly notice it, even with lemon."

"If he drank a cup of it, could it kill him?"

"Absolutely! But where's the teacup?"

Miller motioned to the teacups on the table on the other side of the room. "Over there."

The coroner fixed his sights on the table then shook his head.

"He could not have made it to the bed. The chloroform would have dropped him in a matter of seconds. Especially at his advanced age."

A long silence hung in the room. The coroner spoke up again.

"If it is chloroform, it's not what killed him."

"What then?" asked Miller.

"I can't be certain until I do an autopsy, but I think it's heart failure."

"Could the chloroform stop his heart?"

"Sure, if he consumed or inhaled enough of it but then he would have discolorations around his lips and fingertips. And as you see, that's not the case."

Again, silence as Miller considered this information. Then he fixed his sights on the plush pillow.

"If he were smothered with a pillow could that bring on a heart attack?"

"That with the chloroform? Yes."

"The maid last saw him alive at six last night. What do you make the time of death?"

The coroner looked at his watch.

"I'd say a few hours ago. Last night, around 10:30 or so."

Just then Calvin Rutherford returned with a gentleman carrying supplies to make a death mask. He hastily did so and then Miller stepped aside as they rolled in a stretcher to remove Tesla's body.

∞

Downstairs, the lobby was rapidly filling up with police, FBI, and reporters. Despite the late hour, even some of the hotel guests had come out of their rooms to see what the commotion was about.

Finally, Mayor La Guardia made his grand entrance, accompanied by the New York City Police Commissioner Timilty.

Behind them stood a line of police officers acting as a buffer between them and the crowd.

"It's ridiculous, Joseph!" shouted Mayor La Guardia.

"What do you want me to do, arrest the whole lot of them?" asked Timilty.

La Guardia nodded. "It's our city!"

Timilty grimaced. "Tell that to FDR, he gave them all this power!"

"No, not Roosevelt. It's that dammed Hoover!"

The two men now approached the hotel desk and began their own questioning of the staff.

∞

Agent James Miller trudged homeward in the twilight hours of the summer evening, his weary bones aching with the weight of an unsolved mystery that had consumed him for months.

The Tesla case, a labyrinth of enigmas and half-truths, clung to him like a second skin, refusing to release its tenacious grip on his psyche. For months, Miller had pursued the truth with a fervor that bordered on obsession. It felt and smelled like a homicide to him. Behind closed doors and away from prying eyes, he had tugged at threads that connected Tesla's final moments to possibly a conspiracy that led to the highest powers in the land.

The inventor's waning health and the conspicuous absence of groundbreaking inventions and discoveries in his twilight years only deepened the mystery — what sinister motive lurked beneath the surface of this apparently straightforward case?

Even though the powers that be officially determined and closed the case as a natural death over a month ago, Agent Miller remained unconvinced and continued his investigation.

On that fateful night, when he had first set foot in Tesla's hotel suite and discovered the opened safe, the moved furniture, the tea for two and the lingering stench of chloroform — all were pieces of a macabre puzzle that had haunted his every waking moment since.

What secrets had the brilliant inventor taken to his grave? What forces were at play, manipulating the strings of fate from the shadows?

Miller felt the FBI and police investigations into Tesla's death were shoddy, whether intentionally botched or not. There was no full-time security either in Tesla's rooms or the various other locations, including storage units that were searched for any of his papers.

Within two days of Tesla's death, the FBI ordered the Alien Property Custodian to seize all of Tesla's belongings. With the scrambling and disorder that followed, Miller felt the potential crime scene was compromised. A parade of people had passed through Tesla's rooms, searching for everything from a will to sensitive documents. Tesla's safe had been opened and cleaned out before Miller even arrived on the scene; so who knew what else was missing?

Despite Tesla's public statements that he had worked on a "death ray" and hidden the paperwork, it seemed no precise schematics were found to that effect. Had Tesla himself destroyed his research on it? Or had it mysteriously vanished as well?

Nearly three weeks passed after Tesla's death before they found an expert to sit down and go through what remained of his confiscated possessions and papers. They chose the most brilliant mind they could find to study all of it, one who could confront and understand the technicalities of Tesla's writings.

John G. Trump was an MIT professor, an electrical engineer and physicist. His area of expertise was developing rotational radiation therapy, and he invented the first million-volt x-ray generator.

Being chosen to oversee Tesla's work would not be John Trump's only claim to fame; his nephew, Donald John Trump, born three years after Tesla's death, later became both a media personality and United States President.

After two days of intensive study, John Trump summed up his findings in writing: there was nothing in Tesla's papers that should remain secret, no precise schematics that might prove useful to the United States, Germany or Japan in their possible development of atomic bombs. He turned over a file to the military, written by Tesla in later years, in which Tesla discussed possible use of such weapons.

Trump also directly highlighted in his findings a paper written by Tesla in 1937, an extensive description submitted with filing a patent for what amounted to a particle-beam weapon capable of destroying airplanes, army tanks and for igniting bombs remotely from many miles away.

Still, Trump found no precise schematics to such a weapon anywhere in Tesla's papers. Following up a lead, Trump gained access to a safe deposit box in the Hotel Governor Clinton where Tesla himself had claimed his particle beam weapon prototype was stored for safekeeping. Others who knew Tesla made the same claim, insisting Tesla had told them that the key to that box was kept in Tesla's room safe at the New Yorker Hotel. However, that safe was opened and empty long before Trump ever had access to it. When Trump finally had the safety deposit box opened, he found no particle beam prototype or paperwork inside, just a standard piece of electrical equipment.

While Miller accepted the integrity of John Trump's findings, there was still the fact that so much time had passed before Trump was asked to examine what purportedly was all of Tesla's documents. Additionally, it was later found that dozens of crates, boxes and trunks of Tesla's earlier research were scattered in storage around the city, many not even found or known about for Trump's investigation. Based on the evidence remaining at hand in less than three weeks after Tesla's death, how could Trump have come up with any other conclusion?

Miller didn't appreciate the FBI dismissing Tesla's claims about the death ray and other inventions as exaggerations or an old man's fantasies. Several of the interviewed hotel staff considered Tesla's behavior beyond eccentric in his last years, thinking him irrational and showing the beginnings of senility.

As the dust settled on the investigation, Miller learned that his agency indeed had Tesla papers labeled Top Secret. But since the FBI had no jurisdiction over Tesla's property, it seemed the military stepped in and demanded the papers.

Miller next turned to a friend in the newly formed Office of Strategic Services. The OSS was a secret organization, later to change its name to the Central Intelligence Agency. The little information Miller could learn was that Tesla's secret papers did exist and there was concern they could be — or had been — leaked before or after his death by persons unknown, to foreign countries.

What might have been in those papers, overreaction or not, troubled Miller. Nor was it easy to think that his agency, or someone in his agency or elsewhere, was complicit in some kind of cover-up.

In fact, after some time passed, his OSS friend hinted that there was indeed another agent there, under disguise as a "civilian", who likely not only swapped out the "particle beam" from the safety deposit box, but had both early and later access to Tesla's notebooks and other writings, and had literally torn out notebook pages or confiscated papers deemed sensitive.

John Trump did find documentation that Tesla had, in 1935, sold Russia "complete information" about the particle beam weapon. This was based on a written agreement, for which Tesla received $25,000. James Miller learned from his OSS friend that it was likely the United States government had also received identical details but was suppressing the fact. Why? And since Tesla had long ago suggested he would provide seven nations with the same information, what other countries had he reached out to?

Miller concluded there remained serious gaping holes in the entire Tesla investigation and he was not amused.

As he made his way closer to his humble abode, the soft, radiant illumination from the streetlamps stretched the shadows across the tranquil evening.

The summer night air hung heavy with an unnatural stillness, as if in anticipation of some impending calamity.

Miller's seasoned instincts, honed by years of FBI service, prickled with an unsettling awareness that something was amiss.

As Miller approached his front door, an eerie silence enveloped him, broken only by the rapid pounding of his heart. Each step towards the threshold became a measured calculation, his senses heightened to a fever pitch.

He reached for the door handle, only to recoil as if scorched by an invisible flame. A chill ran down his spine, and the hairs on the back of his neck stood up. Something was wrong — terribly wrong.

In one fluid motion born of years of training, Miller withdrew his weapon, its familiar weight offering little comfort against the unknown threat that lurked. He retreated slowly down the steps backwards, his eyes locked on the foreboding entrance, his mind racing through plausible scenarios.

Suddenly, the silence shattered with a deafening bang — a gunshot tore through the night, the bullet entering the back of Miller's head. This was followed by the sickening thud of his body hitting the ground. And then a second gunshot rang out, also piercing the back of Miller's head, obviously an exercise in good measure.

A wisp of smoke curled around Miller's crumpled body as he lay on the unforgiving concrete, his life extinguished in a blink of an eye.

From the depths of his home emerged a shadowy figure, his silhouette a chilling testament to the brutality of the act just committed.

Behind Miller, another shadow, the one that ended his life, stood briefly over the fallen agent's body, peering down at him with cold, calculating eyes hidden behind the veil of darkness.

The neighborhood stirred, awakened by the gunshots. Lights flickered on in nearby houses, curious faces peering out from behind hastily drawn curtains, as if summoned by some unspoken signal.

With chilling composure that spoke of extensive training and experience, the pair calmly and quietly made their way towards the curb. A sleek dark sedan, its engine purring with quiet menace, materialized from down the street.

In a matter of seconds, the mysterious assailants had vanished into the night, leaving behind only questions and a cooling corpse.

As sirens wailed in the distance, screaming the arrival of authorities, not soon enough, agent James Miller lay lifeless on his doorstep. The truth he had relentlessly pursued had exacted the ultimate price, snuffing out the life of a man who dared to peer behind the curtain of power and influence.

In the days and weeks that followed, those in positions of authority left the investigation into Agent Miller's murder unsolved and buried beneath mountains of bureaucratic red tape.

But in society, whispers persisted. Conspiracy theorists and truth-seekers alike latched onto the case of Agent Miller's murder, spinning elaborate tales of government cover-ups. The truth, elusive as ever, remained trapped in a labyrinth of shadows, forever out of reach.

Perhaps one day another brave soul will risk everything in pursuit of the truth.

Part Eight

36

BACK TO THE FUTURE

Queens, New York — August 2024

"Hey, some good news, Mr. Tesla!"

"What, John?"

"I've seen a real Tesla Coil in action!"

"How can that be? Surely technology has advanced in more than a century."

"An original Tesla Coil was used in an old movie, *Frankenstein*, in 1931. It was a big hit and is still considered one of the greatest horror movies ever filmed!"

Tesla was puzzled. "I am familiar with the novel, so how was it used?"

"For electricity, strong enough to bring the monster to life. They switched it on, and we could see exactly how it worked. It's a great scene! Apparently, the special effects guy, Kenneth Strickfaden, got the machine directly from you!"

"I am glad to hear it was demonstrated even in a fictional way," said Tesla, sounding pleased.

"But what's really cool is this: in 1974 Mel Brooks made a comedy spoof of the film, called *Young Frankenstein*. They wanted to use the same Tesla Coil as in the original movie. Turns out Strickfaden was still alive! And he had your coil stored in his garage all those years, and it still worked! They wanted to rent it for the movie, and he said he'd charge a grand for it. Mel Brooks said that wasn't enough; he paid the guy twenty-five hundred to use it in the new movie."

"I am not surprised that it still worked," said Tesla.

"The movie is hilarious," John laughed. "When the monster does his song-and-dance number... and when he hooks up with The Bride, you know they're getting laid because you can hear her singing 'Ah, Sweet Mystery of Life' at the top of her lungs."

"Getting laid?"

"You know, having sex."

"And audiences found this hilarious?"

"It was a huge hit! And it's considered a classic today, along with the original film. Mr. Tesla, you made movie history!"

"I'm assuming from your enthusiasm, John, that this is a good thing?"

"Definitely. Film buffs of every generation rediscover these movies. There are film festivals everywhere now and people can stream movies over the Internet. It's a different way of immortality but in a good way, Mr. Tesla. For us to actually see how a Tesla Coil worked is a miracle, really." John's voice crackled through the static of the time radio, his excitement palpable even across the years.

"This is pleasing to hear indeed, young John." Tesla's distinctive accent carried warmth and pride.

John shifted in his chair, his fingers fidgeting with the radio dial. "Mr. Tesla, I should also mention something that happened recently. We went through a global pandemic, a coronavirus."

Tesla's voice became distant, as if he'd suddenly moved away from the transmission receiving parameter. The silence that followed was heavy, oppressive.

John felt his heart rate quicken, the cold metal of the radio's casing beneath his fidgety fingers. "Mr. Tesla? Are you there!?" John's voice cracked with worry, the static seeming to grow louder in the silence.

When Tesla's voice finally returned, it was barely above a whisper, laden with an emotion John had not heard from the usually composed inventor.

"Yes, John... a coronavirus, you say?" His voice trembled, each word seeming to cost him great effort. "I... I lost a dear friend to such a virus."

John's throat tightened as he heard the pain in Tesla's voice. He shot a look over at Sara, who sat nearby curled up in a chair, reading a book. She glanced back at him and shrugged in surprise. John's palms grew clammy against the radio dials as Tesla spoke again.

"We called it different names then, but medical science has since confirmed it was indeed a coronavirus." Tesla paused, his breathing audible and unsteady. "She was a brilliant mind. The symptoms were devastating – the fever, the breathing difficulties. It spread across Europe and America like wildfire, just as I imagine it did in your time, John."

John slumped in his chair, his own memories of lockdowns and loss of basic freedoms washing over him. "Yeah, it was pretty bad," he replied, recognizing that the subject was particularly hard for Tesla.

"I'm so sorry, Mr. Tesla. I didn't mean to bring up painful memories." John's voice was thick with emotion as he imagined Tesla alone in the park in 1913, reliving such personal tragedy.

"No, no," Tesla said, and John could hear him taking a deep breath, gathering himself. There was a rustling sound, as if Tesla was straightening his jacket, trying to physically reset himself. "It's important to remember." His voice grew stronger, though John could still hear a slight quaver beneath the composed exterior. "Though perhaps we could speak of something else?"

∞

John had barely switched off the Time Radio when Sara spoke excitedly.

"Who do you think he was talking about? A dear friend.... Did he have a girlfriend?"

"I don't know," John said slowly, puzzled. "Maybe Katharine Johnson? I think she did get sick with the flu epidemic, but that was later, in 1918..."

"We gotta find out!" Sara declared, her eyes sparkling with excitement. She carefully set down the hardcover novel she was reading. It was a heavy book, the ninth and most current volume in the *Outlander* time travel series, over 900 pages.

"Maybe it's like *Outlander*," she suggested, "A love story. If Tesla can change history, maybe he can fix whatever happened to Katharine and save her. By the way —" She jumped up and pulled out a printed sheet of paper from her purse. "Here's our confirmation for Comic Con in October. Can't wait to see the *Outlander* cast again." She was referring to the long-running television series, based on the books. "Especially Caitríona Balfe... and dreamy Sam Heughan," she sighed, referring to the show's hunky male star.

"Should I be jealous?" John chuckled, already knowing the answer.

Sara threw her arms around John's neck, gave him a gentle kiss on the cheek and answered with surprising softness in her voice.

"Of course not, silly," she declared. "You're my dreamboat."

She settled herself on his lap. John held her close for a tender moment then frowned. "Sara, it doesn't make sense. Tesla can only change what happens from 1913 on..."

"So ask him what happened, next time you talk to him. Unless you think it will be too upsetting."

"Maybe," John replied. "I don't want him to stop talking to me."

"Yah, I get it. It's a mystery, all right. Or as your grandmother would say, 'Ah, Sweet Mystery of Life'!"

∞

John used his key and entered his grandmother's house.

He found Ruth sitting in the living room, reading a book.

John glanced at it; it was a biography of Jeanette MacDonald and Nelson Eddy, her two favorite singers from the Golden Age of Hollywood. John had bought it for her as a birthday gift and from the happy look on her face, she was obviously enjoying it.

He gave her a welcoming hug.

"*Sweethearts*... and they were in real life?" he asked.

"Yes. As a child watching their movies, I always thought they loved each other off screen. Even though they married others, your mom and dad agreed with me. There was something special there between those two, it wasn't just acting. And now this book documents the truth. We were right all along."

"I'm glad, Grandma."

She nodded. "Sometimes, if you live long enough, the correct history is revealed when there's no longer a reason to cover it up. Come on, let's get dinner ready."

John followed her into the kitchen and helped her set the food on the table. "I get it. The world was different then, the studio system ruled over their stars. Mr. Tesla was alive then too, when you were a kid."

John leaned back in his chair, his eyes distant as he tried to imagine the world in which his grandmother had grown up.

Ruth nodded, a wistful smile playing on her lips. "It was a different time, indeed. Hollywood was a dream factory, and Tesla... well, he was a genius ahead of his time." She paused as a thought occurred to her. "Speaking of Tesla, I wanted to ask you, did you ever figure out that radio?"

John's eyes lit up and he sat up straighter. "That's actually why I came over tonight. I wanted to tell you about it." He took a deep breath, knowing what he was about to say would sound incredible.

He retrieved from a thin briefcase he'd brought with him, two large heavyweight plastic sheet protectors containing the letters his grandfather and Tesla wrote. Ruth watched as John carefully placed them on the table in front of her.

"Grandma, you need to read these." He pointed to Henry's letter. "This one first."

Ruth picked it up, curiosity washing over her. She put on her reading glasses and silently read her husband's writing. When she finished, she took a moment to digest it and then, saying nothing to John, began reading Tesla's letter. Halfway through that one she gasped, her right hand placed on her chest, as she exclaimed,

"Oh heavens!"

"I spoke to him, Grandma!"

"In 1913?"

"Yes."

"Your grandfather and I weren't even born." Ruth removed her glasses and looked dazed.

"I know it sounds crazy. I didn't believe it at first either. But it's true. Tesla wants me to research what happened to some of his inventions. That way, he knows whether to destroy the documentation or make it available for posterity."

Ruth's brow furrowed. "John, I'm worried."

"No need to be, Grandma."

"I know I should trust Tesla. He's all your grandfather ever talked about, and I trusted your grandfather with all my heart. But still..."

"Grandma, this is an opportunity of a lifetime to help the greatest mind that ever lived. What can go wrong?"

By now Ruth was flushed with worry. "Everything!"

John took hold of Ruth's hand and explained in detail how he had managed to get the radio working, describing the strange frequencies he discovered, the first time he heard Tesla's voice crackling through the speaker, and the confusion Tesla experienced on their first communication.

This caused Ruth to briefly laugh. And as John continued, Ruth's expression gradually shifted from concern to curiosity. She listened intently, asking questions about the technical aspects of the radio and the nature of John's conversations with Tesla.

"So you're saying that Tesla is using you as a... what, a future informant?" Ruth asked, her tone less concerned now.

John nodded eagerly. "Exactly! He's trying to make the best decisions about his work based on what I can tell him about the future." They sat in silence for a moment, the gravity of the situation settling over them.

Finally, Ruth spoke again. "If you read anything about Tesla, you know there were several inventions he mentioned in his writings, and yet no one has found his research on them. Historians wonder why he discontinued work on them. Maybe what he's asking of you has already happened and the reason those inventions vanished."

John nodded slowly as he considered the implications. "It's fascinating, Grandma. Truly. If this is indeed true... then... all of this becomes a loop, doesn't it?"

"That's an interesting point, dear. I hadn't considered that." Ruth took a moment to consider it. "I wonder... if Tesla would agree to save your parents from the car accident that took them from us. He could tell Henry in 1942 about the date and time of the accident in the future."

John slowly shook his head. "I thought of asking Mr. Tesla that very question. But after he explained things to me about causing a paradox, I knew it wasn't possible. I told him on what day and year he would die and his reaction to that was to still die on that date but in a way of his choosing."

"I guess you're right," said Ruth, wiping a stray tear from her eye. "I know a thing or two about a paradox. You know, *Star Trek* was your grandfather's favorite TV series. They were always playing with time travel and parallel universes. "The Tholian Web" was his favorite episode. It's funny how yesterday's sci-fi becomes today's reality."

John nodded. "I can't tell anyone about this. Sara knows, that's all. Mr. Tesla asked me not to, maybe to protect me, I don't know. But that's another reason I wanted to tell you, since you're a part of this. You're the heroine who saved the Time Radio all these years. But please don't mention this to anyone else."

Ruth reached across the table and squeezed John's hand. "I won't, John. We're partners in crime, aren't we?" Her expression grew more serious. "And you be careful too."

"I will," John assured her.

He set down his fork, having cleaned his plate. A mischievous grin spread across his face. "And now, can I have a large piece of that strawberry rhubarb pie you baked?"

Ruth laughed, the sound warm and comforting. "Of course, my dear. After all, time travelers need their strength." She chuckled and added, "It seems Shakespeare was right."

"What do you mean?"

"Hamlet. *There are more things in Heaven and Earth, Horatio, than are dreamt of in your philosophy.*"

"Ain't it the truth, Grandma!"

They both laughed as she cut him a generous slice of pie. Her mind whirled with the implications of what John had told her. Part of her still couldn't quite believe it. But as they sat there, enjoying their dessert and each other's company, both of them felt the weight of the secret they now shared.

∞

FBI Headquarters, Washington D.C. — August 2024

The summer heat reached its zenith on this sweltering August afternoon, the air heavy as if weighted by the very secrets that permeated the halls of the J. Edgar Hoover Building. As the glass doors slid open with a soft hiss, a blast of artificially chilled air washed over Alan Xavier, offering momentary relief from the punishing temperatures outside.

At fifty-four years old, Xavier was a seasoned veteran of the Federal Bureau of Investigation and recently promoted to deputy director of the Bureau.

His two decades of service etched into the stern lines of his face and the steely glint in his eyes. Standing at an impressive six-foot-one, with an athletic build, he had a formidable physical presence. He commanded respect and as he strode through the lobby and made his way towards the elevators, heads turned and conversations hushed. Junior agents straightened their postures, senior staff offered respectful nods, and security personnel snapped to attention. Xavier acknowledged them with curt nods.

Most of his day passed, uneventful. The Deputy Director stretched in his chair, his joints protesting after hours of poring over reports and surveillance briefings. He glanced at his watch — 3:39 p.m. — and decided it was time for a very late lunch.

Xavier rose slowly from his desk, his hand already reaching for his suit jacket draped over the back of his chair. He was halfway to the door when the shrill, insistent ring of his secure line shattered the room.

For a moment, Xavier froze, his hand suspended in mid-air. That phone rarely rang, and when it did, it was never something good. With a resigned sigh, he turned back to his desk, the promise of pastrami on rye and a tall glass of bitter lemonade fading as quickly as it had come.

With a resigned sigh, he turned back to his desk. He lowered himself back into his chair and answered the phone.

The voice on the other end spoke rapidly and urgently. Xavier's expression shifted from mild curiosity to intense focus as he listened, his free hand hovering over his keyboard.

"Yes... hold on..."

His fingers flew across the keys, navigating through layers of classified databases. Suddenly, he encountered an unexpected barrier, causing him to lean in closer to his monitor.

"This is a locked Hoover file," he said to the caller. "Do we have this key it's asking for?"

The voice on the other end rattled off a series of numbers. Xavier's fingers danced across the keyboard, typing the sixteen-digit key with practiced precision. For a moment, nothing happened. And then, the screen flickered and Xavier's eyes widened.

"I'm in!" he exclaimed.

A labyrinth of folders flooded his screen. The parent folder's name caught his eye; it was labeled 'Nikola Tesla'.

"What am I looking for here?" asked Xavier.

The person on the other end of the phone read the sub-folder name to him. Xavier found it, titled 'Queens Seagull to Manhattan Dove'. He opened the folder to find hundreds of files inside but one file stood apart from the rest: it was labeled in red color 'Atwater 1913'.

When Xavier opened this one, he found dozens of documents and a photo of Walter Atwater, likely taken shortly after his encounter in Central Park with the talking oak tree and his encounter with Nikola Tesla.

Part Nine

37

A Truth Revealed

Central Park, New York — October 1889

Tesla sat on a park bench, as was his habit during his years in New York City. As always, he found a strange peace there, sitting in the quietness and beauty of this oasis.

On this occasion, he silently read a letter from Anya. She was still living in Paris, and the two corresponded by letter. Reading her words usually brought Tesla pleasure, but on this day, it was the exact opposite.

He slowly read the letter aloud:

My darling Nikola, I regret any pain I caused you and hope you find it in your heart to forgive me. Yes, I want to join you in New York, and I know that is also your wish.

I have fulfilled all my life desires here in Paris except for one, to meet President Carnot and have him choose one of my paintings to hang in the Louvre. This is my dream as an artist, but strangely it means little if I cannot be with you.

My love, do you think it possible to come here to help me? I have been ill, not to worry, but with your assistance perhaps my strength will return.

Tesla set the letter down and after a few minutes of reflection, he picked it up again and returned to his hotel to answer it.

∞

Paris, France — December 1889

A respiratory viral epidemic, identified as a coronavirus, had broken out in Russia earlier in the year, in May. Over the next many months, it swiftly traveled worldwide. With its ebbs and flows over the following years, the epidemic finally ended in early 1895. About one million people had died in a world population of 1.5 billion.

By November 1889, the pandemic had spread through Sweden, Norway, Denmark, Germany, and Austria. In December it spread to Italy, France, Spain, and the United Kingdom; and by the end of the year, it attacked the United States. This would come to be known as the last great pandemic of the nineteenth century, and one of the deadliest pandemics in history.

Anya Ivanov was one of the victims. She fell ill in Paris, was hospitalized and struggling to recover when she received Tesla's written reply.

A sympathetic nurse handed the letter to Anya and, feverish and deteriorating in her bed, she eagerly read it.

Dear Anya, it is I who must beg your forgiveness for my harsh display of disappointment. But now my heart is filled with joy, and I impatiently await your arrival. Much has happened, misfortune has befallen me, so it is not possible for me to travel to you this month. My workload is heavy.

Remember, for a time I was digging ditches, hard but honest work and allowed me to plan my next step, to find a new sponsor and open my own electric company. As you know, a kindly gentleman, George Westinghouse, came to my rescue. I am doing better and have moved into an elegant hotel.

My sponsor is generously covering the expense for that; but unfortunately, my current income does not allow me to take a leave from work.

At the moment, my thoughts are leaning towards next year as a viable option. Meanwhile, you must recover your health and come instead, so we need not wait to be together. I can take care of you and help you get well again.

You will live with me and create your art. To have you at my side will make my heart complete. I will care for you and support you for the rest of my life, my darling girl. I count the hours until I hold you again in my arms.

Anya read and reread Tesla's lengthy letter. She was lost in her thoughts until the kindly nurse spoke up.

"Would you like me to get you paper and pen, so you can answer this letter? I will be happy to send it off for you."

"Yes, please," Anya whispered. "Actually, perhaps a telegram would better serve."

She dictated to the nurse:

Again, my trip was delayed. Dearest, hurry, I need you. I am certain that your presence would help me recover. Please advise if your schedule would allow it.

In the coming days, Anya focused on trying to regain her strength and for a short time, her determination seemed to be conquering her illness. She felt a burst of strength and clarity of mind. When Tesla's return telegram arrived promptly, she eagerly snatched it from the nurse and read it.

My darling Anya, I will examine all options and endeavor to make the trip.

∞

Central Park, New York City - one month later

The park was awash in the golden hues of late afternoon, its tranquil beauty a stark contrast to the turmoil in Nikola Tesla's heart. He found

Paris, France — December 1889

A respiratory viral epidemic, identified as a coronavirus, had broken out in Russia earlier in the year, in May. Over the next many months, it swiftly traveled worldwide. With its ebbs and flows over the following years, the epidemic finally ended in early 1895. About one million people had died in a world population of 1.5 billion.

By November 1889, the pandemic had spread through Sweden, Norway, Denmark, Germany, and Austria. In December it spread to Italy, France, Spain, and the United Kingdom; and by the end of the year, it attacked the United States. This would come to be known as the last great pandemic of the nineteenth century, and one of the deadliest pandemics in history.

Anya Ivanov was one of the victims. She fell ill in Paris, was hospitalized and struggling to recover when she received Tesla's written reply.

A sympathetic nurse handed the letter to Anya and, feverish and deteriorating in her bed, she eagerly read it.

Dear Anya, it is I who must beg your forgiveness for my harsh display of disappointment. But now my heart is filled with joy, and I impatiently await your arrival. Much has happened, misfortune has befallen me, so it is not possible for me to travel to you this month. My workload is heavy.

Remember, for a time I was digging ditches, hard but honest work and allowed me to plan my next step, to find a new sponsor and open my own electric company. As you know, a kindly gentleman, George Westinghouse, came to my rescue. I am doing better and have moved into an elegant hotel.

My sponsor is generously covering the expense for that; but unfortunately, my current income does not allow me to take a leave from work.

At the moment, my thoughts are leaning towards next year as a viable option. Meanwhile, you must recover your health and come instead, so we need not wait to be together. I can take care of you and help you get well again.

You will live with me and create your art. To have you at my side will make my heart complete. I will care for you and support you for the rest of my life, my darling girl. I count the hours until I hold you again in my arms.

Anya read and reread Tesla's lengthy letter. She was lost in her thoughts until the kindly nurse spoke up.

"Would you like me to get you paper and pen, so you can answer this letter? I will be happy to send it off for you."

"Yes, please," Anya whispered. "Actually, perhaps a telegram would better serve."

She dictated to the nurse:

Again, my trip was delayed. Dearest, hurry, I need you. I am certain that your presence would help me recover. Please advise if your schedule would allow it.

In the coming days, Anya focused on trying to regain her strength and for a short time, her determination seemed to be conquering her illness. She felt a burst of strength and clarity of mind. When Tesla's return telegram arrived promptly, she eagerly snatched it from the nurse and read it.

My darling Anya, I will examine all options and endeavor to make the trip.

∞

Central Park, New York City - one month later

The park was awash in the golden hues of late afternoon, its tranquil beauty a stark contrast to the turmoil in Nikola Tesla's heart. He found

Part Nine

37

A Truth Revealed

Central Park, New York — October 1889

Tesla sat on a park bench, as was his habit during his years in New York City. As always, he found a strange peace there, sitting in the quietness and beauty of this oasis.

On this occasion, he silently read a letter from Anya. She was still living in Paris, and the two corresponded by letter. Reading her words usually brought Tesla pleasure, but on this day, it was the exact opposite.

He slowly read the letter aloud:

My darling Nikola, I regret any pain I caused you and hope you find it in your heart to forgive me. Yes, I want to join you in New York, and I know that is also your wish.

I have fulfilled all my life desires here in Paris except for one, to meet President Carnot and have him choose one of my paintings to hang in the Louvre. This is my dream as an artist, but strangely it means little if I cannot be with you.

My love, do you think it possible to come here to help me? I have been ill, not to worry, but with your assistance perhaps my strength will return.

Tesla set the letter down and after a few minutes of reflection, he picked it up again and returned to his hotel to answer it.

of awareness. The park grew quiet, the chirping of evening birds replacing the chatter of afternoon visitors.

It took every ounce of strength Tesla possessed to force himself to his feet. His legs felt like lead as he stumbled back toward the hotel, his mind still reeling from the devastating news. Was it even real?

Once back in his hotel room, he took to his bed. Curled up in a fetal position, he rocked himself endlessly and finally cried. His sobs echoed off the hotel room walls, each cry feeling like it was being torn from his very soul. The taste of salt on his lips, the burning in his chest, the way his fingers clutched at the bed sheets until his knuckles turned white — every sensation amplified by grief. His mind, usually so ordered and precise, had fractured like a dropped mirror, each shard reflecting a different memory of Anya.

She had begged him to come to her, but he had not done so.

He was to blame for her death. Guilt churned away at his mind and stomach until he feared he might vomit.

If this was true, she was... Dead — before his return to Paris and before he witnessed her painting being unveiled at the Louvre in the presence of the French President and Serbian King. She was dead when he was summoned to his mother's deathbed. Dead — when he spent those three dreamy days in Belgrade with her. Her love and laughter had carved itself into his bones. That laughter had become part of his skeletal architecture, as fundamental as marrow, as necessary as calcium, structuring the very framework of who he was. Those three days had crystallized in his memory like amber, preserving a moment of perfect happiness now fossilized by grief.

She was dead.

Dead.

The truth of it hammered through his skull with each heartbeat, each breath, each second that stretched into infinity. She was a ghost — nothing more than vapor and memory wearing borrowed flesh. A beautiful lie that had infiltrated every corner of his world, threading itself through the tapestry of his days with such exquisite precision he could no longer unpick the truth from the deceit. The lines had blurred, smeared like watercolors in the rain, until his entire existence felt like a masterpiece painted. He never suspected that she was dead until now.

He heard himself scream and as he rocked in agony, he moaned a desperate mantra. "Anya," he whispered, her name a prayer and a lament. "Anya, Anya, Anya." He clung to the sound, as if by repeating it often enough, he could somehow summon her back from the abyss that had claimed her.

Out of sheer weariness, he finally quieted down and lay staring at the ceiling. He understood that no amount of wishing or pleading could change the cruel hand that fate had dealt. Anya was gone, and with her a piece of his heart that he feared he might never recover.

For the next couple of days, he refused all food or drink. He continually berated himself; could he have saved her if he had rushed across the Atlantic Ocean?

Tesla finally dragged his weary body up and sat at his desk, unshaven, clearly exhausted, wiping away tears from his red-rimmed eyes.

The rescued large light bulb from his old laboratory sat on his desk. He eyed it for a moment; it was just another reminder of his burned down laboratory and his failures in life. For all the work triumphs he enjoyed, such moments of devastation tore away at his pride and self-esteem. A deep depression gripped him, and he felt both worthless and useless.

He rested his weary head on his folded arms, wondering how he could pull himself out of his pain, and whether it was even worth the effort. At some point, his energy exhausted, he acknowledged to himself that he'd himself perched on the edge of his favorite bench, its weathered wood cool beneath his trembling fingers.

The lush canopy of trees above him swayed gently in the breeze, casting dancing shadows across the manicured lawn.

Tesla's eyes darted nervously from one passerby to another, his mind hardly registering their carefree laughter and animated conversations. He had been waiting for what felt like an eternity, his stomach churning with a mixture of hope and dread. The weight of anticipation pressed down upon him, making each breath a conscious effort.

When the news of a fresh telegram had reached him, Tesla instinctively reacted with fear. Instead of having it delivered to the sanctuary of his room, he had made his way down to the hotel's opulent front desk. The marble floors echoed his unsteady footsteps as he approached the concierge, his voice low as he requested the telegram be placed in an envelope.

Without uttering another word, Tesla had taken the sealed envelope and fled the suffocating confines of the hotel. He had sought refuge in the park, as if somehow the beauty of his surroundings could soften the blow of whatever news awaited him.

For a brief moment, his mind flashed back to his childhood, seeing his older brother Dane mounting his horse and starting to ride off. That moment of his premonition of what was about to happen... and his agony at not being able to stop it.

Under normal circumstances, Tesla was proud of his telepathic abilities, but today, right now, sitting on his park bench, a sudden terror seized him.

Now, as the sun began its slow descent towards the horizon, Tesla still found himself unable to muster the courage to break the seal. His fingers trembled as he finally tore open the envelope and unfolded the paper, the crisp edges cutting into his skin. The words seemed to dance before his eyes, refusing to stay still:

We regret... inform you... death... Anya Ivanov...

The letters blurred and swam, melting into incomprehensible shapes. Tesla blinked hard, trying to force his eyes to focus.

...hospital... influenza... lovely, courageous young woman... fought hard...

A ringing filled his ears, drowning out the peaceful sounds of the park. His chest constricted, each breath becoming a desperate struggle. The paper shook violently in his hands, the words fragmenting, scattering like broken glass across his vision.

Death... Anya... death...

No. This couldn't be right. He needed to read it again, to make sense of these swimming letters that refused to form coherent thoughts. But before he could grasp their meaning, a sudden gust of wind tore the telegram from his trembling fingers. He watched, paralyzed, as the paper danced away on the breeze, disappearing out of sight into the golden afternoon light.

What had it said? The words were already fading from his mind. Surely he had misread it. Anya was ill, yes, but she would recover. She had to recover. The alternative was... unthinkable.

His body felt disconnected. The world tilted sideways, colors bleeding into one another. The familiar park transformed into an alien landscape, distorted by the tears he refused to acknowledge. His throat burned with unvoiced screams, while his mind frantically scrambled to reject what he had read — or thought he had read. Had he really seen those words? Without the telegram in his hands, it all seemed like a terrible dream.

He tried to stand, to run, to escape the crushing weight of his grief, but his legs refused to obey. A darkness crept in from the edges of his vision, threatening to engulf him. Time lost all meaning as he drifted in and out suffered a breakdown and that somehow, he had to snap himself out of it and carry on. But just now he didn't seem to care whether they hauled him away, locked him up in an asylum and threw away the key.

Soon after this, he suffered his first bout of amnesia. His memory regarding work remained unaffected. His memory, in terms of his private life, somehow vanished. The pain of Anya's death was too much for his mind to confront. It would be a long time before he could come to grips with it.

∞

She lived on in his mind, his memories. In low moments, he desperately needed to speak to her, needed to discuss his work with her, needed to love her.

He tried to sublimate his needs elsewhere, even becoming emotionally attached to a few of the many pigeons he fed and cared for. One in particular reminded him of a pigeon Anya had spoken to all those years ago at Parc Monceau. He remembered how they had interacted, with an understanding, a special communication between Anya and the bird. Now he had his own experience, which made him wonder whether Anya's spirit had inhabited this special bird now reaching out to him.

In a heartbreaking reveal, he surprisingly shared the following with two close friends:

I have been feeding pigeons, thousands of them, for years. But there was one, a beautiful bird, pure white with light gray tips on its wings; that one was different. It was a female. I had only to wish and call her and she would come flying to me. I loved that pigeon as a man loves a woman, and she loved me. As long as I had her, there was a purpose to my life.

∞

It was not enough.

Whether the spirit of Anya returned and inhabited that bird, he needed and wanted her back in his life in a more tangible way.

In his fantasies, he envisioned her coming back to him, to have her by his side again, never to leave him.

So it was no surprise when one day, the soft chime of the doorbell pierced the heavy silence of Tesla's suite, startling him. For a moment, he remained motionless, his weary eyes fixed on the ceiling above.

He shuffled towards the door, each step a monumental effort. As he reached for the handle, a fleeting thought crossed his mind — perhaps it was all a mistake, perhaps Anya was alive.

He shook his head, banishing the foolish hope. He had read the telegram, felt the crushing weight of its words. There was no mistaking the finality of death.

Tesla opened the door, his eyes downcast, bracing himself for whatever awaited him on the other side.

And there she stood.

Anya, radiant and alive, a small suitcase clutched in her delicate hand. Her lips curved into that familiar smile that had haunted his dreams and waking moments.

Tesla blinked once, twice, certain that his mind was playing a cruel trick on him. He stood frozen, unable to comprehend the sight before him. Was this a hallucination born of grief and desperation? Had he finally succumbed to the madness that had always lurked at the edges of his brilliant mind?

"Niko?" Anya's voice, soft and melodious, cut through the fog of his disbelief. "May I come in?"

Wordlessly, Tesla reached out and took the suitcase from her hand, setting it down with trembling fingers. Then, as if pulled by an irresistible force, he drew her into his arms.

"My love," he sobbed, his entire body shaking with the force of his emotion. "You have come at last."

He held her close, breathing in the familiar scent of her hair, feeling the warmth of her body against his. If this was insanity, he decided, then he would gladly surrender to it.

"I am in disbelief to see you here," Tesla whispered, his voice thick with emotion. "Like an angel come to my rescue. Can this truly be real?"

Anya's arms tightened around him, her voice soothing as she murmured, "Darling, I shall never be apart from you again. I'm here, I'm real."

Tesla pulled back, his eyes searching her face, drinking in every detail.

"Last night, I dreamed of you," he confessed. "It felt just as it does now, so vivid, so real."

A soft smile played on Anya's lips. "Dreams do come true, my love."

"Am I dreaming now?"

∞

He had taken her into his bedroom and indulged in the sexual fantasies he so needed. At last emotionally and physically sated, and as sleep began to claim him, Tesla's rational mind made one last attempt to assert itself.

Was this real? Could he trust his senses, his experiences? But as he looked down at Anya, her face serene in sleep, he made a conscious decision.

Real or not, this was what his heart needed. This was the balm to soothe his wounded soul. And if it was a delusion, it was one he would gladly embrace for the rest of his days.

From that moment on, Tesla remained committed to his promise. Whether Anya was a miracle, a figment of his imagination, a ghost or something in between, she became his anchor, his muse, his reason for being.

In his mind and heart, she was not dead.

And in her presence, real or imagined, he found the strength to continue his work, to push the boundaries of science and imagination.

Until his last breath, Nikola Tesla held onto this reality he had chosen, finding in it the peace and love he had always sought. In his own private world, he found he could, at choice, be a "normal" man; free of fears, phobias, compulsions, and the choking responsibility of trying to save the world.

In his mind, it all made perfect sense and helped him keep his sanity for the rest of his life.

38

THE FUTURE REVISED

Queens, New York — August 2024

Tesla and John Watt were speaking again via the Time Radio. John was pleased with himself at how much he had learned about Tesla's work and history since their last conversation.

Sara was again at his side, and she had brought them sandwiches and drinks. She ate and listened as the two men talked.

Tesla was asking, "Did they use my work on wireless transmission of electric energy?"

"Yes," said John excitedly. Then paused and continued again... "But not to power cities or anything very big but instead small devices, mostly wireless phones."

"Hmmm, they could never figure out how to charge fees for it, even after so many years," Tesla said with notable disappointment in his voice.

"Also, you should know that you invented something you called a Death Ray and since then it has advanced considerably by America and Russia," John interjected.

"And I gave it such a diabolical name?" asked Tesla.

"Well, it is kind of diabolical. It's a weapon. But a good weapon if there is such a thing."

"Please explain!?"

"Mr. Tesla, you designed a defensive weapon that could knock thousands of enemy planes out of the air all at once; for that matter, knock anything airborne out of the air. Unfortunately including birds but in the greater interest of world peace.

"And then there is the earthquake machine that could split the planet in half. You probably shouldn't invent that one."

Tesla reacted with dismay. "I am to be a mass bird killer and the one who split the planet in half!? This is precisely why I created this radio, to stop myself from inventing such insanity."

John chuckled. "Actually, sir, Colonel Sanders is the mass bird killer. Your Death Ray is a good thing, and future scientists figured out how to spare the birds. And they don't call it the Death Ray anymore."

"I should have named it the Peace Ray," Tesla commented, "because all I ever hoped to achieve is peace on earth."

"Well, it's called Star Wars now. And it's purely a defensive weapon, we have it and so do the Russians. Maybe the Chinese too. But the Germans don't have it, and they haven't caused anymore wars after Hitler."

"Who is Colonel Sanders?"

John laughed, "He invented Kentucky Fried Chicken fast food. But aside from killing so many chickens, he's also indirectly responsible for killing many humans due to cholesterol."

"A culinary madman, there's that too, then?"

"I'm afraid so," John quietly laughed.

"World War II, what was the outcome?"

"Hitler killed himself. Germany surrendered, so did the Japanese. And more or less, the world after that had two superpowers, the U.S. and the Russians."

"And I am surely the reason for the birth of these superpowers?"

"Actually sir, a man called Oppenheimer is responsible, well not exactly him alone, there were others involved too. They created the nuclear bomb for our side and used it on Japan, a terrible bomb capable of wiping out entire cities. For those who didn't die in the blast, they would die of disease later."

"Good God!" Tesla gasped.

John continued, "A couple of years after its first use the Russians developed their own version – just as deadly, maybe even worse, but to this day they have not used this weapon. It's probably the reason there isn't a third World War. If there were another one, it would for sure be mutual destruction of both America and Russia and most of the world."

"My God, what was this man Oppenheimer thinking!" Tesla said, flabbergasted.

"There was a movie about him recently. An excellent one, actually. Oppenheimer was a decent man and he later spoke out against using such weapons. But the thinking of the good guys back then was this: if the enemy is developing such weapons and killing masses of innocent people, you have to be able to respond in kind, to put a stop at it as quickly as possible."

"That is always the dilemma," agreed Tesla.

"They say that the last fifteen years or so of your life, you did very little work of importance. Is that because of our conversations now, in that you understand the future implications of your inventions? So that you can undo whatever could prove dangerous?"

Tesla chuckled. "This is hard to know, since it hasn't happened yet. But yes, I imagine in my old age they will think me a doddering fool, while in reality I shall strive to preserve and hide such work. It may yet prove invaluable to those with honorable intentions in your century. Assuming, of course, that people do learn from historical mistakes."

"I'm afraid that's not always true," John admitted. "Every few generations, for example, a group of people rise up, proudly identifying themselves as Nazis. We're going through that right now, in fact."

At Tesla's silence, John quickly changed the grim subject.

"The good news is that as best as I can figure, sir, more than 40% of your patents have been used to better mankind."

"I am glad some of my work proved valuable. But what of the other 60%?"

"Oh, some have never been further developed after your patent filings, and others have been used in combinations of other people's patents to develop questionable things, but nothing as horrible as the nuclear bomb."

"I am pleased to hear this, John. I was afraid that future generations would remember me as a madman responsible for humanity's many evil deeds."

"Are you kidding?" John looked at Sara and they both laughed.

"In today's world you are a superhero! Like Batman and Superman! They were around in your day, in DC comic books. Well, they will be, in the late 1930s."

"I am not familiar with comic books. John, is that your young lady I hear?"

"Yes, it's my girlfriend Sara."

"Hello, Mr. Tesla," Sara called out. "It's a pleasure to meet you."

"The honor is mine, Miss Sara."

"One thing you should know, Mr. Tesla," John said cheerfully. "You know how Marconi screwed you over, taking full credit for inventing the radio?"

"I prefer not to dwell on that subject," Tesla replied.

"I intend to sue him for patent infringement."

"And eventually you'll win, sir. First in the Court of Claims but later on, in the United States Supreme Court. They rule that Marconi's most important patent was invalid, acknowledging your earlier and more significant contribution as the inventor of radio technology."

"I suppose that is some consolation," Tesla said dryly. "When does this happen?"

"The Supreme Court? A few months after your death. I wanted you to know because, at least now you finally have the credit you deserve."

"Good to know, I suppose."

"Getting back to your inventions that we use today... Electric cars, energy sources, disposable razors, microwave, radio, smart phones, sonar, spark plugs, robots, lasers, ozone therapy, microscopic surgery, ultrasound, Wi-Fi, Star Wars Defense System. And social media, you know, like Twitter and Facebook."

"Facebook, Twitter?" Tesla seemed puzzled.

"Like broadcasting your thoughts to the masses," John explained. "Well maybe not the masses, depends on how many people are following you. Elon Musk, the man I told you about before, he bought Twitter and renamed it "X". But most people still call it Twitter."

"This social media, does it help humanity?"

John gave a hearty laugh. "Jury's still out on that. But yes, I think so." He hesitated and then asked, "Mr. Tesla, you've invented so many things for health and healing. Is that because of... your friend you mentioned before?"

Silence. John shot a worried glance at Sara then quickly said, "I don't mean to upset you, Mr. Tesla, I just wondered. Another thing, I am curious, are you an atheist?"

"No. An atheist believes in nothing. I believe in a higher power, however not in the traditional sense of organized religion. This Twitter you mentioned. Surely people are not—"

John interrupted him. "Yes, they are tweeting."

"We have become like birds?"

"Yeah, sort of, I guess. We text our thoughts out loudly so others can read it. Like your Thought Camera..."

"Outstanding! Just last month I began work on the Thought Camera. And yesterday, I had doubts about its feasibility and was considering terminating further research."

"You won't terminate it, because it's alive and well today." And then John had a burning thought. "But sir, had I not told you this just now, would Facebook and Twitter be alive today?"

"In all probability they would."

"How?"

"Someone other than me would have initiated its first development. What's interesting is I believe the timeline would still be the same even though the originating source is different."

Tesla fell silent...

"Mr. Tesla, are you there?"

"Yes, yes young man. Just absorbing what you've told me and what my next move must be. Thank you."

∞

The sun-drenched streets of John's muted suburban neighborhood buzzed with an undercurrent of tension, unnoticed by John and Sara as they remained engrossed in their conversation with Tesla. Outside their modest five-story apartment building, an unprecedented scene was unfolding.

A convoy of sleek, black government vehicles materialized with practiced precision. The fleet was comprised of ten Chevrolet Suburban SUVs and four Ford Taurus sedans, their tinted windows concealing the occupants within. At the center of this dark assemblage sat the crown jewel of the FBI's mobile operations: a state-of-the-art Tactical Command Vehicle (TCV).

The TCV, a behemoth of technology disguised as an innocuous semi-truck, housed the most sophisticated mobile communication monitoring center in the world. Its exterior, a nondescript gray, belied the cutting-edge equipment that filled its interior.

Inside the climate-controlled confines of the TCV, seven operators from the FBI's Special Technologies and Applications Section (STAS) hunched over banks of monitors, their fingers flying across keyboards. The air hummed with the low whir of powerful servers and the urgent murmur of voices.

Special Agent Gregory Selinger, a veteran of countless high-stakes operations, stood at the center of this digital nerve center. His steely gaze swept over his team, each member handpicked for their expertise in fields ranging from quantum computing to electromagnetic field analysis.

"Status report," Selinger barked, his voice cutting through the ambient noise.

Agent Yates, the team's signals intelligence specialist, responded without taking his eyes off his screen. "Sir, we're picking up unusual EM readings. They're unlike anything in our database."

"Triangulation?" Selinger pressed, moving to peer over Yates's shoulder.

"In progress," Agent Chen, the geospatial analyst, chimed in. "The signal's erratic, but we're narrowing it down."

Selinger nodded then tapped his secure comm link. "Sierra Actual to all units. Maintain position. No one moves without my order."

A chorus of affirmatives crackled over the comm system.

Outside, curious neighborhood children on bicycles gathered at a safe distance, their young eyes wide with excitement at the unusual spectacle.

The FBI agents in the surrounding vehicles remained stoic, their hands never far from their concealed weapons.

Back in the TCV, the tension ratcheted up as Agent Ramirez, the quantum mechanics expert, called out, "Sir, we're detecting a spike in tachyon particles! This shouldn't be possible with current technology!"

Selinger narrowed his eyes and a subtle smile appeared on his lips. "Cross-reference with Project Atwater 1913."

"Checking now, sir," Ramirez replied, his fingers a blur on the keyboard.

Suddenly, Agent Chen's voice cut through the controlled chaos. "Got it! Signal source located!"

Selinger leaned in, his heart rate quickening despite years of field experience. "Where?"

Chen's finger stabbed at his monitor. "Sixty-nine yards, north-northeast. It's coming from that building, sir."

All eyes in the TCV turned to the monitor displaying a real-time satellite image of the neighborhood. At its center, a pulsing red dot marked their target: John and Sara's unsuspecting building.

Selinger straightened, his mind racing through protocols and contingencies. This was no ordinary operation. Whatever was happening inside that building had the potential to rewrite the laws of physics — and possibly history itself. The immediate problem now was which apartment in the building. There were five floors with three apartments per floor.

If they stormed them all systematically the element of surprise would be lost. But those present on the street were already stirring too much attention anyway, so surprise was not on their side in any scenario.

He keyed his comm once more. "Sierra Actual to all units. Target confirmed. Prepare for breach on my mark. All apartments. Non-lethal tactics only. I repeat non-lethal tactics only!"

As acknowledgments flooded in, Selinger turned to his team. "Gentlemen, whatever's in that building, it's our job to secure it. Let's make it count."

With a final nod to his team, Selinger moved towards the TCV's exit, ready to lead the operation that would today change the lives of John, Sara, and even Tesla in 1913.

Meanwhile, back in John's apartment, John was explaining to Tesla, "There is a lot of theory that some Nazi called Otto Skorzeny killed you, but nothing was ever proved and the official cause of death by the coroner was natural causes."

"Nazi?"

"Yes, Hitler's followers; he was head of the Nazi party. But honestly, Mr. Tesla, the more I read up on this theory the more I believe it. In your day natural causes could be faked easily to make it appear like your heart just gave out. January 7th, 1943. You can prevent it, sir, you have the date now."

Tesla disagreed. "My death must happen on that date. But with what I know now, I can choose how to die which would not cause a paradox."

John shot a glance at Sara. "Oh man, if I knew the exact date I was going to die and how I–"

Tesla interrupted him. "John! Let's move on to something else."

"Okay. They said you believe in aliens."

"I do, there have been sightings and documentation to suggest earlier civilizations visited here. Have events in your time born that out?"

John replied, "Many more people believe it now. We have space travel, but NASA would never have come about without your research and a bunch of ex-Nazis. And of course there's Area 51."

"They have found evidence of life elsewhere?"

"At least conditions that support life, yes. But no Martian invasion yet like in *The War of the Worlds*."

"It has always been my belief that this information was suppressed by governments," said Tesla.

"There's something I want to ask you, Mr. Tesla, but before that, your views on life and death?"

"When I was younger, I thought the soul died at death but now I—"

Suddenly a thunderous crash from the hallway cut him off mid-sentence. The sound of splintering wood and shouted commands drowned out the gentle hum of the radio.

Both John and Sara jolted upright. Tesla's voice on the radio abruptly fell silent. John leaped to his feet, his heart hammering against his ribs like a trapped bird.

"What the hell?" he hissed, eyes darting frantically towards the door.

Sara scrambled behind him, her trembling fingers digging into his shoulders. "John," she whispered, her voice quivering with fear, "What's happening?" Her eyes were wide with terror.

The commotion in the hallway echoed loudly. Gruff voices barked orders, punctuated by the ominous metallic clicks of weapons being readied. John's mind whirled, grasping for an explanation. Was this the police? The FBI? Were his neighbors being arrested, or were they here for him and just broke into the wrong apartment?

His eyes frantically searched for an exit, but there was no escape. They were on the third floor, too high to jump from the window. The only other option was the front door.

"FBI! Open up, now!" a commanding voice boomed from the other side of John's door.

"Oh God!" John gasped, as he finally realized they were here for them!

"What did we do?!" Sara cried out, her nails digging deeper into John's flesh.

The Time Radio crackled to life, Tesla's concerned voice cutting through the chaos.

"John? Sara? What's wrong? What's happened?"

"Mr. Tesla!" John shouted towards the radio, his voice tight with panic, "It's the FBI — the Bureau of Investigation in your time. They've found us!"

"The Bureau?" Tesla's voice rose in pitch, a mixture of confusion and alarm. "But how? John, you must protect the device at all—"

His words were drowned out by the deafening crack of the door being breached. It exploded inward in a shower of splinters and drywall dust, revealing half a dozen armed agents in dark suits and tactical gear. They entered the apartment, with nearly another dozen agents outside in the hallway.

"FBI! Hands where we can see them!" bellowed the lead agent, his weapon trained squarely on John's chest.

"Get down on the ground, now!" another agent shouted, advancing into the room with practiced efficiency. John and Sara lay down on the floor flat their hands open and spread apart.

"We're not resisting," John said, his voice surprisingly steady despite the fear coursing through him.

Several agents swarmed around John and Sara and immediately secured their hands with tactical zip ties.

"Mr. John Watt and Ms. Sara Elise Parker," a stern-faced agent in a suit announced, stepping forward with a tablet in hand. "You're under arrest for violations of the Espionage Act and unauthorized possession of classified technology.

"You have the right to remain silent," the agent continued, reciting the Miranda rights with practiced ease. "Anything you say can and will be used against you in a court of law…"

"Clear!" shouted one of the tactical officers. The tension in the apartment eased and guns were lowered.

Special Agent Selinger entered the apartment, and stared at John and Sara, his focus interrupted by Tesla's voice emanating from the Time Radio:

"John? Sara? What's happening?" Tesla's voice had a mixture of confusion and concern.

John's heart leapt. He opened his mouth to respond, but Sara beat him to it.

"Mr. Tesla!" she cried out, her voice thick with desperation. "They're arresting us! Please, you have to—"

Selinger interrupted her sentence by interjecting: "To the speaker on the radio. This is the FBI. Will you confirm that you are in fact Nikola Tesla, broadcasting from the year 1913?"

At first, no answer… just the hum of the radio… and then Tesla spoke.

"I concede no such thing, my good man."

"Speaker, identify yourself!" ordered Selinger.

"The past controls the future. I will change this outcome. I promise you, John! The future is mine!"

Selinger yanked on the power cord, releasing it from the electrical outlet. The radio powered off, emitting a high-pitched squeal. Selinger fished his mobile phone from his pocket and dialed, tension evident in his movements. After a moment, he spoke curtly into the device.

"Secured," he announced, his voice clipped.

A pause, then his tone turned defensive. "In the time we had, there was no other way." Frustration crept into Selinger's voice as the conversation continued. "Contact failed, sir." He exhaled sharply before adding, "Two in custody."

As Selinger spoke on the phone, John's mind raced. What would happen now? Had they changed the future? Or had they set in motion something far worse?

Selinger ended the call. He looked like a man who had been chewed to pieces and spit out. "Take them in," he barked to his team. "Seal the premises, create a buffer. The target stays on site, five men back, everyone else out!"

As Sara and John were roughly led from the apartment, a silent promise passed between them. This wasn't over; somehow, someway, Tesla would find a way to set things right.

39

GROUNDHOG DAY

New York City - November 18, 1942

As Tesla sat at his desk, the once inconceivable idea of the Time Radio in the hands of the FBI played relentlessly on Tesla's mind. He reached into his desk drawer and retrieved a crisp piece of parchment, then began writing a new letter to accompany the Time Radio.

Anya emerged from the bathroom, holding a sizable French hairbrush in her hand.

"It all worries me so, darling." She elegantly positioned herself into one of the comfortable armchairs, placed the brush in her lap, and poured herself a glass of water.

"And your friend Adler. How will saving his life affect the paradox of time?"

"It won't, he'll simply live awhile longer, and we will talk of days gone by. I owe him my life." Tesla stopped writing, his eyes welled up for a moment. "History owes him my life."

"Your argument is contradictory," said Anya.

"How so?"

"Adler's death is caused by 'Skorzeny' whom you will allow to later take your life. But if Adler is saved then surely Skorzeny's path does not lead him to taking your life."

Tesla nodded in agreement. "Very good. That's correct."

"I don't understand?" Anya shook her head.

"My life is meant to end January 7th, 1943," explained Tesla. "Whether it be by Skorzeny's hand or by some other way is irrelevant."

"But why!? Why then?"

"Because my father would have thought that date to be fitting-"

Anya softly interrupted him. "Of course, Christian Orthodox Christmas."

Tesla nodded. "But more importantly, if I live past the first month in 1943, that would be a paradox of time. Adler is quite right in that the Nazis would not stop until they acquired me."

An uneasy silence from Anya; then she asked the question Tesla was anticipating.

"How will it end?"

He met her gaze with a weary sadness. "Luciano will dispatch someone to administer chloroform on me while I sleep. It will induce a state of unconsciousness." He shifted his gaze to the window. "And then...suffocation. It will be swift, painless."

Anya's voice trembled. "And the contents of your safe?"

Tesla's expression softened. "The safe," he murmured, his voice thick with a somber resolve, "shall be left open. Luciano's emissary will retrieve my life's work, that which is truly important, entrusting it to the Don's own hands. From there, it will embark on a secure journey to Yugoslavia where I have already made arrangements with the King for a sanctuary untouched by the evils of men to take possession of the contents. They will hide it and guard it."

He paused, his gaze distant, as if peering into the future itself. "A monastery is like a fortress of faith. The secrets of my science will remain safe, shielded from those who would wield them for darkness."

Anya's brow furrowed in concern. "Why not simply destroy your work the night before your death?"

Tesla's eyes flashed with an unwavering conviction. "That would be a betrayal of my purpose, of my being, a halt to mankind's progress towards a better world."

"But darling," Anya protested, her voice laced with desperation, "Having your work hidden will achieve the same result, will it not?"

"No, my love," Tesla replied, a gentle smile gracing his lips. "It will be given to the right person, at the right time."

"And who shall decide who is the 'right person'?" Anya asked, shaking her head in confusion.

"That," Tesla said, his eyes twinkling with a mischievous glint, "would of course be me."

"But how is this possible?"

"The Time Radio. But first, I must alter the future. Young Mr. Watt's freedom hangs in the balance, and the Time Radio — it must not fall into the hands of the FBI. The potential consequences are catastrophic."

"What good is it to them? All they have is a transmitter. You're the receiver, darling."

Tesla replied, "When Marconi left, we had only really developed the transmitter but yet he managed fine without me to develop the receiver."

"Yes, but that was different," Anya argued. "That was a transatlantic transmission. This is time and space. Niko, we are talking about more than one hundred years! How can someone who will not be born until the twenty-first century give instructions to someone now, in our time?"

"We must never underestimate man's genius," was Tesla's answer.

While still engaged in conversation with Anya, Tesla shifted his focus away from her and directed it back to the letter, seamlessly continuing his writing and speaking with Anya.

"Our conversations had scarcely begun before this calamity with the FBI struck. Many of my queries were not heard, much was left unsaid. The purpose of the Time Radio was not fully served, my love."

His pen flew across the page, his handwriting growing increasingly frantic as the urgency of his thoughts spilled onto the paper.

"Darling, after you are gone how can you be sure Luciano will do as you have instructed. After all, he is a criminal."

"Indeed, a criminal, but no ordinary criminal. One that is bound by a sacred code of honor. He will do as he promises." The scratching of his pen was now more measured, each word chosen with deliberate care.

"And the King, he is exiled from Serbia, are you sure the monastery will be faithful to him?"

"Absolutely," Tesla said without wavering.

A knock on the door echoed in the room.

Tesla paused his writing and with weariness evident in his every movement, he pushed himself up from his desk and embarked on a slow and laborious trek towards the door, as Anya disappeared from sight into the bedroom.

"Mr. Tesla, I have your tea?" called the maid through the door. He opened the door and motioned her in.

"Good evening, Mr. Tesla," Alice said cheerfully.

Tesla nodded and Alice entered the room, careful not to stand too close to him. She put the tray with the tea on the table that was nearest to the window. Then she made sure everything on the platter was neatly arranged as Tesla did not like disorder. Satisfied with the presentation, Alice turned to Tesla.

"Will there be anything more, Mr. Tesla?"

Tesla shook his head.

"Well then, I'll be saying goodnight, sir."

Tesla nodded. Alice retraced her footsteps and left the suite. Tesla returned to his desk and resumed writing the letter.

"Darling, this second letter you're writing," said Anya, while coming out of the bedroom. "If I understand it correctly," she went through it again in her mind... and then continued,

"You are now instructing this young man to keep the conversations short and assure the radio is powered off when the two of you are not talking, because in 1913 you will not know this information to tell him." She paused again, collecting her thoughts. "This should prevent the future authorities from finding him out and arresting him."

"Yes, my love, that is correct."

Tesla paused writing the letter... He set down his pen, leaned back in his chair and let out a sigh as he lifted his gaze to meet Anya's. A gentle smile tugged at the corners of his mouth.

"But darling, what I don't understand is how is it possible that after the conclusion of this day, I... nor you, will remember the first letter you wrote, and the conversation we had then."

"Because, my love, it didn't happen."

"What do you mean it didn't happen? How is that possible? It did happen. We are speaking of it now!" Anya anxiously clasped her hands tightly.

He placed his hand on hers and gave it a reassuring squeeze.

"I know this must all seem terribly confusing and perhaps even frightening, my love. I promise to provide you a detailed explanation once we retire for the evening. For now, please allow me to complete this letter. The bellboy will be arriving shortly to collect it and the Time Radio."

"Alright, but darling, is it not too much of you to ask of him to carry that trunk home in this wretched weather? He is only a boy."

"The storm has not reached its peak yet and I have arranged for a taxi to take him home," Tesla explained.

Anya nodded, still clearly puzzled but willing to wait.

"Very well, Niko."

Tesla lifted her hand to his lips, pressing a gentle kiss to her knuckles. "Thank you, my dear." He then picked up his pen once more, its weight familiar and comforting in his hand. With a deep breath, he bent over the paper, ready to continue writing.

The scratching of nib against the parchment filled the room, punctuated only by the ticking of the clock on the mantle.

A few moments later, a knock on the door interrupted his focus and diverted his attention, but he forced his focus back to the letter. The final words he was writing would not wait.

His pen scratched out the last sentence, and Anya once again disappeared into the bedroom.

The door swung open, revealing the bellboy. Henry Watt.

As Henry approached, Tesla merely gestured towards the small leather travel trunk beside the bed. With a final flourish, he sealed the letter, rose from his desk, and moved toward Henry.

"We have discussed this." Tesla's voice was low with concern. "You understand the instructions. You understand the importance."

"Mr. Tesla, I won't fail you," Henry replied, his voice firm, a flicker of resolve in his eyes.

A brief smile touched Tesla's lips. He placed the envelope in Henry's waiting hand and said, "Conceal the letter in the trunk's lining."

"I understand, sir." said Henry, placing the envelope into his deep side pocket. He picked up the trunk and left without another word. Tesla returned to his armchair by the window and sipped his tea, while Anya quietly rejoined him.

Outside, the storm raged, a symphony of chaos against the rain-lashed glass. Tesla gazed at the fury unleashed outside his window. A feeling of accomplishment washed over him – a sense of finality, a mistake corrected, a quiet peace.

"The future," Tesla began, his voice barely a whisper yet charged with the weight of his vision, "belongs to me now."

His gaze through the window diverted to Anya, whose smile held a bittersweet understanding. No further words were needed. She felt the shift in the air, the culmination of his relentless pursuit. After a lingering moment, she spoke, her voice soft and grounding.

"Drink your tea, dear."

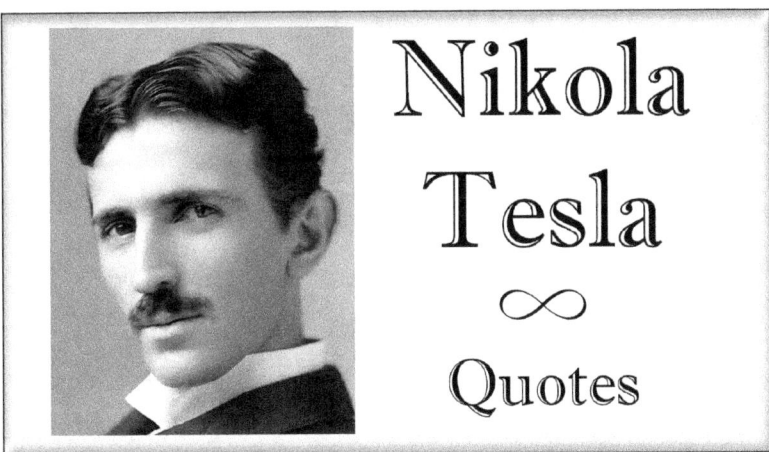

Nikola Tesla ∞ Quotes

"In the twenty-first century, the robot will take the place which slave labor occupied in ancient civilization."

∞

"I don't care that they stole my idea . . I care that they don't have any of their own."

∞

"The day science begins to study non-physical phenomena, it will make more progress in one decade than in all the previous centuries of its existence."

∞

"Be alone, that is the secret of invention; be alone, that is when ideas are born."

∞

"If you want to find the secrets of the universe, think in terms of energy, frequency and vibration."

∞

"The present is theirs; the future, for which I really worked, is mine."

∞

"My brain is only a receiver, in the Universe there is a core from which we obtain knowledge, strength and inspiration. I have not penetrated into the secrets of this core, but I know that it exists."

∞

"I hope this is the invention that will make war impossible."

∞

"My mother understood human nature better and never chided. She knew that a man cannot be saved from his own foolishness or vice by someone else's efforts or protests, but only by the use of his own will."

∞

"From my childhood I had been intended for the clergy. This prospect hung like a dark cloud on my mind."

∞

"The Buddhist expresses it in one way, the Christian in another, but both say the same: We are all one."

∞

"How extraordinary was my life an incident may illustrate... [As a child] I was fascinated by a description of Niagara Falls. I had perused, and pictured in my imagination a big wheel run by the Falls. I told my uncle that I would go to America and carry out this scheme. Thirty years later I saw my ideas carried out at Niagara and marveled at the unfathomable mystery of the mind."

∞

"Of all things, I liked books best."

∞

"One must be sane to think clearly, but one can think deeply and be quite insane."

∞

"I do not think there is any thrill that can go through the human heart like that felt by the inventor as he sees some creation of the brain unfolding to success . . . Such emotions make a man forget food, sleep, friends, love, everything."

∞

"All that was great in the past was ridiculed, condemned, combated, suppressed — only to emerge all the more powerfully, all the more triumphantly from the struggle."

∞

"If you only knew the magnificence of the 3, 6 and 9, then you would have the key to the universe."

∞

"I do not rush into constructive work. When I get an idea, I start right away to build it up in my mind. I change the structure, I make improvements, I experiment, I run the device in my mind. It is absolutely the same to me whether I operate my turbine in thought or test it actually in my shop. It makes no difference, the results are the same. In this way, you see, I can rapidly develop and perfect an invention, without touching anything."

∞

"I am trying to awake the energy contained in the air. These are the main sources of energy. What is considered as empty space is just a manifestation of matter that is not awakened."

∞

"All peoples everywhere should have free energy sources."

∞

"You may live to see man-made horrors beyond your comprehension."

∞

"The desire that guides me in all I do is the desire to harness the forces of nature to the service of mankind."

∞

"Women will ignore precedent and startle civilization with their progress."

∞

"I do not think you can name many great inventions that have been made by married men."

∞

"I could only achieve success in my life through self-discipline, and I applied it until my wish and my will became one."

∞

"Sometimes I feel that by not marrying, I made too great a sacrifice to my work."

∞

"In a time not distant, it will be possible to flash any image formed in thought on a screen and render it visible at any place desired. The perfection of this means of reading thought will create a revolution for the better in all our social relations."

∞

"The scientific man does not aim at an immediate result. He does not expect that his advanced ideas will be readily taken up. His work is like that of the planter - for the future. His duty is to lay the foundation for those who are to come, and point the way."

∞

"The future will show whether my foresight is as accurate now as it has proved heretofore."

∞

"The opinion of the world does not affect me. I have placed as the real values in my life what follows when I am dead."

∞

"It's not the love you make. It's the love you give."

ABOUT THE AUTHOR

SHARON RICH is a best selling author, film historian and screenwriter. She has written, edited, annotated or ghost written dozens of books, penned Hollywood-related magazine articles and was a contributing editor for an opera magazine. She has lectured about writing and film history internationally, at AFI East Coast and on theme cruises. Based on her friendship with Jeanette MacDonald's older sister, actress Blossom Rock, Rich was authorized to write *Sweethearts*, the acclaimed, candid biography about her sister's tragic love affair with Nelson Eddy.
IMDB: imdb.com/name/nm6955722/
Website: sharonrich.com

"The opinion of the world does not affect me. I have placed as the real values in my life what follows when I am dead."

∞

"It's not the love you make. It's the love you give."

About the Author

Sharon Rich is a best selling author, film historian and screenwriter. She has written, edited, annotated or ghost written dozens of books, penned Hollywood-related magazine articles and was a contributing editor for an opera magazine. She has lectured about writing and film history internationally, at AFI East Coast and on theme cruises. Based on her friendship with Jeanette MacDonald's older sister, actress Blossom Rock, Rich was authorized to write *Sweethearts*, the acclaimed, candid biography about her sister's tragic love affair with Nelson Eddy.
IMDB: imdb.com/name/nm6955722/
Website: sharonrich.com

About the Author

D. D. Vujic is an international film producer, screenwriter, and author. Creative writing professor and English teacher. He is also a popular writer for hire and story and production consultant. His works include various international feature films, TV films, and TV series, as well as novels, short stories, and articles for producers and publishers in Europe, North America, and Asia. He has ghost written many personal memoirs, books, and screenplays, published in several languages and is a favorite guest speaker among many international literary clubs.

IMDB: imdb.com/name/nm1729423/

Website: ddvujic.com

About the Author

D. D. Vujic is an international film producer, screenwriter, and author. Creative writing professor and English teacher. He is also a popular writer for hire and story and production consultant. His works include various international feature films, TV films, and TV series, as well as novels, short stories, and articles for producers and publishers in Europe, North America, and Asia. He has ghost written many personal memoirs, books, and screenplays, published in several languages and is a favorite guest speaker among many international literary clubs.

IMDB: imdb.com/name/nm1729423/

Website: ddvujic.com

About the Author

D. D. Vujic is an international film producer, screenwriter, and author. Creative writing professor and English teacher. He is also a popular writer for hire and story and production consultant. His works include various international feature films, TV films, and TV series, as well as novels, short stories, and articles for producers and publishers in Europe, North America, and Asia. He has ghost written many personal memoirs, books, and screenplays, published in several languages and is a favorite guest speaker among many international literary clubs.

IMDB: imdb.com/name/nm1729423/

Website: ddvujic.com